HUMAN INQUIRY IN ACTION

HUMAN INQUIRY IN ACTION

Developments in New Paradigm Research

edited by
Peter Reason

SAGE Publications
London • Thousand Oaks • New Delhi

First published 1988
Reprinted 1990, 1992, 1994, 1995, 1998

SAGE Publications Ltd
6 Bonhill Street
London EC2A 4PU

SAGE Publications Inc
2455 Teller Road
Thousand Oaks, California 91320

SAGE Publications India Pvt Ltd
32, M-Block Market
Greater Kailash – I
New Delhi 110 048

British Library Cataloguing in Publication data

Human inquiry in action : developments in
  new paradigm research.
  1. Social sciences. Research. Methodology
  I. Reason, Peter
  300'.72

ISBN 0–8039–8089–2
ISBN 0–8039–8090–6 Pbk

Library of congress catalog card number 88–061780

Printed and bound by Antony Rowe Limited, Eastbourne

'If you have not lived through
something, it is not true'

Kabir

Contents

Notes on Contributors

Ian Cunningham is Director of Roffey Park Management College. He has been a research chemist, management trainer, lecturer, and has run his own business. He is currently researching organizational culture and change.

Peter Hawkins is a psychotherapist, trainer, and organization consultant. His PhD dissertation explored ways of creating learning environments in different work situations, and he now works with a variety of organizations and individuals helping them learn from their experience and seek to bring about fundamental change. He is a founding partner of Bath Associates.

John Heron was Founding Director of the Human Potential Research Project, University of Surrey, and Assistant Director of the British Postgraduate Medical Federation, University of London. Author of *Confessions of a Janus Brain*, he is now travelling, researching altered states of consciousness.

Robert Krim has served as Assistant Director of Personnel for a large US City as well as consulting for the Commonwealth of Massachusetts and New York City on labour-management co-operation. He has worked as union organizer and president as well as public sector manager, and holds a PhD in Sociology with a focus on action research from Boston College.

Judi Marshall is a Senior Lecturer in Organizational Behaviour at the School of Management, University of Bath. Her main interests are women in management, issues of gender in organizations and organizational culture. These are strands of a continuing fascination with change and transformation.

Adrian McLean was until recently Lecturer in Organizational Behaviour in the School of Management at the University of Bath. He is now a privatized academic and organization development consultant specializing in cultural change. He is a founding partner in Bath Associates.

Peter Reason is Director of Postgraduate Research in the School of Management, University of Bath. He works partly in the field of management education, using self-directed learning methods at undergraduate and postgraduate levels, with particular emphasis on research training. He also works with individuals and groups using humanistic approaches to psychotherapy and personal growth.

Marja-Liisa Swantz is Director of the Institute for Development Studies, University of Helsinki, and Senior Fellow at the United Nations University World Institute for Development Economics Research. She has been engaged in participatory research work in Africa for many years, and has been a central figure in the international participatory research network.

Arja Vainio-Mattila is presently completing her PhD dissertation using participatory research at the Department of Geography, School of Oriental and African Studies, London. She is also affiliated as a researcher to the Institute of Development Studies, University of Helsinki.

Acknowledgements

My thanks go first to the contributors to this book. Many are very close personal friends and colleagues – John Heron, Judi Marshall, Adrian McLean, Peter Hawkins – with whom I have shared significant parts of the inquiry, and who know how fully I appreciate the love and struggle of our work together. Others I know less well, although we are all part of the community of people who are working to develop new approaches to research. I have known Ian Cunningham for many years, and have much appreciated the challenge of his contribution. Marja-Liisa Swantz I have met on a few occasions both in Finland and England, and have always been impressed with the depth of her understanding of the countries in which she has worked, and her compassionate applications of participatory inquiry. Bob Krim I have not met personally, but through an open and enjoyable transatlantic correspondence. Arja Vainio-Mattila I have only met through her writing. Thank you all; I particularly appreciate the way all of you have responded to my editorial comments and suggestions.

Thanks too go to the co-researchers in the many projects that are described or mentioned: Kenyan villagers, managers in City Hall, doctors, nurses, health visitors, consultants, teachers, co-counsellors, members of various organizations. I hope participating in the inquiries stimulated your lives, and that you enjoy reading about them here.

My gratitude is due also to members past and present of the Postgraduate Research Group at the University of Bath, and to other research students with whom I have discussed ideas. If I have taught you as much as you have taught me, we have indeed done well.

My work over the years has been well supported by members of the School of Management at the University of Bath, and particularly by close colleagues in the Centre for the Study of Organizational Change and Development. I particularly want to thank Iain Mangham for using his professorial position to create an environment in which creative work is welcomed and encouraged; David Sims for his quiet appreciation and support; Steve Fineman for a conversation that helped me pull together the framework of this book; Joan Budge for delightful colleagueship and practical help with word processors, spelling, and grammar; Diana Stoddart for real help in the library over many years, and specifically for helping with the references of this book.

More formally, I wish to acknowledge the support provided by a variety of organizations and their officers for the projects reported in this book. Thanks are due to: the Director of the British Postgraduate Medical Federation (University of London) for the Holistic Medicine Research Project (Chapter 5); the Finnish International Development Agency which supported the Bura project (Chapter 6); the School of Management, Boston College, Boston, Mass. (Chapter 7); the Director of the Centre for Alternative Education and Research (CAER) which hosted the Altered States of Consciousness project (Chapter 9); and the Officers of Wrekin District Council and the Local Government Training Board who supported and funded the cultures inquiry (Chapter 10). Thanks to John Rowan personally, and formally to John Wiley and Sons Ltd, for permission to quote at length from 'A Dialectical Paradigm for Research', which originally appeared in *Human Inquiry: a sourcebook of new paradigm research*, 1981.

Peter Reason
University of Bath

Introduction

Peter Reason

In 1981 John Rowan and I edited *Human Inquiry*, subtitled 'a sourcebook of new paradigm research', in which we put together both existing and new articles representing the emerging paradigm of co-operative experiential inquiry: research that was *with* and *for* people rather than *on* people.

The simplest description of co-operative inquiry is that it is a way of doing research in which all those involved contribute both to the creative thinking that goes into the enterprise – deciding on what is to be looked at, the methods of the inquiry, and making sense of what is found out – and *also* contribute to the action which is the subject of the research. Thus in its fullest form the distinction between researcher and subject disappears, and all who participate are both co-researchers and co-subjects. Co-operative inquiry is therefore also a form of education, personal development, and social action.

Although co-operative inquiry in its several forms is a relatively novel approach to research, it has developed considerably since the publication of *Human Inquiry*. Several of the originators of the approach have initiated and taken part in projects, and a second generation of researchers, many of them Masters and Doctoral students, have used and adapted the basic ideas for their own purposes. We have now several developments in methodology and a range of examples of co-operative inquiry in practice.

Thus the new volume is truly *Human Inquiry in Action*. It is the result of taking the co-operative inquiry model out into the field of research practice, and responding to the practical requirements of research with people. This has resulted in several new methodological proposals, which are included in Part One, and a number of examples of actual research projects. Five of these latter are included in Part Two, each taken from a different field of endeavour and representing a different primary purpose in conducting human inquiry.

The idea of co-operative inquiry

I tend to use 'co-operative inquiry' as an overall term to describe the various approaches to research with people. Others have used different terms, and in doing so have emphasized different aspects of the overall process. Thus those who work within a development context, often in the Third World, use the term *participatory research*; they are represented here by Marja-Liisa Swantz and Arja Vainio-Mattila. The emphasis of participatory research is in establishing a *dialogue* between research workers and the grass-roots people with whom they work, in order to discover and realize the practical and cultural needs of those people. Research here becomes one part of a developmental process including also education and political action. Participatory research has also been termed dialogical inquiry (Randall and Southgate, 1981).

Emerging more from a tradition of critical theory, humanistic psychology and organizational development in the USA are the terms *collaborative inquiry* and *action science*, represented here by Bob Krim's chapter on work within a city government. Many of the fundamental ideas in this tradition were developed by Bill Torbert, whose concern has been to establish an action science useful to the practitioner at the moment of action, rather than a reflective science about action. This concern has led practitioners in this mode to be concerned about ways of learning from experience, and with the high-quality attention which is needed if this kind of inquiry is to be successful.

In the United Kingdom the developments in co-operative inquiry have been closely linked with experiential learning and humanistic psychology. John Heron's original contribution, *Experience and Method* (1971), was written as an exploration of the relationship between personal development and inquiry, and he called this approach *experiential inquiry* to emphasize the fundamental importance of honouring personal experience as the touchstone of valid psychological inquiry. Much of my own work with John Heron and with my colleagues and students at Bath has involved integrating the methods and insights of humanistic psychology and what we used to call the 'growth movement' with experiential research.

Another aspect of our work has been the development of the *co-operative inquiry group*. While participatory research was developed for work within existing social settings such as Third World villages, in experiential inquiry we have often chosen to establish groups entirely for the purpose of research. In establishing such co-operative inquiry groups we have drawn on our skills as group facilitators and educators, and we have attended to the integration of the inquiry process into the development of the group as a learning community. Again, the differences between inquiry, learning, and action in the world become indistinct and unimportant, as we consider collaborative inquiry as a holistic human learning process.

Thus it is likely that co-operative inquiry processes within these three different 'schools' will look rather different. Participatory researchers will be engaging in dialogue with groups in their natural settings; action-inquirers will be reflecting on their experiences of social action; experiential researchers will be setting up and working with inquiry groups. Others, like Ian Cunningham in Chapter 8, will borrow from all schools so as to develop a method to suit their particular needs. But the commonality in all the approaches is that they are all working openly, directly and collaboratively with the primary actors in their various fields of interest.

According to Maxwell (1984), orthodox science operates within a 'philosophy of knowledge', that is to say it is primarily concerned with intellectual problems of knowledge and technology. Maxwell regards these as subordinate and peripheral to the main issue of human existence, which is to 'articulate... the basic problems we wish to solve, and... propose and critically assess possible solutions'. All forms of co-operative inquiry can be seen as working within what Maxwell terms a 'philosophy of wisdom', in which the primary attention is given to the promotion of human welfare.

> The basic (humanitarian) aim of inquiry, let it be remembered, is to help promote human welfare, help people realize what is of value to them in life.... But in order to realize what is of value to us in life, the primary problems we need to solve are problems of *action* – personal and social problems of action as encountered in life. (Maxwell, 1984: pp. 47–8)

My personal belief is that our basic philosophical stance for a new approach to human inquiry has been established. It is part of a new world-view which is emerging through systems thinking, ecological concerns and awareness, feminism, education, as well as in the philosophy of human inquiry. It has been articulated partly by those associated with the development of co-operative inquiry; partly by authors such as Lincoln and Guba (1985), who have provided a quite excellent summary of 'post-positivist' thinking; and partly by books and articles by a whole range of critics of the mechanical and reductionist scientific world-view. Among those who represent this perspective are Bateson, 1972, 1979; Berman, 1981; Bohm, 1980; Capra, 1982; Hainer, 1968; Koestler, 1978; Macmurray, 1957; Maslow, 1966; Mitroff, 1974; Mitroff and Kilmann, 1978; Polanyi, 1958; Reinharz, 1981, 1983; Roberts, 1981; Schwartz and Ogilvy, 1979; Skolimowski, 1985, 1986; Stanley and Wise, 1983; Wilber, 1981b.

In saying that our basic stance is established I am saying, to use John Rowan's version of the inquiry cycle (1981; see also below) that 'Thinking is not enough....Philosophizing any further would be sterile and useless.' This is not to say that there are no interesting debates to be conducted or puzzles to be solved. But it does mean that the emphasis of our task has become one of establishing the approach in practice, and developing varied methodological approaches suitable for different situations (in Rowan's terms PROJECT and ENCOUNTER). From this follows the form of this book: there is no section on the philosophy of new paradigm research, although there are philosophical discussions where they seem to be appropriate. Rather the book focuses on developing methods and developing practice.

The co-operative inquiry method

It will be helpful to readers not familiar with *Human Inquiry* to include, as part of this Introduction, a more detailed description of the methodology of co-operative inquiry. I will therefore summarize John Heron's model, since that is the one with which I have been most associated. I will also include John Rowan's account of a dialectical cycle of research, since this provides a helpful model within which to compare different approaches. These descriptions will provide a more detailed introduction to the method; however, the serious student of these methods is referred to the earlier writings.

Heron's basic argument (1971, 1981a) is that orthodox research methods are inadequate for a science of persons, quite simply because they undermine the self-determination of their 'subjects'. He argues that what above all distinguishes the human person is the ability to choose how they will act, and the capacity to give meaning to their experience and to their actions. This self-directing ability is at least latent in all human beings; the extent of its possible development is unknown. Orthodox scientific method (particularly the formal experiment, but following this surveys, questionnaires, and observation) aims quite systematically and intentionally to exclude the subjects from all choice about the subject-matter of the research, all consideration of appropriate inquiry method, all the creative thinking that goes into making sense; and it therefore excludes from the field of research just that aspect of being – self-determination – which particularly characterizes the subjects as persons.

In doing so these inquiry methods are not only epistemologically unsound, but contribute also to the impoverishment of our world, and to the quite frightening consequences of the mechanical world-view, which in the end treats all living beings as things to be manipulated and exploited.

Heron's response to this problem is to point out that whereas orthodox researchers presuppose that they are self-directed while requiring their subjects to be other-directed, it is possible to conceive of another approach in which *all* those involved are self-directed, contributing both to the creative thinking and to the research action. Such an approach would involve all actors in three forms of knowing: propositional knowing, or knowledge *about*, which takes the form of ideas, propositions, and theories; practical knowing, or knowledge *how to* which takes the form of skills and abilities; and experiential knowing, or knowledge *by encounter* from sustained acqaintance face-to-face, which is tacit, intuitive, and holistic.

One way of describing the cycle of co-operative inquiry is shown in Figure 1. A group of co-researchers meet to inquire into some aspect of their life and work. (Only two are shown in the figure for simplicity. 'R' indicates each person in their capacity as co-researcher; 'S' as co-subject; this is of course a bit arbitrary, but helps the explanation). At Stage 1

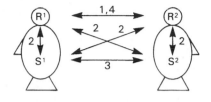

Figure 1

they discuss and agree *what* it is they wish to research; what *ideas* and *theories* they may bring to the inquiry; what kind of *research action* they will undertake to explore these ideas; how to observe, record, measure, and otherwise gather their experience for further reflection. Stage 1 is primarily in the realm of propositional knowledge.

In Stage 2 they take these decisions about research action into their lives; they engage in whatever behaviour has been agreed, note the outcomes whether these be physical, psychological, interpersonal, or social; and record their discoveries. Stage 2 may involve self-observation, reciprocal observation of other members of the inquiry group, or other agreed methods of recording experience; it is primarily in the realm of practical knowledge.

As part of this application the co-researchers (Stage 3) become fully immersed in their practice. They encounter each other and their world directly, as far as possible without preconception, bracketing off any prejudicial influence of the ideas they started with in Stage 1, and so opening themselves to novel experience and discerning so far as possible what is actually happening. They may actually forget that they are taking part in an inquiry. This deep engagement with the subject of the inquiry is in the realm of experiential knowledge, and is the touchstone of the method; it is to be contrasted with the superficial engagement of a subject in orthodox inquiry, who responds to a questionnaire or who is paid to take part in an experiment, while having at most superficial knowledge of, and interest in, what is being studied.

Having engaged deeply with their practice and experience in Stages 2 and 3, the co-researchers return in Stage 4 to reflect on their experience and attempt to make sense of it. This will involve revising and developing the ideas and models with which they entered the first cycle of inquiry, even discarding them and starting anew. This reflection involves a whole range of both cognitive and intuitive forms of knowing; its expression may be primarily propositional, but may also involve stories, pictures, and other ways of giving voice to aspects of experience which cannot be captured in propositions. When this making sense has been completed, the co-researchers can consider how to engage on further cycles of inquiry.

Thus the essence of co-operative experiential inquiry is an aware and self-critical movement between experience and reflection which goes through several cycles as ideas, practice, and experience are systematically honed and refined. It must be self-evident that this method is much more complex to carry out then to describe.

John Rowan (1981) approached similar questions from a perspective of alienation. He argued that 'pure research' of orthodox inquiry alienated experimental subjects in all four forms identified by Karl Marx: they were alienated from the product of the research; from the work of the research; from other people; and from themselves. He also pointed out that this did not need to be so, and drew up a list of inquiry methods ranging from most alienating to least alienating, the latter including what we here call co-operative inquiry. John also explored the ways in which different research styles engaged actively with problems of action in the world. From these reflections he drew up his dialectical research cycle (Figure 2), commenting that it would be convenient to have some way of comparing and contrasting these methods more easily.

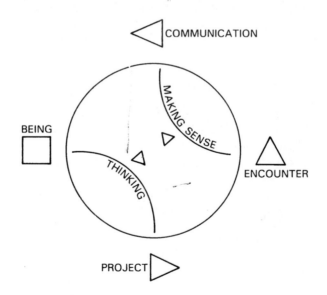

Figure 2

He uses the research cycle first as a perspective on the 'standard alienated research project':

> One is working in a particular field (BEING) and finds or is given a problem. One searches the literature to find if anyone has already tacked it, and mentally combines the information to refine the problem (THINKING). One then designs

a research plan and discusses it with one's supervisor or colleagues (PROJECT). One then conducts an experiment, or carries out the survey or observations (ENCOUNTER). One does one's data processing, content analysis, statistical manipulation, etc. (MAKING SENSE). And one writes the paper, or dissertation, or thesis (COMMUNICATION) and perhaps talks about it at conferences and other meetings, or writes an article about it, before returning to one's normal work in the field again (BEING). (p. 97)

In contrast to this he describes the same cycle as a dialectical engagement with the world:

I start by resting in my own experience. But at a certain point my existing practice seems to be inadequate – I become dissatisfied. So the first negation arises; I turn *against* old ways of doing things. A real problem has arisen. . . .

So I move into a phase of needing new thinking. Perhaps I start by finding out what others know already – gathering information through conversations, phone calls, meetings, libraries or whatever. Ideas start churning around. THINKING in this model is not the application of a technique to inert material – it is a creative process of invention and testing. It continually asks the question – 'Will this do?' It is essentially an *inward* movement, gathering in information; but it is also a processing movement, adding and combining the new information into unfamiliar relationships, and trying it against some template of what would be acceptable. . . . The major contradiction here is between always needing more information ('Maybe that new paper will have the answer') and feeling that there is too much information already, and it needs to be cut down. It is only when this contradiction is transcended that movement takes place to the next stage.

At a certain point I *abandon* gathering more and more information. Thinking is *not* enough. I have to make a definite decision as to what to aim for. . . . Philosophizing any further would be sterile and useless. Some action plan has to come into being. This may require some daring, some risk-taking, some breaking of bounds. I need to involve others at this stage in the process. PROJECT is essentially an *outward* movement. This is where I take a risk, and form an intention. . . . It essentially involves plans and decisions. The major contradiction of the formal moment itself is between the need for more and better plans and satiation with plans. 'Plans should be adequate' *versus* 'No plan can be perfect'. Again, this contradiction has to be overcome before movement can take place to the next point on the cycle.

But again, at a certain point, plans are *not* what is needed. Action itself is the thing to get into. In action I am fully present, here now. Plans are a mere distraction from the past, and can only hamper and impede. I must be ready to improvise if unexpected reactions occur. I have to really be *with* others. ENCOUNTER is a moment of height and depth, like BEING, though it involves regular inward and outward moments. (The rhythmic nature of the cycle is now becoming more apparent.) This is where I actually meet the other. There is some action, some engagement, such that some other reality can get through to me. I may get confirmed or disconfirmed: and it appears, paradoxically, that disconfirmation is actually more valuable as a learning experience than is confirmation. An experience of unfreedom can be very stimulating to further effort. . . . The major contradiction of this moment is between the need for perseverance and assiduity, and the plethora of too much activity. 'I am just here and now' *versus* 'I am not just here and now'. This is the place for test, for experiment, for comparison. It is also a place for involvement, for commitment, for spontaneity – to the extent that I am not genuinely open to experience, to that extent I am not genuinely encountering reality, and hence not likely to learn.

This goes on until I get to the point of feeling that action is *not* enough. I must withdraw and find out what it all *means*. How can I understand what I have been through? And what others have been through? Perhaps there is more than one message, more than one way of seeing it. What does it *all* mean? What are the contradictions, and can they be resolved? MAKING SENSE in this model involves both analysis and contemplation.... The contradiction here is between reducing the data to an understandable simplicity, and adding more and more connections to the data to make them more understandable in that way, expanding them until they say everything.

But at a certain point, after I have been immersed in this for some time, I begin to get dissatisfied. Analysis is *not* enough. I must start telling people what it means and how I have understood what we have been through. What have we actually accomplished or achieved? Can I explain it to somebody else? Can others learn from our mistakes and false starts? From our successes? I or others may write papers, give lectures, go to conferences, go on the radio, on television, in the popular press, or whatever, either individually or collectively. COMMUNICATION is again an *outward* movement. This is the stage where we have digested what has happened, and made it part of our new accommodation to reality. Our mental structures become richer and more complex. Our consciousness expands. I communicate with myself about what it has all meant for me. I may communicate with others who were not involved with me in it. The major contradiction at this moment is between the need to get data more finely processed and accurately and clearly expressed, and awareness of the impossibility of communication to anyone outside the experience. The main thing it to understand what we have been through.

At a certain time, however, I do *not* want to turn into a communicator, I want to get back to some real work. Now that I have learned what I have learned, I can go back to my field and continue to practise, only now on a higher level. BEING is neither inward nor outward, but represents a dimension of height and depth. It is here that I am a full three-dimensional human being most truly and most fully. Existence, perception, identity are all involved here.... The major contradiction here is between cultivation of the everyday and dissatisfaction with it. 'Everything is (now) all right as it is' *versus* 'Everything is not all right as it is'. Implied in any movement from this point is a negation of one's existing practice – one turns away from old ways of doing things. This is essentially a resting place, a place of contentment. It always hurts to leave. It always feels good to come back. It can represent one's daily work in the field. One only leaves under some form of pressure. I am who I am here. (Rowan, 1981, pp. 97–100)

John Rowan makes a particularly important contribution here in showing how inquiry is an *alive* process of engaging in the world. His model also provides a helpful way in which we can map out different ways of engaging with other people as we go round the research cycle. In classic experimental research the researcher goes through all the stages alone (or in a professional research team), making contact with 'subjects' only at the point of encounter, and then in an alienated fashion. In 'full blown' co-operative experiential inquiry a group of co-researchers engage in every point of the cycle in a fully collaborative fashion. Between these idealized extremes are of course a wide variety of possible relationships.

At a minimum, for a research strategy to claim the term co-operative inquiry, I would argue that the nature of the involvement of all participants should be openly negotiated, that all should contribute to the creative thinking that is part of the research, and that relationships should aim to be authentically collaborative. Thus it may be quite appropriate for, say, professional medical researchers engaged in the exploration of disease to invite patients to join a co-operative inquiry group to explore the outcomes of particular forms of treatment. This does not mean that the co-researcher patients have to develop technical expertise comparable with the medics, nor that the latter have to experience the same dis-ease symptoms as the patients. Rather, they may all join together in the research project some-where around the point of PROJECT and probably separate somewhere around MAKING SENSE and COMMUNICATION. Their relationships during this time can be fully co-operative.

Given this view, the form of co-operative inquiry can range from full collaboration through all the stages of inquiry, to genuine dialogue and consultation at the moments of PROJECT, ENCOUNTER, and MAKING SENSE. But I think that moving towards the fully collaborative model is the most challenging, both personally for those involved, and as a contribution to the emergence of a genuine practice of new paradigm inquiry. In my Reflections on Part Two I use Rowan's dialectical cycle to map out the form of inquiry of each of the examples in this volume.

The idea of a new paradigm for research

In giving this book the subtitle 'Developments in new paradigm research' I am making the claim that in co-operative inquiry we have a genuine new paradigm for human research. I am aware of a certain delightful outrageousness about this claim, and can imagine some critics snorting, 'New paradigm, indeed! Who does he think he is?' Indeed, my much-loved old teacher, Nathan Grundstein of Case Western Reserve University (for whom I wrote my first 'new paradigm' essay entitled 'Out of the scientific prison'), gently took me to task for this when *Human Inquiry* appeared. I have over the past years more modestly taken to referring to 'the paradigm of co-operative inquiry' and eschewed the bolder 'New Paradigm Research'.

However, the essential quality of a paradigmatic shift is that it presents a discontinuity with the previous world-view and methods; I believe that collaborative forms of inquiry do this. As mentioned above, the post-positivist or post-modern philosophy has been developing in many places for some time, and the co-operative inquiry methodologies offer one way – maybe the most developed way – of putting this emerging philosophy into research practice.

There are three interrelated aspects of the shift that are important: the move to participatory and holistic knowing; to critical subjectivity; and to knowledge in action.

Participatory and holistic knowing
The first change, towards knowing based on a participative and dialogical relationship with the world, is also a move away from the distance and separateness of objectivity. Skolimowski (1985) sees the history of knowledge in terms of a series of world-views or cosmologies, each of which has held sway for a while, to be replaced by one more adequate for its time. He points out that since about the time of Newton we have seen our world in terms of a mechanical cosmology, a world of material cause-and-effect which can be manipulated and exploited. This has brought enormous material benefits through the development of science and technology; but it has also a dark side – 'ecological devastations, human and social fragmentation, spiritual impoverishment'. He argues that this mechanical metaphor is breaking down, and that our society is in epistemological crisis because, while we may fear to acknowledge it consciously, we are all aware that 'official knowledge' is inadequate.

A replacement for this mechanical metaphor has not yet fully crystallized, but new themes do seem to be emerging quite consistently as aspects of a new world-view. One of these is wholeness – while the mechanical metaphor is 'piecemeal, atomistic, fragmentary and fragmenting' (Skolimowski, 1985), the variety of new visions are holistic and unitary. Another is the idea of evolution, that whole systems may spontaneously shift to higher levels of complexity (Teilhard de Chardin, 1959; Jantsch, 1980; Prigogine, 1980).

An important aspect of wholeness is that is *requires* participation:

> Wholeness means that all the parts belong together, and that means that they partake in each other. Thus from the central idea that all is connected, that each is part of the whole, comes the idea that each participate in the whole. *Thus participation is an implicit aspect of wholeness.* You cannot truly conceive the structure of wholeness unless you grant that the meaning of wholeness implies that all parts partake in it, or put otherwise – participate in it. (Skolimowski, 1985, p. 25; emphasis in the original)

Just as wholeness implies participation, so participation means empathy, 'an almost complete identification with the subject of our attention'; and empathy implies responsibility, since we 'cannot truly participate in the whole unless we take responsibility for it'. This perspective is so different from that of positivist science, which was originally based on Bacon's idea that we should 'Put Nature herself on the rack and wrest her secrets from her' (Griffin, 1984). It is more like Heidegger's proposal that we should 'tarry alongside' with an attitude of astonishment.

Thus in co-operative inquiry we work with our co-researchers, establishing relationships of authentic collaboration and dialogue; ideally we care for each other, and approach each other with mutual love and concern. While not ignoring the necessity for direction and the role of expertise, we eschew unnecessary hierarchy and compulsive control.

The emphasis on wholeness also means that we are not interested in either fragmented knowing, or theoretical knowing that is separated from practice and from experience. We seek a knowing-in-action which encompasses as much of our experience as possible. This means that aspects of a phenomenon are understood deeply because we know them in the context of our participation in the whole system, not as the isolated dependent and independent variables of experimental science. Our holistic concerns lead us to a form of theory-building and understanding which is descriptive and systemic, what Geertz (1973) would call a 'thick description', or Kaplan (1964) a 'concatenated' theory. The essential quality of a pattern model is that it creates a dense of web of knowing.

This kind of non-hierarchical thinking-in-action is quite foreign to formal Western thinking: we tend to see the world in terms of hierarchical cause-and-effect, rather than in networks of understanding. This point is nicely illustrated by the following account of Inuit hunters:

> Hunters make thousands of critical decisions each year. The processing of this information leads into the domain of spirituality and metaphor, where accumulated knowledge, intuition and the subtlest of connections with the natural world can generate choices on a basis that is quicker and surer than a narrow rationality. In this way, the decisions of hunters are close to the certainties of artists. By denying a reduction to a limited set of variables, the fullness of both culture and consciousness come to bear on each day's activities. The mobile and flexible behaviour of hunters is inseparable from this state of consciousness, this form of decision-making. (Brody, 1987, p. 93)

Critical subjectivity

This leads us to the second major change: the shift from an objective consciousness to a quality of awareness I have called critical subjectivity (Reason and Rowan, 1981a; Reason, 1988). As I have argued before, the process of inquiry can be seen as starting in a naive inquiry based on our primitive subjective experience of the world. This kind of knowing, like the knowing of a small child, is very prone to distortions arising from our biases and prejudices, from anxieties, and from the pressures of the social world. But it also has a lot of good qualities because it is alive, involved, committed, it is a very important part of our humanity, and we lose a lot if we try to throw it out altogether.

The move from this subjective and active knowing to the objective knowing of orthodox inquiry does just this: in order to get away from the confusion and potential error of naive inquiry, we develop the objective consciousness of scientific method. This parallels the development of ego and of what Freudians call the secondary process based on the reality principle. Skolimowski calls this a 'yoga of objectivity':

> The yoga of objectivity consists of a set of exercises specific to the scientific mind. These exercises are practised over a number of years, sometimes as many as fifteen. . . . The purpose of these exercises is to see nature and reality in a selective way. It takes many years of stringent training . . . before the mind *becomes* detached, objective, analytical, clinical, 'pure'. (1985, p. 12; emphasis in original)

A very similar and more detailed argument is put forward by Berman in his delightful book *The Reenchantment of the World* (1981).

This objective approach to inquiry deals with many of the problems of naive inquiry, but because it is separated from our subjectivity we are left with essentially dead knowledge, alienated from its source. It has been argued that this epistemology is a root cause of the fundamental problems which appear to beset our civilization (Bateson, 1972; Griffin, 1984).

So one of the features of the emerging new paradigm is that we seek to go beyond this split between subjective and objective. Critical subjectivity is a quality of awareness in which we do not suppress our primary subjective experience; nor do we allow ourselves to be overwhelmed and swept along by it; rather we raise it to consciousness and use is as part of the inquiry process. John Rowan, drawing on Hegelian thinking, has referred to this as a leap to the Realized level of consciousness, so that

> because we now see the world as *our* world, rather than *the* world, we can see clearly through our own eyes. Being rational . . . at this stage, is doing justice to the whole thing – to all that is out there in the world and all that is in here, inside ourselves. (Rowan and Reason, 1981, p. 116; emphasis in orginal. See also Rowan, 1979)

Thus all co-operative inquiry honours individual experience, and at its best works to enhance that experience towards a critical subjectivity. This may involve practices that free our attention from the constrictions and distortions of past distress (Chapter 2), or from political oppression (Tandon, 1981); or it may involve exercises that expand our attention into multiple domains of experience (Chapters 3 and 7; Torbert, 1981b; Reason, 1988). All the examples in Part Two of this book explore this issue to some extent.

Knowledge in action
The third major shift is to the view that knowledge is formed in and for action rather than in and for reflection. This idea has been around for a

good time, at least since Kurt Lewin pointed out that 'There is nothing so practical as a good theory'. Macmurray (1957; Reason, 1988) argued that 'it is the practical that is primary. The theoretical is secondary and derivative'. Maxwell (1984) identifies a philosophy of wisdom based on offering solutions to practical human concerns. From a feminist perspective it is argued that an over-reliance on analytical, theoretical knowledge contributes to an oppressive patriarchy, and is part of the alienation of Western Man; what is needed is a recovery of the muted feminine which is both more intuitive and more grounded and practical.

Co-operative inquiry seeks knowledge in action and for action. Co-operative researchers may write books and articles, but often the knowledge that is really important for them is the practical knowledge of new skills and abilities: a more holistic practice in the surgery (Chapter 5), or more efficient and safer stoves for cooking (Chapter 6). And thus in co-operative inquiry, education and social action may become fully integrated with the research process.

My argument is that these three changes constitute a paradigmatic shift. The old world-view, with its fragmented and alienated mechanical metaphors, is discarded as we move into a participatory universe. But I think that this move can be seen as a synthesis in which, while much is negated and discarded, significant aspects are retained and re-integrated. For what we keep of the old scientific view are the ideals of critical and public knowledge. Indeed, the notion of critical subjectivity means that we are more demanding than orthodox science, insisting that valid inquiry is based on a very high degree of self-knowing, self-reflection, and co-operative criticism. Good co-operative inquiry is both wholeheartedly involved and intensely self-critical.

> What it is important, in this transition to post-positivism, is that we keep hold of and develop this quality of critical knowing. We are not in the business of lapsing back into naive inquiry, nor of resting with objective consciousness with all its epistemological errors; rather we are seeking ways to move forward to a new form of integrated consciousness and critical awareness. (Reason, 1988)

In my experience as one strongly identified with this emerging paradigm, I have lectured to and discussed the ideas with very diverse groups of people. I have noticed three kinds of response. First there are those who hear and receive the ideas with what appears to be uncritical joy. These are often people who hold humanistic values and feel strongly the dehumanizing influence of mechanical science. Second, there are those who reject the ideas with either incomprehension or hostility. These are usually people who are working as scientists in a traditional mode, or who have been educated within a scientific profession. The proposal for a co-operative research paradigm does not fit with, or threatens the ideas of, objective knowledge on which their work is based. The third response, which usually only comes about after some immersion in the new paradigm ideas and acquaintance with them in use, is a critical acceptance of the new paradigm. People are then able to integrate the ideas with their own field of activity, and to develop the methods to fit within their own personality and inquiry needs.

Finally, if I am right and co-operative inquiry can be seen as an emergent paradigm, we must remember, as Feyerabend (1978) pointed out so clearly: paradigms are incommensurable; it is not possible to judge one paradigm in the terms of another. We will need to develop new criteria appropriate to the co-operative world-view – a task that John Heron tackles in Chapter 2.

The postgraduate research group

Just as the New Paradigm Research Group was a central forum for discussions which led to the publication of *Human Inquiry*, so in many ways parts of this book were conceived and developed in discussions and seminars over the past seven years with members of the Postgraduate Research Group at the University of Bath. This group, composed of three members of staff and their research students, is part support group, part intellectual seminar, part research laboratory and part encounter group. All members are committed to some form of co-operative inquiry, and all have taken the fundamental ideas of the new paradigm, chewed them over and developed them for their own purposes. Some of them have left with higher degrees by research; some of them have left for other reasons; some are still members of the group. All have taught me something, and their contributions are evident in the pages of this book, some acknowledged, some not.

This group has also been an important place in which we have experimented with the development of training methods for co-operative inquiry. Obviously we have read and discussed various pieces of literature, and explored and criticized each other's writing and ideas. But maybe more important than this has been the collaborative ethos that we have developed over the years: the group is to a very large extent a peer learning community, and an on-going inquiry into new paradigm research.

It has been particularly important for us to learn how to integrate personal needs with the inquiry process. Many university seminar groups are tense and competitive places, in which the main purpose of interaction is either to show how smart you are, or to demonstrate that you have read more than the others present. We have realized that when a member (staff or student) presents a piece of work in the group they will nearly always feel vulnerable. And we have had to learn at these times how to establish vigorous dialogue around both the ideas and the personal vulnerability, how to challenge without attack and defence, and how to support without being suffocating.

We have also realized the importance of not over-structuring ourselves. It is easy to feel short of time, and to put pressure on ourselves to use it efficiently – to plan and have carefully structured agendas. But equally useful has been the time spent in loose conversation, which allows the free associations and spontaneous connections to arise; and the informal time over lunch and coffee in which personal links can be forged. The group recently discussed how its process is often characteristically female rather than male in this way, tending towards the chaotic rather than the compulsively ordered.

We work hard to keep a collaborative and personal ethos alive. To do this we continually re-affirm the peer principle, exploring how the inevitable power and expertise of the staff members can be used creatively rather than oppressively. We often face the problem of integrating the needs of new members tentatively starting on their inquiries with the needs of those in more advanced stages who are beginning to break new bounds. We try to be open to rivalry and competitiveness on the one hand, and friendship and love on the other. We have not always done any of this as well as we would wish.

It is very important to us that research is a personal process; our paper on this (Reason and Marshall, 1987) drew directly on experiences of group members. We have included in our work together experiments to explore the personal aspects of inquiry, some of which have been similar to the psychodrama discussed in Chapter 3 and the role play in Chapter 7. In addition to this some group members have chosen to work in psychotherapy, or attend personal growth workshops in order to take their personal exploration further. As staff we have encouraged our students to include accounts of this personal process in their dissertations because they are part of the exercise of critical subjectivity: we have argued that the reader of a research report needs to know as much as possible about the perspective of the primary researchers.

Thus Gill Robertson (1984, 1987) included an account of her 'hidden agenda' in doing the research, and how it burst uninvited and unexpected into her awareness. Peter Hawkins' (1986) applications of psychodrama are discussed in this book. Elizabeth Mellor-Ribet (1986) used a sub-personalities exercise (Assagioli, 1965) to identify and work with all the different internal 'voices' that were trying to have a say in her research. Angela Brew (1988) includes in the first section of her dissertation a philosophical critique of positivism and an exploration of alternatives based on phenomenology, while the second part – the real research – is an exercise in personal phenomenology in the form of a story.

Many of the other activities of the research group have been experimental. Thus the storytelling methodology developed from a spontaneous suggestion in a seminar that we might better understand our experience by telling it as a story than by trying to analyse it. This suggestion was taken up, and over several sessions some members tried out different ways of using stories. Other experiments have included looking at the possible relevance of astrology as a way of throwing new light of personal aspects of inquiry: to do this we invited Liz Greene, a well-known astrologer and Jungian analyst, to run a workshop for us. We have from time to time embarked on small co-operative inquiry ventures – looking, for example, at our own learning and at the ways of giving each other personal feedback. And we have used the group as a workshop where members can try out approaches they may wish to introduce to other inquiry groups.

In *Human Inquiry* John Rowan and I wrote, 'we strongly advocate that all new paradigm researchers should build themselves a support group of some kind' (p. 486). We started the Postgraduate Research Group on the basis of this advice. Seven years of experience confirm our opinion. Doing co-operative research well is enormously demanding; we all need well-informed friends who can and will support us, challenge us, and travel some of the road with us.

Introduction to the chapters

In chapter 1 I draw on the experience of several inquiries to discuss the issues involved in setting up and being part of a co-operative inquiry group. The chapter is primarily practical in its intent, offering guidance to anyone wanting to work in this fashion. There are many links between this chapter and the others written by myself and my close associates, particularly Chapters 2, 5, 9, and 10.

In Chapter 2 John Heron continues the debate about validity in co-operative inquiry. This debate started in the New Paradigm Research Group, when we first discussed the many ways in which co-researchers might mislead themselves. We borrowed the notion of validity from positivist inquiry, and included a chapter on the issue in *Human Inquiry*. However, the use of the term validity begged several epistemological questions. For the term implies, within a positivist world-view, that valid knowledge provides some kind of accurate representation of an 'objective' world (or at least in a Popperian view can approach such a representation through falsification). Since the paradigm of co-operative inquiry holds that we live in a participatory universe in which we co-create the world we seek to understand, this form of empiricism is unacceptable. This exploration of the issues was contained in John Heron's earlier statement on validity (Heron, 1982) and in my critique of this in Reason (1988). John now offers a complete revision of his 1982 article with a brief new exploration of the meaning of validity based on the notion of *coherence*.

This chapter also contains a set of interdependent procedures for exploring issues of validity in co-operative inquiry. These procedures were developed and tried out in several inquiry ventures, including the holistic medicine inquiry reported in Chapter 5 and the altered states of consciousness inquiry in Chapter 9. While they are designed to be used in the context of a co-operative inquiry group, researchers engaged in other forms of inquiry within the broad co-operative paradigm will doubtless find the suggestions helpful and be able to adapt them to their own style of inquiry.

Peter Hawkins, in Chapter 3, illustrates one of the important links between the fields of experiential learning and psychotherapy, and co-operative inquiry. Peter came to research as an accomplished psychodramatist. He developed his practice of phenomenological psychodrama for his own PhD research in learning communities (Hawkins, 1986), and extended it in practice with the Bath Postgraduate Research Group. His chapter is a semi-fictional account of a phenomenological psychodrama workshop, based on real workshops which have taken place in our research groups and conferences over the years. The chapter is presented in this form so that readers may actually *use* some of the psychodramatic exercises in a research group. It is a chapter that needs to be used (enacted) to be fully understood.

Chapter 4 offers another example of a methodological development in the use of storytelling as a way of exploring meaning – a practical co-operative hermeneutic. Again, I invite readers to try the storytelling exercises for themselves, and to play with the ideas to develop their own approaches.

Part Two of the book contains reports of six co-operative inquiry projects. These are drawn from very diverse fields of human action – the practice of medicine; problems of wood for fuel in Kenyan villages; ways of facilitating learning; altered states of consciousness; and interventions to change and develop organizations. At the end of Part Two are my Reflections on these examples. There are also many connections and cross-references between the various chapters, and I have tried to point these out when they seem important.

PART ONE

DEVELOPMENTS IN METHODOLOGY

1

The Co-operative Inquiry Group

Peter Reason

One way to conduct inquiry within the overall collaborative paradigm is to establish a co-operative inquiry group in which the intent is that all members work together fully as co-researchers. In this chapter I explore some of the issues that such a co-operative group might run into in their work, and suggest some solutions, or if not solutions then at least 'ways forward'. My aim is to offer a practical 'How to do it' chapter, and in doing this I have drawn on the experience of several inquiry groups whose reports are available in various forms, many of which I am familiar with at first- or second-hand.

The idea of co-operative inquiry is simple: fundamentally it is that people work together as co-researchers in exploring and changing their world:

Who was that research
I saw you with last night?
That was no research,
That was my life!

as we wrote on the cover of *Human Inquiry*. But since the initial idea of co-operative inquiry arose in its various forms, much attention has been paid, particularly by academic writers such as myself, to locating it within 'new paradigm' thinking and to exploring issues of knowledge, validity, critical subjectivity, and all that (Reason, 1988). We have got at times into some deep philosophical waters in trying to understand what we were up to, and in doing so may at times have lost sight of the simple idea of doing research with people, rather than on people. This chapter is an attempt to redress any imbalance, to provide straightforward practical guidance for the practice of co-operative inquiry, both for students and those professionally committed to research, and indeed for any group of people who want to understand better some aspect of their life and work, and who maybe want to find new ways of practice. It would be a shame if the essentially libertarian aims of co-operative inquiry became sunk underneath too many conceptual considerations.

Towards co-operative inquiry

The design for co-operative inquiry which I outlined in the Introduction is simple in concept, yet is a formidable challenge in practice. It is of course an ideal to which we can only approximate however hard we strive: even translating the simplest form of the model, with its iteration between action and reflection, into the complexity of interaction of a live inquiry group is difficult. When we consider also the inclusion of validity procedures such as those suggested in Chapter 2, the challenge may seem daunting. But more than this, the practice of co-operative inquiry requires skills which are in short supply in our world today – particularly the skills of working in genuine collaboration on a complex task with a group of peers; of managing the anxiety which arises as we genuinely examine our world and our practice; of paying critical attention to our experience as we act in our world. All these skills are important; the last calls for a subtle rigour of consciousness which is particularly unusual.

Thus the idea of co-operative inquiry starts with a paradox: the label implies equality and a democratic process in which we can all engage; yet it is not a causal and unstructured process, and to do it well demands intense commitment and subtle skill of those who would undertake it. These skills can only be learned through the doing: inquirers may already be able to work in democratic groups; they may be skilled practitioners in the area under scrutiny; they may have experience of other forms of inquiry; they may be competent conceptualizers; they may have developed exquisite attention. But the inquiry process brings all these (and more) together in a complex endeavour, and one which will place unique demands on the participants.

It is therefore helpful to regard co-operative inquiry as an essentially *emergent* process. You can't just *set up* a co-operative inquiry group, because co-operative processes have to be negotiated and re-learned by every group in every new instance. You may be able to establish a group in the spirit of collaboration, with the intent to become a 'full-blown' co-operative inquiry group. But there is nothing mechanical or automatic about whether this intent can be realized: that is up to the goodwill and hard work of the people involved. The establishment of authentic collaboration is one criterion of the validity of an inquiry (see Chapter 2); as we wrote when we originally reviewed our work on the holistic medical project:

> our judgment is that a first stage of genuine collaboration was achieved. That is to say we passed over that imaginary dividing line that separates an other-directed group from a self-directed group. Nevertheless there were clearly further degrees of collaboration which could have been achieved: there could have been a much more thoroughgoing internalisation of the research paradigm; there could have been greater participation in decision making, a less steep influence hierarchy, and a more even gender balance in the culture of the group . . .

> One conclusion from this is that the establishment of full collaboration in an enterprise of this kind would be a remarkable achievement given the educational, political, research, and professional conditions out of which people emerge in our society. (Heron and Reason, 1985, p. 105)

So my first invitation to those thinking of setting up a co-operative inquiry group is to trust yourself and get on with it. If your hearts are in the right place you will have an exciting time, and even if the process is at times stormy and difficult, it is most likely that you and your co-inquirers will learn a lot. In this chapter I have tried to provide some practical help and some examples, starting with considerations of how a project might be initiated, and working through the issues that may arise through its life until it is eventually wound up. But whatever I write can serve only as a guideline and hopefully inspiration; it cannot substitute for the inventiveness and application of the people actually involved.

Initiation

How does a co-operative inquiry start? How does an inquiry group get off the ground? Experience so far shows that such groups are usually initiated by one or two people who have an idea and passion for an inquiry project and wish to recruit others to join it. These initiators are the ones who in the first place identify the problem they wish to solve, or the issue they wish to explore. Often these initiators are committed both to the issue and to the method of inquiry. The challenge is, therefore, to set up a group which can work co-operatively, given that the initial ideas for content and process are owned by one or two people.

> P.J. Hawkins (1986) wanted to explore the effects of catharsis in psychotherapeutic work for his PhD dissertation. He writes that personal experience had led him to believe that catharsis is beneficial, and that he wanted to use co-operative inquiry because he was personally involved in the subject-matter and committed to this approach to research.

This kind of personal commitment is typical, and sets up the possibility of a tension between initiators and the group: if one person strongly wants to pursue a particular line, can they genuinely co-operate with a larger group of people? Obviously the answer is 'Yes', but the process may need some careful attention and management.

So it is a good idea at this stage to consider carefully questions such as, 'Who is this research *really* for?', and 'Is there a genuine possibility of a co-operative endeavour?' If there *is* an inquiry task around which a group of people can genuinely join to explore, then any problems of initiation, ownership, and power can be resolved through authentic negotiation and confrontation. But if there is no such possibility of a shared inquiry task, then the group will have been set up on a phoney basis, and the possibilities of co-operation remote.

Gill Robertson (1984) was interested in her own and other people's capacities for learning and development in their everyday lives, and in finding ways in which people could help themselves with their everyday choices and possibilities. She was in the middle of a major life change herself. To explore this she invited people to join inquiry groups that would help them explore and better understand their experience of change in their everyday lives.

Gron Davies (1986), a senior lecturer at a college of higher education, wanted to explore student experiences of that college. In doing this he was academically motivated to explore contradictions between new and old paradigm thinking, and by his own feelings of alienation in his work. He invited students to join inquiry groups, facilitated by himself, which would explore these experiences.

In Robertson's inquiry groups there was a good match between her experience and interests and those of the groups she set up, and thus they had the potential of success from the beginning. On the other hand, I believe there was a fundamental mismatch between Davies's position on the staff of the college and the students' position, and in his existential and theoretical concerns and theirs. This contributed to a difficult and alienated group experience:

> I wanted the group to 'do things' and they wouldn't....I talked a great deal....I wanted them to produce a form of data I could capture and record. As I became more anxious about 'my' data I talked more and became frustrated by the long shuffling silences I met....(Davies, 1986, p. 82)

The important point here is to be sure that the project the initiator wants to do is one that makes sense to potential group members; and to be careful that any differences in power or status deriving from organizational or social position do not make it impossible to negotiate an open contract. Davies was not able to conduct successful co-operative inquiry, in my view, because his relationship with students in his college made it impossible to negotiate a clear and unambiguous contract.

These kinds of questions can be well explored with help from someone not too closely involved – a research supervisor if the research is part of a degree, or a colleague or friend who is prepared to probe and challenge, to help the initiators get clear about what they want and what may be negotiable.

Finding a group

It may be that the research group comes together quite naturally as a development of some other kind of activity. But more likely the initiators, once some of these early questions have been explored, need to find a way to recruit and form an inquiry group. There are two basic strategies – to work with an existing group, or to advertise and set up a group for the purpose of the inquiry project.

One difficulty in working with an existing group may be that they already have their business together, and that this takes up all the time they have available for their activity together; and there may be different views as to how relevant an inquiry is for the group in relation to other activities. If this is the case, time may be given to the inquiry only grudgingly and inadequately. Another problem will be their history and existing group dynamics, which the initiator will need to find time to understand. On the other hand, a ready-formed group does offer the obvious advantages: it is there and may be ready to work. As a rule of thumb, an existing group is likely to be a good co-operative inquiry group only if members are already looking for a way to solve a current problem in their life and work, and if co-operative inquiry appears to be an appropriate strategy to explore this problem. Certainly, if an existing group is chosen for the work, much care should be taken in exploring issues of ownership and commitment.

> Peter Hawkins, in describing his reasons for wishing to work with a particular Centre, points out that its members were interested in having him work with them. They sensed that the Centre was going through changes and that there were questions of direction and of organizational and personal relationship.
>
> Having met initially with a small group of members, he visited the Centre and explored with all current members how they could jointly engage in the research. He then wrote up the outcome of this discussion, and they agreed to proceed. (See Hawkins, P., 1986, pp. 211–12)

A new inquiry group can be set up through some form of advertising with a likely population:

> For the co-counselling projects (Heron and Reason, 1981, 1982) the initiators wrote to members of local co-counselling communities outlining the proposed topic and method for the inquiry and inviting interested people to join.

> For his study of catharsis, P.J. Hawkins invited psychology students at the college where he worked to a meeting to discuss the project.

Robertson advertised her study of life changes through her network
of acquaintances, through discussion in pubs and bars, and was able
to get a small feature describing the project in a local paper.

Contracting

Once a group has been established, or more likely once a group of people
have expressed a degree of interest, it is really important to explore carefully the different expectations people bring to it, and to work out whether
there is a sensible basis for working together. It is usually worthwhile
holding one or two initial meetings at which people can discuss the project,
have some influence on its design, and decide whether or not to join.
Joining an inquiry group may involve a lot of commitment of time, energy,
and maybe money. People will come with different ideas, hopes and fears,
and they need to know what they are letting themselves in for. Also, the
co-operative inquiry method, as a way of doing research, is not well
known. People expect, when asked to help with some research, that they
will simply have to answer some questions, or take a test, and that is the
end of it. So is is important that people understand the method and know
what they are letting themselves in for.

All the inquiries reported in this book offer evidence of their concern
for clear contracting. One way to facilitate this stage is to design and
organize an introductory workshop, which might proceed something as
follows:

1   Welcome. People are helped to feel at home. Some sharing of names
    and some kind of 'icebreaking' activities may help, depending on the
    subculture of the group.
2   People in pairs or trios to 'talk and listen' with equal time for each
    person, responding to a question such as, 'How I got to know about
    this project and what interests me about it.' This helps to get potential
    participants talking before the initiators. You may choose some short
    sharing of the pairs discussion, but I would suggest keeping this
    brief.
3   One initiator explains the thinking that has gone into the activity so
    far: the whys and wherefores of proposing the project, and what is
    likely to be expected of people who join. This is followed by questions
    and discussions about the topic. This activity may get as far as sketching
    out some of the questions which need to be addressed in the project,
    all of which can be profitably recorded on blackboard or flipchart.
4   One initiator explains briefly the ideas behind the co-operative inquiry
    method, and suggests how the group might proceed. It is important
    to point out both the logic of the method – all involved working as
    both researchers and subjects, going through a number of cycles, etc;

and to emphasize the personal involvement in the inquiry and the demands of this – the importance of shared power and responsibility, the possibility that people may get upset as their pet ideas get tested, that there may be conflict in the group to work with, and so on. I believe that inquiry members should be asked to contract into some kind of interpersonal and emotional work to keep the inquiry process relatively sweet (see for example Chapter 5).

Again, these ideas can be discussed and explored. It may be helpful to have people form small groups to air their reactions before holding a group discussion. This section can be expanded, if there is time, to include some kind of experience of co-operative inquiry. I have invited seminar groups to inquire into their capacity to use a pendulum for dowsing as a demonstration inquiry – this is a suitable topic because it is relatively compact and so can be undertaken in one place, and also because a group can go through several inquiry cycles in a relatively short period; it can also get people quite excited and worked up so they can see the personal involvement in the process.

5   These introductory discussions will lead into consideration of practical details – who wants to be involved? how much time, money and commitment will it take? when and where shall we meet? do we need to actively invite other people to join? what are criteria for membership of the group? will people take particular roles in the project, and how will these be negotiated? and so on. If the session has been set up so that people have plenty of time to express their views and be heard, there is no need at this stage to worry about the creativity needed – there will be lots of ideas. It may be necessary to set up a second meeting of those intending to join the project to sort out the details.

6   Summary of decisions. It is really important to be clear at the end of the session as to what has been decided and what next steps have been agreed.

7   Closing. An opportunity for people to say how they feel about the session, whether they are intending to continue with the project or not. A useful form is a round of 'resentments' – 'I was annoyed that some people had more to say than others'; 'I think this is a really interesting project and I am fed up that I can't take part' and so on; followed by a round of 'appreciations' – 'I really liked the care you took to explain all this to us'; 'I am looking forward to working on this with you all'; and so on.

At this contracting stage there is an important tension to manage. If the initiators are already very clear about what they want to do and how they want to do it, there will be little room for negotiation. As a consequence the group will not, at this important formative stage, be able to have much influence on method or on objectives, and it is unlikely that a genuinely co-operative climate will flourish: the group will either form in a dependency mode, doing the inquiry *for* the initiators; or will be resistant and argumentative; or will simply not get off the ground at all. On the other hand, if the initiators are completely open and flexible the forming group will have nothing to get its teeth into at this early tentative stage, and so may flounder around in ambiguity and confusion. A third possibility, if the initiators are too vague about their proposals, is that the group will take over and formulate an inquiry project completely different from the wishes of the initiators, who are then left having done a lot of work but not having their own needs met.

My recommendation is for a combination of clarity and flexibility. The attitude of the initiators should be: 'This is our idea about what we want to look at together. This is an outline of co-operative inquiry. Let's talk about all this and see if we have a basis for co-operation.' They should answer questions openly and straightforwardly, and give people a genuine opportunity to choose whether to get involved or not.

P.J. Hawkins (1986) describes the preliminary meetings for his second inquiry as follows:

> 26 students attended this meeting. Although this was quite a large number I decided to ask everyone to say who they were, and to very briefly state why they had come along. Responses included, 'I wanted something practical from the course, and this seems to be the only way to get it'; 'The chance of doing a co-counselling training course for nothing'; 'Being involved in a research inquiry'; 'I know someone who was a member of the first research group, and they seemed to enjoy it and get something out of it'; 'Just to find out what is involved'; 'To help me sort out some of my own personal problems'. In other words, those present were there for a whole range of individual reasons. I also introduced myself, and declared my interest in the research inquiry. I also declared my 'ideological bias' towards humanistic psychology and its attendant strategems for change, and experientially-oriented methodology.
>
> Having completed the introductions, I briefly described the first research inquiry, including the theoretical rationale, the methodological procedures, the results, and the tentative conclusions. Before proceeding to introduce the proposed second research inquiry, a short discussion occurred.... I was asked to elaborate, and justify, the new paradigm experiential method. There was at this stage a certain atmosphere of 'suspiciousness' of such approaches....
>
> I then presented my general thoughts about a second research inquiry, emphasizing that they were not definitive, and that those who chose to participate would be fully involved in early discussions about the content of the research. It was agreed, however, that a co-counselling training course would be run on two consecutive weekends, and that attendance at these would be necessary for further involvement in the research project. (P.J. Hawkins, 1986, pp. 191–92)

In this project, of the 26 who attended this introductory meeting, 18 completed the co-counselling training, and 13 subsequently joined the inquiry group.

While clear contracting with the inquiry group is a first essential, it may also be important to pay attention to contracting with key members of institutions within which the inquiry is to take place. Even with the holistic medicine project (Chapter 5) whose members were self-employed and presumably self-responsible professionals, the inquiry activities brought about conflict and change within both personal and professional partnerships to a degree we had (maybe naively) not anticipated. For other projects the institutional context is more acute:

> Hilary Traylen's initiative to set up an inquiry group of health visitors in her district of the British National Health Service raised several issues with her colleagues who were managers of potential group members. While many welcomed the inquiry, it was seen by some as a potential threat and carried the implication that they were out of touch with the needs and views of their staff. This response was both surprising and alarming to Hilary, who was primarily keen and excited to get on with her venture. She was forced, with some reluctance, to explore these issues and to negotiate and contract more clearly and openly with managerial staff. (See Traylen, in preparation)

Devising an overall research plan

Once a group of people have agreed to work together as a co-operative inquiry group they need to agree some basic outline of their working arrangements. Co-operative inquiry is not an unstructured process, but involves a rigorous iteration between action in the world and reflection. The basic outline of this iteration usually needs to be worked out fairly early on: it is most important, at this stage, to arrange the project so that several stages of action and reflection can be undertaken.

Inevitably this involves some pragmatic guesswork in arriving at an appropriate balance between action and reflection. If the topic involves some kind of action in the outside world – some kind of social or organizational change project, for example, then the group will need to arrange a series of meetings for reflection interspersed with periods of action (Chapters 5 and 10 provide examples of this). If, on the other hand, the inquiry is more introspective, for example into experiences of the self or states of consciousness, it may be more appropriate to organize an extended meeting or series of meetings at which time can be taken to practise the disciplines involved (see, for example, Chapter 9). If those involved are busy people, as is so often the case, then the project needs to be organized in a practical way to fit in with their other concerns.

Roles

Just because we are setting up a co-operative inquiry group does not mean that all those involved participate in identical ways. An inquiry is a pluralistic endeavour, in which different people with different skills and interests come together to collaborate. Usually all members will share skills and interest in the actual topic of the inquiry, although some may be more skilled and experienced than others. But there are other important skills needed to help the inquiry run successfully, which are not universally shared. Some of these, such as administrative and organizing skills, do not need particular exploration here. However, facilitating roles are of particular importance. For example, some members may be skilled at facilitating the development of a co-operative group, others may have clarity about the co-operative inquiry model, and some may have skills in facilitating personal distress management. What is important is that these differential roles are recognized and negotiated in the first instance, and that opportunities are provided for re-negotiation as the project proceeds.

Group facilitation
An exceptionally sophisticated group may work in a completely leaderless fashion (see, for example, the television programme which showed an inquiry into reactions to the threat of nuclear war, Postle, 1983); this may be particularly true if they all have some experience of co-operative group working, or if they are a successfully established co-operative group.

However, it is more likely that the group will need some democratic leadership which is both facilitative and educative – facilitative in the sense of offering structures and processes which may help the group in its work; educative in teaching members about effective group working. A number of books are available which offer guides for such facilitation (Ernst and Goodison, 1981; Randall and Southgate, 1980; Donnan and Lenton 1985; Heron 1977a, 1986), and many institutions offer short courses in group facilitation (for example, the Human Potential Research Project at the University of Surrey).

Most theories of group development suggest that a successful co-operative group goes through three primary stages in its life. During the first stage there is a need for the group to come together, to nurture and help individual members feel that they are safe and that they have a place in the group. If this does not happen people will feel isolated and anxious, and they are unlikely to be able to contribute creatively to the life of the group. Leadership at this stage needs to attend to these inclusion needs of members by offering ways in which people can get to know each other and feel comfortable with each other, and can get some measure of clear agreement about the nature of the task they have joined to undertake. All the suggestions I have made about contracting are in one sense to do with inclusion needs.

Once these early inclusion needs are adequately satisfied, the group is able to move into a more energetic phase of actually working on the inquiry task. As this happens there will probably be more differences of opinion, and the group may develop opposing cliques or sub-groupings. The atmosphere is likely to be more argumentative, and group members may struggle for control of the group and its task. If the initial inclusion work of the first stage has been well enough completed, these disagreements will not threaten the life of the group, but rather provide energy and excitement. The facilitation task is to allow and encourage the expression of different opinions, to help people listen to each other, give and receive negative and positive feedback, and to help the group find ways of working which include these diverse perspectives. It was for these purposes that we held regular encounter group sessions during the Holistic Medicine Project.

The successful completion of this second phase, which is about control, can then open the way to a more fully co-operative relationship. If the arguing and the power struggles have been engaged with wholeheartedly, the cliques may then be able to give way to a more open network of affectionate relationships, in which each individual has a unique place and is seen as making a unique contribution to the group. The group is able to engage in a mature way with its task, using fully the contribution of each member. Facilitation of the group and its task becomes more fully shared, so there is less need for a normal facilitation role (Srivastva *et al.*, 1977).

Distress facilitation

Co-operative inquiry is an exciting business; it can also be an upsetting business. It is my experience that research which is genuinely co-operative and which authentically challenges the way those involved conduct their lives raises all kinds of emotional issues which are ignored or denied by conventional research doctrine. It is an essential aspect of co-operative inquiry that these emotional issues are addressed.

Emotional distress arises in several ways. It can be the restimulation of old emotional hurts that have their roots in childhood experiences, as John Heron points out in Chapter 2. It can be that the learning and new understandings emerging in the inquiry process are challenging members to make new choices and take new risks in their lives, so that they have to turn away from old and comfortable ways of doing things and move in new domains. It can be that the very business of collaboration with others confronts people with restrictions and distortions in their behaviour and feelings in ways that they cannot ignore. Some illustrations of these kinds of disturbance can be seen in Part Two of this book, and also in our discussion of research as personal process (Reason and Marshall, 1987).

Gill Robertson writes in the closing chapter of her thesis

> Now, in retrospect, five years on and in the wake of inquiry, I am aware of a hidden agenda coming to light, and painfully so at times. Now I see that my own agenda was idealistic, and one with the object of avoidance; with hope that in throwing myself into the inquiry I would be able to avoid what was

going on in my life outside the research. I found of course that this could not be so! Not only did I find the processes of inquiry revealing to me some of my values and characteristics, limitations and abilities. Conducting the inquiry taught me also some unwelcome truths or realities that I did not particularly want to face up to. (p. 274)

I learned that I myself had a deep seated need to keep going cheerfully, and was fearful of falling into the depths of distress myself. I realised that there was a great deal in my life that I was unhappy about, that I had developed a philosophy of keeping going at all costs, not letting the distressing experiences catch up. Exactly what I was unhappy about did not really surface until later in the day. (1984, p. 278; see also Robertson, 1987)

Gill writes that she 'learned to face up to the complexities and conflicts' in her life. The inquiry process can be a vehicle for this kind of deep personal learning if we allow it. But more than this, unless the co-researchers develop some degree of critical subjectivity, so that underlying conflicts and distresses are acknowledged and worked with, they will muddy the waters of the inquiry so they cannot see their truths clearly.

Skills at working with emotional distress are not very widely available in our culture. We are more likely to close down, deny or otherwise defend ourselves against distressing feelings, than we are to bring them to awareness, work with them, abreact and understand them, and allow ourselves to move beyond them. It is therefore a clear advantage if an inquiry group has available to it a degree of emotional competence so that personal distress can be appropriately managed.

One way to do this, and probably the most satisfactory, is to compose a group in which every member is competent in some form of personal growth process such as co-counselling (Heron, 1977b, 1979), so that members can explore their psychological states and discharge any distress both at regular times within the inquiry, and when distress comes welling up unexpected. However, to adopt this as a rule for inquiry members would exclude most people from participation.

An alternative is to have, as a member of the group, one or more persons prepared to facilitate the psychological work of other group members. They might be counsellors or personal growth facilitators, and their role would be to lead sessions for exploration of personal distress, both facilitating directly and offering structures for members to work in smaller groups.

At a miminum the inquiry group needs to establish a culture in which the exploration of distress is accepted as appropriate, in which people can express feelings of anger, grief, fear, and so on when these arise, and be supported in so doing. It is important that the group allocates time to consider seriously questions such as, 'How am I being upset by this inquiry' – maybe initially in 'talk and listen' pairs – and that the impact of such distress on the inquiry group is taken seriously. A lot can be accomplished if people learn to listen to each other fully.

Hilary Traylen, who as I write this is right in the middle of a co-operative inquiry, has pointed out that the reverse side of the anxiety that may arise in doing co-operative research is the joy and sense of breakthrough when new practice is achieved. The example she suggests is from her own research with health visitors in the British National Health Service. The group had come to the conclusion that in order to improve their practice they needed to find ways of being more open with their clients about difficult issues such as child abuse, incest, drug-taking – the kind of intimate things that may go on in families without anyone ever feeling able to discuss them. The decision to be more open raised all manner of anxieties within the group, and Hilary herself, as the initiator of the research, was frightened by what might happen, and 'so worried that I telephoned each member and shared my concern'.

At the next meeting the group shared their experiences. The following is one example

> I was really spent by four o'clock...and one of my priority families came into the clinic. I thought I just don't want to see this lady. So I avoided her because I really couldn't cope. But she heard my voice and had me out...and burst into tears on me....So I went round [to her house] and was there for two hours, and it was the best two hours I have ever spent with them.
>
> The first thing I said when I walked in (because my temper was short) was, 'I have nothing to offer you, I am here to listen. I can give you no money. The only support I can give you is for the next hour.' I put a time limit on it. I was really very very cross and they could see I was. So they made me a cup of tea and made me sit down and they just talked to me for two hours. They were so *honest* because I had been very honest with them. It was *great*. It *really worked*....My honesty just produced a lot of honesty in them. We had no hidden agendas....We just talked all about child abuse and wife battering and his illegal drugs and how many time he breaks into the meter and it was just *incredible*...it has been a *great relief* and it's really *reduced my stress*. But my main thought when she came into the clinic was, 'I cannot cope with them because my stress would be too high.' So it was very very useful.

As Hilary reflects on the session,

> the personal accounts were full of life and energy almost effervescent, it gave everyone a tremendous feeling of confidence....There was general acknowledgement that these experiences were helping them to feel stronger and more confident, not only with their clients but in their personal lives too....I think this was probably due to the group focussing on an aspect of their practice which they were particularly anxious about....(Traylen, personal communication, 1988)

Inquiry facilitation

It is of enormous help if someone or some sub-group keeps an eye on the inquiry process and helps the group develop some clarity about where it is within that process. It may be particularly important to help the group clarify its movements between reflection and action, and also to help it develop and review its validity procedures.

This may be quite simply done by proposing activities in a consultative manner. For example, early interventions might be

'I suggest we spend some time getting clear about what exactly it is we want to look at.'

'We have spent quite a time developing our ideas about this, can we move on now to see how we might put these into practice and record what happens.'

At a second meeting, following time allowing the group to reform and rebond,

'Let's take the next hour to have a look at our experience over the past few weeks.'

And maybe later

'I think we need to spend some time discussing whether we should focus our inquiry on X, or whether we want to keep looking at Y as well.'

On the other hand, the inquiry facilitation may be more complex. It may be necessary to point to some methodological or epistemological issue and invite the group to consider how to manage it. To do this the inquiry facilitator might offer a short lecture and lead a subsequent discussion. For example, in the holistic medicine project, in the third cycle of inquiry the initiators offered a review of validity issues, focusing in particular on issues of convergent and divergent inquiry (see Chapter 2). In the subsequent discussion the inquiry group, clearly (but hopefully authentically) influenced by this intervention, chose to focus the inquiry on power and spirituality in medical consultations, and formed two sub-groups for this purpose (see Chapter 5).

In one enquiry I planned, but which did not actually take place, I intended to offer two facilitators for the group, one of whom would primarily attend to the group process, helping group members work together authentically, while the other would pay attention to the inquiry process. I think this model has a lot to recommend it because it honours the needs of both aspects of the inquiry.

Of course, if the facilitators get stuck in their role as facilitators, then they will no longer be participating members of the inquiry group, and this may be regarded as a problem. There seem to be two possible ways out of this. This first is to accept that the facilitators are facilitators and just that; that their contribution to the content of the inquiry may be minimal (indeed they may not actually count themselves as full members of the inquiry group), but that their contribution is nevertheless important and maybe essential. A second possibility, more in keeping with the ideals of the co-operative inquiry model, is for the facilitators to aim to work themselves out of a job. In other words their role is to bring the group together, to facilitate its development, educate members in effective group work, and at an appropriate stage pass the facilitation over to group members and to become ordinary group members themselves. Again, this is easier to say than to do.

In the holistic medicine inquiry, the roles of the initiating facilitators were not explicitly negotiated. While we took an active part as facilitators in the early stages, by the third cycle it was accepted that the management of business, the 'chairing' of the group, should be rotated among members, and we took a lower profile role, regarding ourselves more as group members. However, we implicitly retained much of our power as experts in co-operative inquiry and as skilled facilitators of group and personal process.

Toward the end of the inquiry we were severely criticized by some group members because of this ambiguity of role. It was argued that the inquiry would have been more orderly and thus more successful if we had kept a higher and more consistent facilitator profile.

In retrospect my own view is that we failed to negotiate and re-negotiate our roles clearly enough, and that the confusion did not help the group work either authentically or efficiently.

The progress of the inquiry

Formally, a co-operative inquiry can be seen as going through a series of logical steps from identifying the questions or issues to be researched, developing a more or less explicit model of practice, putting this model into practice and recording what happens, reflecting on this experience and making sense of the whole venture. These logical steps run alongside the group and emotional processes so that there is an integration of systematic inquiry with human interpersonal and emotional development. It is this that makes the whole venture a truly human inquiry and makes co-operative inquiry uniquely different from other forms of research.

Formulating a model for research
The first logical step in the inquiry process is for the group to get clear what it is inquiring into. This involves adopting or developing some kind

of a conceptual map or model – not necessarily a very complex or formal affair – which assists understanding of the area in question, and illuminates choices for action. The main point of the model is to help in deciding what questions are to be asked and what experimental actions are to be taken.

The inquiry into catharsis in human development started by adopting a model already developed (Heron, 1977b); the group also had as a starting point the suggestions of the first inquiry group.

> I then presented the suggestions that had been made by the first research group. . . . There was, of course, an assumption on my part that the focus of the project would be the same as the first inquiry, namely into the *effects* of catharsis. We considered each proposal in turn, and initially made a decision to retain or eliminate it (in retrospect I was aware of the strong influence I had on the decision-making process). . . . After some discussion we agreed to research the following area:
>
>> what are the psychological and somatic consequences of emotionally discharging (through catharsis) my distressed feelings? (P.J. Hawkins, 1986, pp. 193–4)

The group continued to agree on a number of detailed procedures to explore this question.

Putting the model into practice
Since the whole point of the inquiry process is to move between, and systematically contrast, reflection and experience, once the model and the questions are as clear as is felt appropriate, the group must develop ways of applying the model in practice and recording its experience.

> The holistic medicine inquiry group spent a session brainstorming ways of applying the five-part model of holistic medicine in the surgery. Long lists of possibilities, some practical and some outrageous, were developed. A similar time was spent developing ideas for recording experiences (see Chapter 5).

This is a time for creative thinking and practical support. If the inquiry is into innovative practice in some field, it will be important for the group to find ways of thinking past the limitations of current practice towards the truly creative. This will be experienced as more or less risky by group members, and some may need the support and encouragement of their colleagues.

It is helpful to have group members make some form of contract with their colleagues: this may be either idiosyncratic, in that each member makes their own decisions about how to apply the model in their lives; or it may be a collective decision to all pursue the same line of inquiry. It is the experimental action defined in these contracts that forms the practical basis of the inquiry.

There are many ways of recording the experience of applying the model. The most obvious is to keep a diary of events and experiences, but there are other possibilities, for example:

1   Making audio/video recordings for later discussion with group members.
2   Visiting other group members and watching them in their new practice and giving feedback.
3   Telling stories to other group members (see Chapter 4).
4   Using questionnaires (either co-operatively designed or borrowed from established sources) to explore aspects of experience systematically.
5   Keeping precise measures where appropriate (the catharsis study measured blood pressure systematically; and the doctors at one stage kept record of prescription rates).
6   Mutual interviewing.
7   Recording dreams or 'stream of consciousness' material, making drawings, and other expressive works. These may tap unconscious aspects of experience.

And so on.

Reflecting on experiences and making sense
After each period of application, and finally at the end of the inquiry, the group needs to take some time to make sense of its experiences and formulate its learning. Typically, a lot of experience of the matter at hand has been gathered, but its form may be confusing, and the group will probably want to find some way to pull all this disparate experience together into a coherent statement.

It is also likely that individual members of the group will have formulated their own theories during the course of their investigations; or that individual members will be committed to particular explanations and theories. What is needed is some systematic comparison of experience with theory. One way to do this is to charge one or more persons with the task of going through the experiences and making sense of them:

In an inquiry into learning in a therapeutic community Peter Hawkins (1986) gathered experiences from an inquiry group of community members and spent time sorting them into a model of members' learning. He took this to a subsequent meeting of the group and invited them to systematically criticize it, and to make sure that their own experiences were represented in the map.

Lyn Goswell (in preparation), exploring the experiences of Western Buddhist monks and nuns, through discussion agreed with them a set of relevant questions, and then interviewed them on the basis of these questions. She transcribed each interview and returned it to the person concerned, asking them to agree its accuracy and to make any additional points. She then sorted the interview material into categories using a grounded theory approach (Glaser and Strauss, 1967), and evolved a descriptive model of their experience. She took this to meetings of the monks and nuns to explore its accuracy. Their response was validating in two ways: first, they agreed that the model appeared to be a reasonable map of their own experiences; second they pointed out that the major categories Lyn had identified explaining why people turned to meditation were exactly the same as the Buddha had pointed to 2500 years ago!

Another option is for the group to stick together and work collectively on members' experiences, sorting them and discussing them until an acceptable agreement is reached. In the catharsis study

> Four of the group felt that it would be appropriate if I [P.J. Hawkins] took away all the information, collated it, and prepared summary statements with respect to the group findings. The other five members (including myself), on the other hand felt that this was unacceptable given the methodological premises of the research project. We felt it would be more appropriate for us to have another group meeting where we would sift through all the individual summary statements in order to generate a 'summary of the findings of the group....'
> Each person read out their summary statement with respect to their own experiential and somatic data.... Their findings were written down on a flip pad, and then an attempt was made to collate the data in a systematic way. The findings were delineated into a number of headings representing the major aspects of the research.... All the statements were worked through, removing redundant material, clarifying ambiguous statements, refining others and so on, until the statements remaining were seen to be representative of the whole group. (P.J. Hawkins, 1986, pp. 206–7)

The first co-counselling inquiry group (Heron and Reason, 1981), spent its final two-day session systematically going through its findings and developing agreement among members. The conceptual outcome of the project was maps of human consciousness as experienced through co-counselling. A number of such maps had been tentatively put forward during the project.

> To refine the maps, we first of all drew them all out on a large piece of paper on the floor in the middle of the room. (On the first weekend we used a chart pad on the wall, which meant that anyone who wanted to write something had to get up and talk down to the group; from the second session we worked on a pad on the floor, which was much more relaxed and collaborative. Among other things it meant that several people could contribute to the same drawing.) We then went over each map in turn, comparing it to our experience of counselling, criticising it, categorising it, discussing its uses and limitations, until we were clear about what it represented, and had modified and developed it to

accommodate criticisms made. Thus all the maps of experience described in this paper were derived and refined through a collaborative process. (Heron and Reason, 1981, p. 20)

There are many methods that an inquiry group can adopt for the making-sense process. Some of these can be borrowed from traditional qualitative inquiry methods: Diesing (1972), Glaser and Strauss (1967), Glaser (1978), and Lincoln and Guba (1985) are my personal favourites. Contributions within the spirit of co-operative inquiry can be found in Rowan and Reason (1981) and Reason (1988), and Judi Marshall's (1981) personal account is invaluable. Reduced to bare essentials these methods involve 'chunking and sorting': discovering categories within the experience – 'chunks of meaning' as Judi Marshall calls them – and sorting these into categories which form the basis of descriptive theory (Bell and Hardiman, 1988).

However, these methods were designed for individual researchers working unilaterally. An inquiry group has the enormous advantage of being a *group*, and so having much more potential life and energy. It is partly because of this that we have developed methods such as psychodrama and storytelling as inquiry methods. Making sense of experience (data analysis is the more traditional term for this!) becomes much more fun and much more creative if co-researchers can tell the story of their experience to each other, or 'become' psychodramatically different categories of an emerging theory, so that the research experience can be understood as it is re-enacted. Our approaches to these methods are described in more detail in Chapters 3 and 4, and we invite interested readers to borrow, adapt, and more importantly to 'invent your own'.

Fundamentally, the making-sense process requires time, energy, patience, and resources. It helps to have plenty of space, lots of large sheets of paper and coloured pens, and a willingness to experiment. The group needs to develop a tolerance for the irritation that comes from thinking too much, and to keep a careful eye out for when members are getting exhausted with the process, and a change of activity is called for to help people relax. The work of systematically making sense appears to be potentially very upsetting for people who consider themselves inarticulate and incompetent conceptually. The conceptualizing work of the co-counselling research project is a good example of this:

> As the proposal [to spend the time conceptualizing] was considered, two members of the group protested their dissatisfaction with the project so far: they were distressed at their inability to conceptualise and communicate with the rest of the group, felt that they didn't understand what the mapping was all about, or the point of it. . . .
>
> After lunch we agreed, having dealt to a great extent with the restimulated distress, so slog through refining the maps, with the ground rule that anyone who felt tired or overwhelmed should say so, and do whatever they needed to take care of themselves. (Heron and Reason, 1981, pp. 18–19)

In view of this difficulty it is important to remember that the outcomes of co-operative inquiry are *not* limited to propositional statements: the validating experiences and competencies of participants are also forms of knowing (experiential and practical knowing), and the findings of an inquiry may be expressed in poetry, drama, and art as well as (or instead of) propositional statements. All these forms and expressions of knowing have their own validity. It may be that inquiry groups are liable to systematic domination at the stage of making sense by those with academic competences to justify and academic careers to follow; if this is true, then other forms of making sense need to be explored and developed.

Designing subsequent cycles

The stage of making sense may occur several times in an inquiry project as the group cycles between action and experience. At intermediate stages the group needs to follow its making-sense activity by exploring questions about what to look at next. Often, when we stand back to make sense of our experience, we are left satisfied with some of our discoveries and concerned by what we still do not know. We may even feel overwhelmed by the enormity of our ignorance – an experience which may be no bad thing if it brings with it a sense of humility and an acknowledgement of the mystery of life that always lies behind our knowledge (Reason, 1988).

We may need to explore and acknowledge such feelings. But once we have done so it is likely that the next steps will be obvious, they will emerge as new and interesting tasks with which to engage. If this does not happen, it may be because some problem in the process of the group is impeding progress: some interpersonal conflict is unresolved; the inquiry experience is bringing up distress which is unacknowledged and not attended to; the making-sense process has been incomplete and unsatisfying; and so on. It is at the point of such difficulties that those members of the inquiry with particular process skills need to be alert and ready to help bring to light those issues that are being overlooked.

Validity procedures

The issue of validity in inquiry is not simply an academic issue but is intensely practical. In exploring questions of validity an inquiry group is looking at the *soundness* of its endeavours and exploring questions such as 'Are we in any way deceiving ourselves in our claims and in our practice?'

John Heron, in Chapter 2, gives one view of validity within a co-operative inquiry group. John Rowan (1981) offers another set of questions. I suggest these are useful starting points for the group to develop its own view of validity, and that some time into the inquiry it is worth taking a longish session to explore questions such as 'What is valid knowing for us in this group?'

and 'How do statements like those of Heron and Rowan help us establish our own criteria and procedures?' Some groups resist this kind of more abstract thinking; others seize upon it and are in danger of sinking into epistemological speculation, never to return to practical inquiry. As Bateson (1972) points out, the most important task for our age is to learn to think in new ways, and some time spent on practical epistemology is worthwhile.

It is particularly worthwhile if the outcome of these discussions can be some set of agreed criteria for validity, expressed by the group in its own terms, and some set of procedures for assessing the performance of the group against these criteria. It is important for the group not to try to be perfect – either by its own standards, or by some academic standards it feels it should live up to. It is not possible to pay full attention to more than five or six validity criteria in any one project, but this is sufficient if they are appropriately chosen.

Once the group has chosen some validity procedures it can apply these systematically at each cycle of inquiry, and in particular at the end. Examples of this process can be seen in the holistic medicine project (Chapter 5) and in the altered states of consciousness project (Chapter 9).

Writing

Presumably co-operative inquiry leads to co-operative reporting, and so the writing of any report should be a shared business. My own experience is that trying to write a report with a group of people is a terrible pain: I can manage on my own or with one or two good colleagues, but more than that is not realistic. There are several solutions, the obvious one being that a (very) small sub-group is deputed to write a report (the form of which may usefully have been agreed in outline by the whole inquiry group) which is then discussed by the whole group in draft form or circulated to them for comment. This was the procedure adopted by the co-counselling inquiry group.

Another solution is for the group to agree that any member can write whatever they like, but that they must clearly indicate the status of the writing, and who has been involved. Thus an article might be labelled 'The findings reported here are the product of the XYZ inquiry group. A draft of this report was circulated to all members and their suggested amendments incorporated as far as possible. The author takes full responsibility for what is written here'; or whatever, as the case may be.

Of course if the inquiry is set up as a part of someone's Master's or Doctoral research, the situation is rather different, because we are confronted with an ideological clash between the normal university requirement for such research to be the candidates's original work, and the ideals of the co-operative paradigm. In practice this problem is surmountable, usually because the student can be seen as the 'primary researcher', and can write their view of the project in some form of consultation with members of the group.

It is worth repeating that writing is not the only outcome of co-operative inquiry. We also talk about it, formally and informally and, as has been pointed out, if successful it informs our practice in our world. For example, apart from changing their medical practice, several of the doctors involved in the holistic medicine inquiry used their experience in lectures and discussion with colleagues and with medical students.

Supervision

Having worked with peer learning communities of several sorts, and discussed inquiry projects with colleagues and students, I am impressed with the importance of having someone to talk to about the work who is interested, experienced, yet not too heavily involved and attached to it. I love Torbert's emphasis (1976) on the importance of having friends prepared to act as enemies.

My suggestion is that long-term inquiry groups, or at least the initiators and facilitators of such groups, should negotiate relationships of supervision with people who have some experience, preferably of co-operative inquiry, certainly of experiential learning and group processes. The issues discussed in this chapter might represent an initial agenda for such supervision discussions, and a useful discussion of supervision in a variety of social enterprises is contained in Shohet and Hawkins (in preparation). In several of the inquiries reported in Part Two of this volume such a supervisory relationship was successfully established.

Endings

Maybe the most difficult part of an intensive group experience – and inquiry groups can be very intensive – is wrapping the business up and saying goodbye. Inevitably some will leave pleased and stimulated by the work while others will be dissatisfied; some will have made lifelong friendships, others may be lonely and hurt. The hopes and aspirations of the beginning have to meet the realities of achievement.

Time must be taken here to acknowledge all the experiences of the members of the group; for members to express their delights and their resentments, and maybe their hopes for the future. And if the group has been any kind of a success, its explorations will live on, not only in dissertations and papers, but also in the lives and work of its members.

2

Validity in Co-operative Inquiry

John Heron

Co-operative inquiry is a new paradigm for research on persons which breaks down the traditional distinction between the role of the researcher and the role of the subject. In the old paradigm only the researchers do the thinking that generates, designs, manages and draws conclusions from the research; and only the subjects – often knowing nothing of what the researchers are up to in their thinking – are involved in the action and experience which the research is about. In the new paradigm this separation of roles is dissolved. Those doing the research as co-researchers are also involved as co-subjects. The same persons devise, manage and draw conclusions from, the research; and also undergo the experiences and perform the actions that are being researched.

A more detailed analysis of and rationale for this paradigm is given in Reason and Rowan (1981a), and in Heron (1971, 1981a,b). Examples of co-operative inquiry in action are given in Heron and Reason (1981, 1982, 1985), Heron (1984), and later in this book. The purpose of this chapter is to deal more thoroughly than previous publications with issues of validity in co-operative inquiry. It is a complete revision and restatement of an earlier paper of mine (Heron, 1982). And for an important initial statement in this field, see Reason and Rowan (1981b).

There are four basic questions I want to consider. Firstly, what does the term 'validity' mean when I talk about the validity of the conclusions of a co-operative inquiry? Secondly, what are the criteria for determining whether such conclusions are valid? Thirdly, what procedures can we adopt during the inquiry in order systematically to apply such criteria? And fourthly, what special skill is central to the use of these procedures?

The meaning of validity

What I mean when I say that the conclusions of a co-operative inquiry are valid is – in accord with standard usage – that they have 'the quality of being well-founded' (*Shorter Oxford English Dictionary*). And what these conclusions are well-founded on are the experiences of the co-researchers as co-subjects. But what does it mean to say that a statement is founded on experience?

I do not think it means a crude empiricism to the effect that the statement corresponds to the real world encountered in experience. For an experience is always an experience of something: it has a determinate content. To have an experience is always to identify its content: indeed, an experience is a way of construing, of giving meaning to, its content. So 'the real world' is already construed by us. We can never get at it outside our constructs to find out whether our statement corresponds to it.

So to say a statement is founded on experience is to say that it coheres with how we <u>construe</u> the content of that experience. And there are at least two basic ways in which we construe this content. One is propositional construing, and the other is presentational construing (Heron, 1981a).

In propositional construing we experience things in terms of the concepts and categories that come with our mastery of language. This kind of construing is tacit: when I look out of my window and see the patio, garden walls, lawns, shrubs, fences and trees, I do not in my mind explicitly name and conceptualize each of these things. Yet I experience them, tacitly, *as* these sorts of things.

In presentational construing we construe immediate appearances in terms of spatio-temporal wholes, distinct processes and presences. So we construe the real shape and size of something from its apparent shape and size; the total temporal form of a process from its serial occurrences; a distinctive presence or entity from its unique signature of form and movement. We share this kind of construing with children before they can talk; and of course with animals, as when I play with my dog and a stick.

Let me summarize the argument so far. To have an experience is to construe its content. Such experiential construing is an interplay of propositional and presentational construing – two basic, interdependent ways of making sense of the world in the process of encountering it. And research statements founded on experience are ones that cohere with these two ways of making sense.

Such coherence has, then, three components: the researchers' explicit, formal statements; the tacit, propositional constructs within experience; and the presentational constructs within experience. For convenience I will refer to these as three kinds of construed world: the researched world, the posited world, and the presented world.

Now if the researched world is to be well-founded on the posited world and the presented world, the co-operative inquirers need to bring them all into active three-way relation. Through their research procedures the researchers continuously modify the impact of these world-constructs upon each other, until they are judged to be sufficiently coherent with each other.

Each of these world-constructs can change as a function of interaction with each of the other two. When as children we learn our mother-tongue and start to create our posited world, this no doubt changes the pre-linguistic presented world. The posited world will have a selective effect upon the presented world: some aspects of it will be brought to a focus and amplified, while other aspects will be ignored and drop into oblivion. And adults may well find it difficult to appreciate the presented world save in the selective terms of the posited world. The purpose of co-operative inquiry is to get these two worlds in active dialogue with each other and with the developing researched world.

Now there is an important sense in which the presented world is the experiential touchstone for the posited world and the researched world: it is the content of that extra-linguistic construing which tells us that some particular conceptual framework that comes from our language, culture and research is inappropriate for a certain experience. But it is a changing touchstone: its is a construct, a content of experience that is creatively framed in a way that will undoubtedly be modified by dynamic interaction with the other two worlds. There is not an unchanging, given, bedrock of pre-linguistic construing that we can all somehow or other uncover and use to test the coherence with it of our post-linguistic construing.

But if the presented world is itself a variable construct, how can we use it as a touchstone, how can we know that its constructs are authentic? I think their authenticity is confirmed through agreement in action or use. We know that the presented world is a world, that we have co-created a working viable version of it, when we can act and interact concertedly within it.

When my dog and I cavort with a stick on the heath, we agree in action that our presentational constructs provide us with a viable world in which to play. Our concerted practical grasp – in throwing and running and chasing – of spatio-temporal wholes, processes and presences, gives us active unanimity about the working status of our world.

So we now have a fourth world, the world-of-action, established through the coherence of concerted deeds. And here the definition of validity in terms of coherence rests. The coherence of the researched world and the coherence of the posited world are modified by, and have their experiential touchstone in the coherence of the presented world (which they also modify) – and this has its touchstone in the coherence of the world-of-action. The subjective–objective reality explored by a co-operative inquiry is a dynamic interaction between these four worlds.

This can be restated in terms of three kinds of knowledge. Propositional knowledge is knowledge that something is the case and is expressed in statements: when formalized in research it tells us of the researched world. Experiential knowledge is knowledge by acquaintance, and is realized in face-to-face encounter with a person, place or thing: its tells us of the interplay between the posited world and the presented world. Practical knowledge is knowing how to do something, and is expressed in the exercise of some special skill: its tells us of the world-of-action.

In a co-operative inquiry the propositional knowledge asserted by the research conclusions is coherent with the experiential knowledge of the researchers as co-subjects, and their experiential knowledge is coherent with their practical knowledge in knowing how to act together in their researched world.

Criteria of validity

This definition of the validity of the conclusions of a co-operative inquiry in terms of their coherence with the inquirers' experience and action, is also, of course, a statement of the criteria of such validity.

The coherence of the conclusions with the inquirers' experience is established by a three-way influence: between the developing research statements and the two components of experiential construing – propositional and presentational. In this triad of constructs, each is brought to bear upon the other two until, through three-way mutual influence, all are coherent with each other. And throughout this process, presentational construing is the experiential touchstone.

This key triangle is the central working criterion of validity: its base the presented world, interacting dynamically with its other two sides – the posited world and the researched world. There is great openness in construing the presented world. This interacts with much ingenuity in trying out alternative conceptual frameworks, during experience, in construing the posited world. And this dialogue is continuously brought to bear upon construing the researched world.

The coherence of the conclusions with the inquirers' experience is consummated through coherence in action – when the inquirers' new-found practical skills are applied concertedly in their researched world. Such concerted action may already be part of the inquiry, and be included in the researchers' agreement about their findings. This could well be the case in an inquiry about some aspect of social interaction or group work.

On the other hand, concerted action in the researched world may lie beyond the confines of the inquiry, in the future. For this world may be too underdeveloped, with too few people construing it, for much coherent concerted action to be taken within it. Yet still some degree of coherent experience of it may be possible. Coherent discrimination may precede coherent action. This could well be the case with an inquiry into extra-sensory states of being.

So we must allow that there can be provisionally valid inquiries, resting simply on the central criterion of coherence with experience, where this does not include coherent concerted action. And where such action necessarily awaits further development of the researched world in question.

There are two further aspects of coherence as a criterion of validity. Firstly, the research conclusions need to be coherent with each other: they are consistent with each other, interdependent and mutually illuminating. Secondly, the inquirers are in agreement about these conclusions.

In a subjective-objective reality the agreement sought between inquirers is not total unanimity, but the illumination of a common area of inquiry by differing individual perspectives. Validity is enhanced by a diversity of views that overlap. It is not found simply in the common properties of the different views, but rather in the unity-in-variety of these views.

Agreement of this sort cannot be absolute, at any rate so far as coherence with experience is concerned, and in the early stages of developing a researched world. It admits of degrees. It is a matter of judgement when the degree of agreement is so low that it constitutes a criterion of inadmissible disagreement. When it is this low, the inquirers must face the fact that distortions at the subjective pole of their reality have obscured their grasp of its objective pole.

When a researched world has developed to the point at which concerted action is possible within it, then agreement in action and use may be highly resolute.

Validity procedures

I now describe a set of interdependent procedures, whose effects taken together enhance the validity of the conclusions of a co-operative inquiry. They are interlocking ways of applying the criteria of validity in the previous section.

Research cycling

There are several overlapping versions of the research cycle for co-operative inquirers (Heron, 1981b; Reinharz, 1981; Rowan, 1981). Each version involves the inquirers moving to and fro between reflection and experience, so that these two poles are in repeated interplay with each other.

In the first reflection phase of the cycle the inquirers generate research propositions to identify and illuminate some area of experience; in the experience phase they open up fully to construe the content of this area; and in the next reflection phase they use this content to modify the research propositions; and so on.

The initial research propositions may be quite elaborate – as with the five-part model of holistic medicine with which we started that inquiry (see Chapter 5). Or they may be quite minimal, outlining a whole area of inquiry in a single broad statement – as with the altered states of consciousness (ASC) inquiry (see Chapter 9).

Once the research cycling gets under way it establishes a two-way feedback loop, that is both negative and positive – and this in both directions, from experience to ideas and from ideas to experience. In negative or corrective feedback the content of experiential construing simplifies, clarifies and corrects the research propositions; and the developing research propositions serve to strip this content of vagueness, ambiguity, illusion and confusion.

In positive or additive feedback the content of experiential construing deepens, diversifies, amplifies, renders more interdependent, the research propositions; and the developing research propositions alert the inquirers to wider, deeper, more subtle or more obvious, aspects of their experience.

Research cycling can be individual, collective or interactive. In individual cycling each inquirer is exclusively their own control on a serial basis: the two-way feedback loops between reflection and experience operate for each person separate from every other. Of course, if there is no interaction between individuals during the bulk of the inquiry, then it is only co-operative in the very first reflection phase about what initial research propositions to adopt and how to explore them, and in the last reflection phase to coordinate the separate individual findings.

In collective research cycling the inquirers function as a group at every phase. They always reflect together; and they always experience together – either interacting as a group, or doing individual things side-by-side in the same space. In the ASC inquiry all the cycles were collective: personal findings were always formulated and shared directly in the group; and experiences were always either interactive or side-by-side. What is essential here is to ensure that each person has a say in the reflection phase; and is fully involved in the experience phase. This is to ensure that co-operation is based on comprehensive individual participation, and does not just reflect the influence of some dominant sub-group.

In interactive research cycling a balance is sought between some individual research cycling and some aspects of collective research cycling. This balance can be struck in many different ways. One or more separate individual cycles of experience and reflection can be followed by collective reflection, in which each person's individual findings are shared for comment, feedback and discussion, and in which the content and method of the next one or more individual cycles is planned collectively. This was the approach adopted in the holistic medicine inquiry; and also in the two co-counselling inquiries (Heron and Reason, 1981, 1982).

In these three inquiries the experience phases – together with minor reflection phases for recording data – were always individual, and the major reflection phases were collective. In another inquiry I initiated in Dublin into 'the energy of the group' (unpublished), all the experience phases were collective and interactive. Then each individual would have a separate reflection phase expressing privately in writing and/or graphics their account of the group interaction that had just occurred. These were then shared and discussed in a collective reflection phase, leading to some broad consensus about what had gone on. And on this basis the next phase of group interaction was collectively planned.

An inquiry is presumably most co-operative if it can maximize both the distinct individual effect *and* the collective reciprocal effect. My reflection needs to be both autonomous, *and* fully open to influence by my experience, your experience, your reflection on my experience, your reflection on your experience, your reflection on my reflection; and vice-versa; and all this in relation to each person in the inquiry group. My experience needs to be both autonomous *and* fully open to influence by my prior reflection, your prior reflection, and by your current experience as immediately encountered.

Of course, this is all a counsel of perfection. For any given inquiry one adopts that form of cycling – usually some version of interactive cycling – that seems best suited to the subject-matter of the inquiry, and that offers an accessible and manageable balance between individual and collective effects.

The balance of divergence and convergence

Divergence is one important way of managing research cycling, so far as the content of the experience phase is concerned. The cycling is maximally divergent when the content which each inquirer explores is a different aspect of the inquiry area – different from everyone else on every cycle. So if there were ten inquirers and six research cycles, then sixty different aspects would be explored, ten of them on each experience phase.

The weakness of such total divergence is that no one aspect of the inquiry area is taken round a research cycle more than once by more than one person. Thus the research proposition about each aspect has been subject to minimal experiential revision.

The strength of such total divergence is that it yields a broad, holistic view of the inquiry area – hopefully as a comprehensive system of inter-dependent parts. Less hopefully it might only yield a disconnected aggregate of ill-co-ordinated bits of information.

Convergence is the complementary principle for choosing the content of the experience phase. The cycling is maximally convergent when each inquirer explores the same aspect of the inquiry area on each cycle. So, again, if there were ten inquirers and six research cycles, then the same aspect would be explored sixty times – six times by each person.

The weakness of such total convergence is that, by refining over and over again just one aspect of the inquiry area, it may become falsely revised because it is considered in complete isolation from other aspects. The effect upon it of its interdependence with other parts of the whole system is ignored. The strength of total convergence is that it does revise that one aspect very thoroughly, with a maximal number of feedback loops.

Clearly, some kind of balance between divergence and convergence is required. We need enough divergence of experiential content to get a good grasp of the interdependent parts of the whole system of our inquiry area. We need enough convergence for each part or sub-set of parts to be taken through two or more research cycles, so that it is more fully validated.

There are innumerable ways of balancing these two complementary claims to understand the whole and clarify its parts.

Divergence and convergence have been applied so far to the content of the inquiry. They also apply to the ways of exploring that content, and to the ways of recording that exploration.

In the holistic medicine inquiry early experience phases were highly divergent, with individuals choosing to explore any aspect of any part of the initial five-part model which took their fancy; and their strategies of exploration and methods of recording were idiosyncratic too. In later experience phases, one sub-group of inquirers converged on power-sharing with patients, and another sub-group converged on spiritual interventions within the surgery. Yet within each of these aspects there was some divergence over sub-aspects (e.g. different sub-group members tried out different kinds of power-sharing, and different sorts of spiritual intervention).

In the ASC inquiry the inquirers converged in each experience phase, exploring the same sort of content either interactively or side-by-side, but the way each person gathered impressions about this same content was highly idiosyncratic and divergent. Furthermore, the content of each successive experience phase diverged into something different.

In the holistic medicine inquiry and the two co-counselling inquiries (Heron and Reason, 1981, 1982), where the experience and initial reflection (recording) phases were done on a separate, individual basis, it seemed best to allow for and encourage a good deal of divergence of content in the early cycles. This both lets each person get up a good head of creative steam, gets them involved, and – when these divergent experiences are shared – brings out the multi-faceted nature of the inquiry area. After a time the divergence becomes uncomfortable, disorienting and unmanageable and the inquirers start to hunger for more convergence.

Theoretically, a good balance divergence and convergence of experiential content would be found by the inquirers dealing with several different aspects of the research area one at a time, taking each of them on its own round the research cycle more than once; then taking these aspects together round the research cycle more than once, in order to study more directly their interplay and interaction.

I have so far spoken of divergence and convergence in relation to the content of the experience phase. But they also apply, of course, to the conceptual maps of the reflection phase; and these two applications are somewhat independent of each other. For the inquirers can all converge on the same sort of content in the experience phase, yet have widely divergent maps of that content in the following reflection phase.

Now some sort of balance, at the conceptual level, is also required between divergence and convergence – at any rate over the whole series of reflection phases. Divergence of conceptual mapping establishes a wide range of differing perspectives on the same content area. Such heterogeneity is essential to honour a subjective–objective reality. But equally, to honour such a reality, it needs to be shown how these diverse conceptual views overlap and converge to illuminate a common content area.

In the early reflection phases inquiries are enriched by divergent conceptual mapping. Of course, in the early shared reflection phases, where individual maps are presented to everyone else, the elements of convergence or overlap among them will be noted. But it is unwise to press for conceptual convergence between individual maps early on; otherwise you may get premature intellectual closure round the experiential content, thus distorting rather than disclosing it.

In the later shared reflection phases, if there are too many idiosyncratic individual maps piling up, then it will be wise to work collectively on conceptual convergence. Thus in the first co-counselling inquiry (Heron and Reason, 1981), in the last shared reflection phase, we took the most coherent maps that different individuals had refined through their own cycles, and all of us took a part in amending each map until all, including its originator, were satisfied with it and with its coherence with the other maps thus treated.

In the ASC inquiry, conceptual convergence started to be developed after the fourth cycle, in the devil's advocate procedure. What then emerged in replies to the devils' attacks on the diverse individual impressions of the other reality, was a set of criteria for distinguishing between genuine impressions and subjective illusions.

The balance between reflection and experience

If validity is enhanced by research cycling, by moving to and fro between reflection and experience, then it also depends on getting a right balance between these two phases. If the inquirers have prolonged experiential phases with only minimal time out for reflection, then their findings have low validity. The inquiry has become supersaturated with experience: no adequate, coherent findings can be distilled out of it, or refined in it.

Conversely, if the inquirers reflect a great deal about a few brief episodes of minimal action, this too will result in conclusions with low validity. The inquiry suffers from intellectual excess: its findings have inadequate experiential support.

What constitutes a good ratio between reflection and experience, one that enhances validity through positive and negative feedback loops, is surely inquiry-specific. There is no general formula. Long hours of contemplative reflection may be needed to clarify the content of a few seconds' experience of a beatific state; whereas a few minutes reflection may be sufficient to describe what happened during many hours in an immersion tank. Or, more prosaically, it may need a lot of consideration to get clear what was going in a brief but elliptical conversation; and only a little thought may illuminate a lengthy period of straightforward co-operative action.

In the ASC inquiry, in several cycles the reflection and experience phases were about equal. In the holistic medicine inquiry each reflection phase covered some hours in one weekend, while each experience phase covered six weeks of daily professional work – with, of course, intermittent times of recording the data from such work.

In the first co-counselling inquiry (Heron and Reason, 1981), each person spent 20 to 30 minutes in the experience phase, 15 minutes in a private reflection phase, then over an hour in a collective reflection phase. In the second co-counselling inquiry (Heron and Reason, 1982), the experience phase was a whole week of daily life (with intermittent recording of data), and the collective reflection phase was five hours in a block once a week. All these different ratios seemed reasonably appropriate to their different subject-matters.

The only guideline I can think of for this procedure is that the inquirers monitor the ratio and discuss it from time to time. They have to judge from within the parameters of their particular inquiry what a good ratio is. Maybe they would have to try out several different ratios before getting a sense of the right one. Maybe a variety of different ratios would itself be fitting; for example if each different cycle requires a different ratio. Maybe it becomes obvious quite quickly, as a matter of common sense, what a good balance is. The inquirers will usually have time-constraints from their other commitments, and these too have to be taken realistically into account.

Aspects of reflection

Peter Reason points out, in Chapter 1, the useful work already at hand in traditional qualitative inquiry methods, about reflecting and making sense. Here I wish to make some very simple and basic distinctions, which in my experience, co-opted inquirers can lose sight of.

After an experience phase there are at least three major forms of thought for the following reflection phase: the descriptive, the evaluative, and the practical. I am here referring, of course, to reflection on the immediate content of experience, not on some already recorded data. When describing, the inquirers are busy with pure phenomenology, seeking to convey to themselves and each other, as fully, coherently, and evocatively as possible the content of the experience phase. They are mapping what went on, framing lucid descriptions.

When evaluating, they are judging how sound and well-founded these descriptions are; that is, how well they cohere with the recollected, presented content of the experience phase. And this will also involve sifting through alternative conceptual frameworks from the wider culture. The researched, presented and posited worlds are being modified and tested for their mutual coherence. Findings from previous reflection phases will be included. This evaluation in the reflection phase refines and extends what was done when thinking on one's feet in the midst of the experience phase.

Sometimes the presented content is ambiguous. Thus in the ASC inquiry impressions that seemed to be of the other world could have been of some not very clear but ordinary state in this world. So judging whether a description of these impressions was well-founded involved finding criteria to distinguish between real and illusory impressions of the other world. Certainly, in early reflection phases of that inquiry, collective reflection got too preoccupied with describing ostensibly occult impressions, and fell short of finding criteria with which to evaluate them.

In the practical part of the reflection phase, the inquirers – on the basis of their descriptions and evaluations, and in the light also of policies from earlier reflection phases to which they may still be committed – are proposing what sort of content to explore in the next experience phase, how to explore it and how to record this exploration. An important part of planning the next experience phase will be some transfer of learning from the previous ones.

In the holistic medicine inquiry this transfer, in the earlier cycles, was at best tacit only. We did not consciously and intentionally use prior findings to influence subsequent planning. We think the transfer happened subliminally and unconsciously. But it only became more conscious, explicit and intentional, when each of the sub-groups converged on its chosen theme over a series of later cycles.

In the ASC inquiry it seemed that almost all the transfer was tacit, or at best the result of some rather vague and unfocused associative or imaginative process. We plunged on from one bizarre cycle of action to another, gathering more and more impressionistic data, with only a minimal conscious grasp of how prior findings affected current planning. Alarmed at this, we set up the devil's advocate procedure after several cycles, and in this way we confronted each other to make explicit the tacit transfer and the tacit learning.

What seems important about reflection is that it is never merely descriptive, but also evaluative in the ways mentioned above; and that there is some conscious transfer from these evaluated descriptions into the practical planning of the content and method of the next experience phase.

Falsification

The basic point about co-operative inquiry is that the inquirers are taking their ideas from the reflection phase both to correct and amplify them through the content of the experience phase. But to take an idea down into experience, whether to notice what it distorts or what is omits, is a tricky business.

Firstly, the inquirers have to be pretty committed to the idea; it must seem in advance to be rather plausible, for them to be willing to make a further commitment of the whole person to explore it in experience. So for this reason, they may be somewhat resistant to noticing inadequacies in the idea that the experiential test throws up.

Secondly, making the experiential test involves them in a change of being. They become different: the idea is no longer just grasped by them intellectually – they have lived through it, they know it connaturally, as the philosophers say. They have worn it as the garment of their doing, and so it becomes warming and endearing to them. For this reason too they have a vested interest in not noticing its shortcomings in the face of experience.

Thirdly, and most crucially, they have to entertain the idea in order to have the appropriate experience: the idea defines the kind of experience they have to have in order to test it. So they have to go along with the idea, believe in it sufficiently in order to get into the relevant kind of action and experience. And this is the most critical reason why they may fail to notice corrective data.

So an important aspect of falsification procedure is vigilance in watching for how ideas fall short when taken in the experience phase. The inquirers need to believe in an idea enough to get experientially involved in it, and at the same time they need to be unattached to it, watchful for shortcomings, noticing more than belief in it entails, and holding alternative ideas available in the mind at the ready.

This is an individual task for each inquirer in each experience phase, and when recollecting experience in the reflection phase. But there is not only individual nescience to take into account. There is also collective or consensus collusion. When this occurs the inquirers are all tacitly agreeing to choose a pseudo-reality. They collude in not noticing, or if they notice, in not mentioning, aspects of their experience that show up the limitations of their conceptual model.

As well as colluding in not noticing corrective aspects of their experience, they can collude in many other ways: in obscuring the false assumptions implicit in their leading ideas and/or in their ways of taking these ideas into action; in lack of rigour in their inquiry methods and in applying vigorously the various validity procedures.

It seems wise to have a special procedure to counter any tendency to collusion of these various kinds. A formal devil's advocate practice works well. When a group decided to adopt this method then any member can indicate, during a group reflection phase, that they wish to speak as devil's advocate. This means that the person is concerned about validity, and wants the freedom to confront fully some possible collusion. This allows anyone to press hard a rigorous attempt at falsification, while merely wondering whether, rather than necessarily believing that, something has gone wrong. And it encourages members to seek out doubts even when the group is most sanguine about its work.

The method can be applied in two complementary ways: on a spontaneous individual basis, and in a full group formal session. It may be wise to use both in the same inquiry. But in the two examples that follow, each inquiry only used one to the exclusion of the other.

In the holistic medicine inquiry any member could at any time take up 'the mace' – a staff – to indicate that they were temporarily adopting the role of radical critic, in order to challenge some possible hidden collusion. This worked well in a piecemeal, impromptu, individualistic way. But it was *en passant*, a spontaneous interlude in some other business. And it sometimes degenerated into mere prankishness, and mischievous boat-rocking. The inquiry as a whole lacked a more systematic use of devil's advocacy, in which a full session involved everyone in a critical review of possible collusion.

In the ASC inquiry we did hold such a full session, driven to it by the mass of divergent, impressionistic data, fraught with ambiguity, which we had accumulated. Each inquirer in turn sat in the 'hot seat' and had read out, from records kept over four cycles, their impressions of the other reality. Any other inquirer could then come forward as devil's advocate, and sceptically attack these impressions, reducing them to some purely naturalistic explanation.

The defendant then had three choices: to give a reasoned defence of the impressions as valid impressions of the other reality; to yield to the devil's reductionist explanation as being the most reasonable; or to stick to their intuitive guns, even though unable to argue the case. This procedure, sustained over some time, did sharpen our awareness of possible criteria for differentiating between extrasensory and naturalistic impressions.

Chaos and order

If the inquirers are really going to be open, adventurous and innovative, to pull all at risk to reach out to their truth beyond fear and collusion, then, especially in the earlier stages of the inquiry, divergence of thought and expression may well collapse into confusion, uncertainty, ambiguity, disorder and chaos – with most or all the inquirers feeling lost to a greater or lesser degree.

About the first co-counselling inquiry, we wrote: 'Accepting chaos facilites the emergence of order. Experiential researchers need to have a high tolerance for ambiguity and confusion. New ideas may be found by allowing, celebrating and encouraging, going through the stages of, confusion which the inquiry generates' (Heron and Reason, 1981). The inquiry process is a bit like a 'dissipative structure' in organic and inorganic chemistry (Prigogine, 1980), in which new order is created by perturbation.

It is paradoxical to call this collapse into confusion and chaos a procedure. The inquirers can't plan for it and programme it in. They can't say: 'Now let's have some chaos.' This is likely to generate only pseudo-chaos. But they can plan to be creatively divergent. And if chaos sets in when such creativity and divergence start to get out of hand and overstep the bounds of everyone's conceptual tolerance, then they can learn to stay with the chaos, recognize it and accept it. And this without anxiously trying to clean it up, without getting trapped by fear into premature and restrictive intellectual closure.

The principle of faith here is that if the inquirers hang in with the chaos *awarely*, it will in its own good time, by the principle of the inter-dependence of opposites, become the seedbed for the emergence of some new, useful and illuminating bit of order. But it is a risky business. There can be no guarantee that order will emerge. The whole inquiry may go down the drain.

Equally, there can be no guarantee that chaos will occur. But there will clearly be some degree of confusion, at least, in the early stages. Issues to do with maintaining adequate divergence, with group interaction and peer decision-making will see to that. And whatever the degree of confusion, the challenge is for the inquirers to go with it for a while, not pull out of it anxiously but wait until there is a real sense of creative resolution.

In the holistic medicine inquiry the degree of real chaos was minimal. The inquiry was characterized more by manageable sorts of minor disorder and messiness. In the original monograph we wrote: 'The group and its members would have to go through an almost psychotic degeneration into disorder if they were to re-create a genuine holistic practice' (Heron and Reason, 1985). The ASC inquiry lived with a good deal of conceptual chaos and ambiguity about the status of the many divergent impressions of the other reality accumulating over the first four cycles. Order emerged out of the chaos, mainly through the devil's advocate procedure after the fourth cycle – and this was overdue rather than premature.

The management of unaware projections

The very process of inquiring into human nature, human interactions and the human condition, may stir up fear and defensiveness in the researchers. The fear is of that which is both unknown and very close to psychological home. The defensiveness is about those aspects of themselves which they have had to repress and deny in order to survive and be accepted when growing up in an emotionally alienated society. Such fear and defensiveness, once stirred up, will reinforce each other, and may distort the whole process of psychological research. Devereaux (1967) puts forward a similar view, arguing that this defensive process is akin to therapist counter-transference in psychoanalysis.

Let's look more closely at the erection of defensiveness. If as a child I want to express my real nature, and this urge is repeatedly interfered with, then I feel – depending on the situation – the distress of grief, or fear or anger. If I am also constrained to suppress such valid distress, then I am conditioned a second time to become false to myself. In order to get whatever kind of restrictive support is available from those who oppress me, I deny both my real self and the pain I feel at its interruption. I erect an alienated self with which I identify. I defend myself against the truth about myself (Heron, 1983).

I become addicted to projecting onto the world the anxiety of my denied distress, seeing the world as a threatening place – which thus reinforces my addiction to my false self. I am stuck in an interlocking compulsion not to identify my real nature and not to see what sort of an exciting and challenging world it is possible to construe. Overlapping versions of this sort of view of what happens to people in our sort of society are put forward in the works of Guntrip, Jackins, Janov, Lowen, Perls, Reich, Winnicott and others.

If researchers are stuck unawarely in this kind of defensiveness, then their research is likely to fall foul of it too. They may compulsively *not* inquire into persons as persons. They may research rats as surrogates for persons. They may use conceptual models that reduce personhood to external behaviour observed by others, or to mechanistic stimulus–response reactions. They may use research methods that reduce persons to objects and to sub-personal functioning. They may research extensively trivial and peripheral bits of behaviour. They may manipulate and deceive their experimental subjects. They may never ask their subjects how they construe the experimental situation and give meaning to their actions within it. And so on. Their research becomes, in part at any rate, a kind of pathological acting out of their own repressive denial of the truth about themselves. Indeed, some writers have argued that the whole scientific enterprise can be seen as a defensive collusion (Maslow, 1966; Griffin, 1984).

Researchers who are aware of this kind of defensiveness, who have started to dismantle it through some personal growth process, will still need to watch for its distorting effect on the research. For even if the co-operative inquiry model is itself outside this effect, the application of the model is likely to stir up disruption from all kinds of unfinished emotional business. Some candidates for such disruption are: the choice of content area; the planning and management of the research cycles; lapses in recording data; neglect of validity procedures; emotional and intellectual difficulty in noticing and reporting important experiences; becoming disgruntled, resistant, bored, distracted, rebellious about the whole enterprise; interpersonal tensions and disruptions; consensus collusion of all kinds; messy peer decision-making; etc. Co-operative inquirers will need to take time out during their research to monitor for the distorting effect of their own fear and hidden distress. Sometimes it may be sufficient simply to identify this effect in order to get free of it. At other times it may be necessary to discharge, by catharsis, some of the underlying emotional pain; or to transmute it through some meditative method.

In the holistic medicine inquiry from the start we had regular group process sessions to identify interpersonal and intrapsychic material that might distort the research, and to give it space at least to be talked somewhat out of the way. We also used regular pair sessions including co-counselling. Both approaches yielded modest gains, but more deep-seated material was rarely reached, there was little catharsis, and a good deal of consensus collusion was unresolved.

In the ASC inquiry there were three in-depth sessions of emotional house-cleaning, involving regression, catharsis and insight. This gave scope for the rigorous use of devil's advocacy. But more house-cleaning was undoubtedly needed. Going into the attic of the psyche calls for a good deal of active sorting out in the basement, combined with a high degree of critical judgement exercised on the ground floor.

Sustaining authentic collaboration
One aspect of validity, discussed above in the section on criteria, is the coherence between the views of different individual researchers: the overlap between well-researched, autonomous and interdependent view-points. Individual viewpoints will not really be authentic unless each person is a fully fledged collaborator, contributing at each stage of the inquiry with a real grasp of what is going on.

There are two aspects of authentic collaboration. First, the relationship between group members and the initiating researchers. And second, the relationships among group members themselves. I will deal with these in turn.

A co-operative inquiry usually starts off with one or more initiating researchers who choose an area of inquiry, co-opt a number of interested persons to become co-researchers, and then initiate them into the research method. If real initiation has taken place the co-opted inquirers internalize issues to do with both the area and the method of inquiry. They will make the whole enterprise their own in a vigorous way.

If the initiation is more apparent than real, then the co-opted inquirers are merely yes-people, being guided and shepherded into appropriate behaviour, without any real grasp of what they are about. They are just followers of the initiating researchers. Any agreement reached is likely to be spurious. Collaboration is inauthentic. The co-opted inquirers simply rubber-stamp what the initiating researchers get up to.

The initiating researchers, while doing the initiation, will quite appro-priately have a high profile about content and method at the outset, and will also, most probably, be the facilitators of the group's work and decision-making. But it is not appropriate for this high profile to continue indefinitely. If it does, the initiation has failed: there has been no effective delegation of knowledge and skills.

The initiation, then, must include an important element of experiential training and consciousness-raising, in which group members are learning through practice new research skills – and the rationale for them. So it helps if the initiating researchers are competent in this kind of training, and know how and when to manage the transition from more directive to more participative forms of decision-making in the group.

There are several signs of successful initiation. The members show by their comments and initiatives their mastery of content and method. They take charge of group decision-making and choose awarely how they make decisions. They rotate the group facilitator role amongst themselves – taking this role over from the initiating researchers. They are as vigilant as the initiating researchers about the use of validity procedures – such as balancing divergence and convergence, the use of devil's advocacy, and so on.

In the holistic medicine inquiry the initiation was adequate but imperfect: all members grasped the broad thrust of the research method, but some remained mystified about its detailed aspects, and were sceptical about its claim to be a genuine alternative to conventional research. In the ASC inquiry the initiation was abducted, so to speak. The group took over the method rapidly and enthusiastically, impatient about its finer points, and blocked attempts by me later in the inquiry to push hard on what I considered to be important methodological issues.

The second important aspect of collaboration is that between individual members. Some may be more fully initiated than others. Even when all are fully initiated, some may hang back for other, psychological reasons. Are there any passengers – group members not putting forth their energy and enterprise, whether in shared reflection, collective planning, validity checks, or even in the experience phases?

In group reflection phases, high contributors may habitually and unawarely push aside low contributors. And such an imbalance in contribution rates may become a fixed pathology of the group. This may overlap with a sexist imbalance, in which male views predominate to the exclusion of female views.

In the reflection phases, verbal skills may be over-valued, to the exclusion of those who could have made an important contribution in terms of non-discursive skills – making sense of their experience in terms of graphics, colour, movement or expressive drama.

And even if all group members contribute fully, influence hierarchies may become established. The views of some may tend to hold more sway than the views of others: everyone speaks but only some are really listened to. It is important to check that views are influential because of their content, not because of some extraneous factors to do with the impact of the speaker; and to ensure that reputation based on past wisdom does not obscure present folly.

Various things can be done by the group to encourage and sustain authentic collaboration among its members. Individual cycles of experience and of reflection guarantee a base-line of equal participation from all inquirers. In group sessions – to do with reflection, planning, validity – the use of rounds, in which each person has a verbal turn, helps to sustain full collaboration. And the interplay between verbal and non-verbal ways of making sense of experience can be used. In open discussion the group facilitator can actively manage contribution rates, drawing in low contributors and shutting out persistent high contibutors; can keep an eye on sexist imbalance, and on improper influence hierarchies.

The inquirers may also need to take special time out, in a formal validity session, to review the issue of collaboration: to look at the developing effectiveness of the initiation; to explore psychological reticence, contribution rates, sexist imbalance, the use of verbal and nonverbal skills, and influence hierarchies; to find out whether the outspoken and influential do voice the genuine aspirations of the more retiring; to devise strategies that ensure that all get a piece of the action and a voice in the reflection.

Open and closed boundaries
Some inquiries, such as the first co-counselling one (Heron and Reason, 1981), and the ASC one, are concerned entirely with what is going on within the researchers' experience – personal and/or interpersonal – and do not include, as part of the inquiry, interaction between the researchers and others in the wider world. Other inquiries, such as the second co-counselling one (Heron and Reason, 1982), and the holistic medicine one, do include such interaction as part of the inquiry.

In the latter case, when members of the inquiry include in it the experience of those who are not members, then there needs to be some personal comment or feedback directly from these non-members – whether written, recorded or whatever. Of course, the inquiry members will report their impressions of how the non-members reacted and responded, and this is clearly important. But on its own it is not enough.

In the holistic medicine inquiry the main part of the experience phases was the doctors' work with patients. The doctors had much valuable data of their own to report on these patients. But direct feedback from the patient concerned was very limited; and in this respect the validity of the inquiry was limited.

Coherence in action
The question here is this: does the coherent viewpoint which progressively emerges out of the inquiry, and which purports to portray a certain field

of subjective–objective reality, does this shared viewpoint enable the inquirers to *act* in a coherent and concerted way within their field? Do their various actions dovetail and interweave so that they agree they have practical knowledge – by the application of their new-found skills – of some part of a *world*?

I refer the reader to the discussion of this issue in the section on criteria of validity earlier in this chapter. As I said there, some inquiries may include this notion of concerted action in their account of coherence with experience, and others may not. It depends on how *developed* the researched world is.

Variegated replication

If a primitive and underdeveloped researched world is to be developed further, to the point at which concerted action can be taken within it, then the design and findings of the original inquiry which focused on that world must be stated with sufficient clarity and thoroughness so that future inquirers can both reconstrue that world, and extend their grasp of it and their action within it.

The same argument applies to a developed researched world, for there will always be more to construe within it, and more extended forms of concerted action to take within it.

So a co-operative inquiry needs to be replicable, not in any crude sense of literal repetition, but in the more imaginative sense of creative metamorphosis. The original study will be done over again, but in a significantly different way, both with respect to research design and initial perspective. Yet there will be enough overlap for the follow-up to be a legitimate development of the original.

Literal and exact replication is inconsistent with the nature of a subjective-objective reality. If the present inquirers are truly going to construe the researched world of the previous inquirers, then they must do so, and plan to do so, in their own autonomous and idiosyncratic way. They will see it better through their own constructs than through the constructs of others.

A central skill

To sustain and interweave such a range of sophisticated procedures throughout an inquiry clearly requires wide-ranging skills – which are all, I believe, different aspects of developing a high-quality awareness. There are several overlapping accounts of these skills (Heron, 1982; Reason, 1988; Reinharz, 1981; Torbert, 1981b). I will identify here a skill which is crucial, and without which validity conceived as coherence with experience is not really possible. I will call it 'bracketing'. It involves the most uncompromising kind of phenomenological discrimination, and is at the heart of a truly radical empiricism. [Heron's discussion of bracketing in this section may be usefully compared with Hawkins' exploration in Chapter 3 – Ed.]

Bracketing is a purely mental skill, central in the experience phase of research cycling. It deal with a critical paradox of research cycling: that I am seeking to validate research propositions by undergoing experiences that are picked out, defined and identified in terms of those same propositions. Bracketing is a competence that prevents such validation from being merely self-fulfilling and circular.

It means that, when I am immersed in the experience phase, I bracket off the research ideas that pick out that experience. And that I also bracket off the tacit concepts involved in my everyday way of identifying the content of the experience. And that I attend to the pure morphology of this content: the form, process and presence that I grasp by my presentational construing.

This notion of bracketing acknowledges that we cannot eliminate explicit and tacit propositional constructs from the content of our experience. But it also means that we can, as it were, hold these constructs in mental suspension, and allow the phenomena to speak somewhat for themselves: or, to put it more precisely, allow our presentational construing a new lease of extra-cultural, extra-linguistic life.

Nor is the bracketing-off procedure a merely passive suspension of the concepts and categories, explicit or tacit, that come from our mastery of language. It also involves an active three-way interaction between the explicit research ideas, a bevy of alternative conceptual frameworks drawn from our language and culture, and the dynamic touchstone of basic extra-linguistic presentational construing.

This composite construing is revisionary. It has active, imaginative power. For the researched world is a dynamic remodelling of the interaction between the posited world and the presented world. This bracketing procedure, in its passive and active modes, is very much at the heart of validity in co-operative inquiry. For if it is not possible to do it, then we cannot really test the research propositions for their coherence with experience.

3

A Phenomenological Psychodrama Workshop

Peter Hawkins

Workshop: day one

I would like to begin by welcoming you to this workshop on phenomenological psychodrama, which I have been developing with colleagues here in Bath over the past four years.

Let me begin by telling you how I got involved in developing phenomenological psychodrama. Years back when I was doing my first degree I was all set for a career in theatre, and was busy directing plays and television programmes. But gradually I got less interested in the finished productions, and more in the dramas of the rehearsal room. Gradually I moved into experimental theatre, then community arts and from there into dramatherapy and psychodrama. This took me into psychotherapy and groupwork for about eight years, before I embarked on research into learning in communities and work teams.

When I came to research I was initially schooled in qualitative research and particularly in the various 'new paradigm' and co-operative research approaches (Reason and Rowan, 1981a). As I began to practise this form of research I became overwhelmed by the complexities in this kind of work and the overwhelming amount of data and interlocking processes. I wanted to develop an approach that would combine both depth and clarity, and that would help in the search for form and essence beyond the welter of data.

I also became interested in the relationship between the myself as researcher when I was engaged in the fieldwork and the me as researcher when I was back in Bath reflecting on the process and trying to make sense of the data. It seemed to me that despite my attempts at a co-operative approach to the research with the groups or teams with whom I was doing the research, there still was a form of *hierarchy of looking.* I (in my fieldwork or encounter mode) was looking at the group and individual processes, and then in my reflective mode I was not only looking at these processes but also at the me that had been engaged in the research encounter process. I was interested in turning this hierarchical pyramid on its head and finding a way that the data and the fieldwork researcher could challenge the reflective researcher. After all, in new paradigm research we have made a big issue of how the researcher is part of the field being studied, and it is important that we also make the reflective researcher part of that which is studied. Out of these interests and concerns I turned to phenomenology and immersed myself in the writings of Husserl, Heidegger, Ricouer and Ihde (see Bibliography for references).

Now one of the difficulties with phenomenology, and why phenomenologists are so hard to read, is that they try and do so many things inside their heads. They sit still in their chairs trying to do six things at once and end up disappearing into a transcendental ego which takes off into a realm of philosophical abstraction. They became unearthed from tangible sensible reality and lost in cerebral formulations. If you try and become your data, reflect on it and reflect on your reflecting on it, all inside your own head, you disappear into a mind-loop. After an hour of trying to think phenomenologically I began to wonder who I was, and nearly wrote phenomenology off as a route to insanity. It was then that I realized that psychodrama was a phenomenological process, and that psychodrama could help phenomenologists to get up out of their chairs and to mobilize the different intellectual processes.

In my own research I found that I was a good researcher when I was with the communities and teams, with exciting feedback loops and creative insights, both for the groups and myself; but when I was back in Bath reflecting on the action, the process and my writing about it was much more flat and less alive than the encounter had been. I wanted to bring the life back from the action stage of the research into the reflection and the writing.

The other thing I realized about phenomenology is that there are two distinct levels. Many American phenomenologists only work with the first level which is what Husserl called *epoché 1*. This is about becoming aware of your preconceptions and assumptions, so that you can 'bracket' them off and encounter the world that is being researched more directly.

The second level of phenomenology is linked to Husserl's *epoché 2*, when, having encountered the world of the research, you stop looking at the 'whatness' of the data, bracket it off, and start looking at 'how' this data has come into being in one's own consciousness. I realized that psychodrama had tools for carrying out both these phenomenological epochés.

More of that later, for I want now to pause from talking about phenomenology and talk about psychodrama, introduce you to Moreno, the founder of psychodrama, who was a contemporary of Freud, also from Vienna.

I want you to imagine that next to me here is a psychodramatic stage. The first scene that appears on this stage is the young Moreno age nine, playing with his friends. He is directing them in creating the universe by building a construction of tables and chairs. Finally Moreno takes his place on top of this furniture pyramid, for he has cast himself as God. The whole edifice collapses and Moreno has a broken arm. This nemesis does not prevent Moreno from his continued attempts to find the God within, and to become a director of his own fate and help others to do the same.

The second scene is Moreno as a young man in pre-first world war Vienna, directing spontaneous theatre events with children in the park, where they produce a living newspaper on the events of the day.

The third scene is in the 1920s, and Moreno has moved to the United States. He is building his psychodrama theatre at Beacon Hill outside New York City. He is also busy writing papers that are laying the foundations for psychodrama, sociodrama, group therapy and sociometry. These papers outlined most of the techniques that later became popular in the humanistic therapies of the 'growth movement' of the 1960s and 1970s, in encounter, gestalt and co-counselling groups. Modern research methods such as the ones represented in this book draw heavily on the approaches of these humanistic therapies.

There is another lovely scene, where Moreno the Founder of Psycho-drama meets Freud, the Father of Psychoanalysis. Moreno says to Freud: 'You analyse their dreams. I try and give them the courage to dream again. I teach them how to play God' (Moreno, 1946).

One of the things Moreno was most interested in was how we each could discover how we are actors in our own dramas, and how we can develop more of the ability to become the author and director of these life dramas. In this he pre-shadows the development of the phenomenological therapists such as Binswanger and Medard Boss. He was also deeply involved in how we can bridge the distance between self and other – a question that was of central importance to many of the phenomenological–existential thinkers, writers, and therapists that followed and developed Husserlian ideas.

Here is a poem of Moreno's, written in 1969:

A meeting of two: eye to eye, face to face.
And when you are near I will tear your eyes out
and place them instead of mine,
and you will tear my eyes out
and will place them instead of yours,
then I will look at you with your eyes
and you will look at me with mine

For Moreno, it is in the 'encounter' that past, present and future become united and one bridges the distance to the other and in so doing also moves deeper in the discovery of the deepest essence of life.

The bridging of this gap is through the process of *tele*, a key but difficult

Morenian concept. Tele is the ability to enter into the lived experience and perspective of the other person, to stand not only in their shoes but also in their emotional body and to see the world with their eyes. This requires not only empathy for the other, but the ability to make an imaginative and intuitive leap into their world. This is how one psychodramatist describes the concept:

> Tele represents insight into and appreciation of feeling for the actual make-up of the other person. It is not merely empathy, the ability to take the role of another in a given situation. It is the ability to assume the feelings of the other in every situation, including the situation involving the self. Tele is responsible for increased mutuality of choices and increased rates of interaction. (Haskell, in Greenberg, 1974)

Thus for Moreno the process is not one of either trying to experience the experience of the other within one's own experience, nor a seeing of the other's experience through the distorting mirror of transference and projection; nor is it an emptying of one's own experience in order to be the blank screen, or analyst without counter-transference. Rather it is a fully entering into the encounter by both client and therapist, in an openness that focuses on the client and their area of 'work'.

This notion of tele can be used to enlighten the research fieldwork and can also be used in the post-fieldwork stage by the researcher exploring the life as lived by the research subjects. To invoke the dramaturgical metaphor, having seen the play, tape-recorded the script, noted the gestures, costumes and props, etc., one can go deeper in understanding the play, by getting inside it and playing the parts oneself.

This taking the parts of the other actor is a form of *research role reversal* which increases tele between researcher and that which is researched. It also frees the knowledge from the facts or relata for within this role reversal one can experimentally further the dialogues that actually happened in the fieldwork by accurate and authentic playing of the roles in the present.

Often it is in playing the role of the other that insight emerges. In research it comes when you stop looking at your data and start looking out from within your data, out by becoming it. Later on I will introduce you to a variety of psychodramatic techniques that I have adapted for research, but at this stage let me tell you about the three stages in all good psychodrama work.

First, there is *the warm-up* when all the group get involved in not just thinking, but moving about, feeling, using their creativity, spontaneity and imagination.

The second phase is *the work*, when as a group we explore in-depth one person's particular issues or research.

The third and last phase is *the sharing* when, having completed the in-depth exploration, members of the group are given the chance to *derole* and then to share any thoughts and feelings from their own life and research that the psychodrama has triggered off.

Now the first rule of warm-up is 'do it, don't talk about it'. I have been talking far too long and I want us all to move into doing some psychodrama about our present research concerns.

Introductory exercise

Step 1. I want you to divide into threes. In each three I want one person to *sculpt* some aspect of their research. This could be a person, a concept, a particular idea you are working on, an organization or the book you are writing.

Sculpting means using another person to physically represent the research. It is done by imagining that the other person is made of clay and you can mould that person into whatever shape feels right in order to imaginatively convey the essence or feeling of that part of your research you want to explore. Don't think it out before you do it. Allow your hands to play around and to experiment. If you think it out you will tend to use digital left-brain awareness; and we are now interested in catching the analogic right-brain thinking which is often less available. That is great.

Step 2. Now I want the person who has done the sculpting to stand behind their creation and put your hand on its shoulder and speak as if you were this being that you have psychodramatically brought to life here today. This is called *doubling*.

Step 3. Now I want the other person in your triad to be the psycho-dramatic *director* and facilitate you in dialoguing with this aspect of your research. What do you want to ask it? or say to it? After you have done this for a while I would like you to *role reverse*, that is change roles and become the aspect of your research that you have sculpted and respond to what you have said. While you are in this role the 'auxiliary' who was playing that aspect now plays you. After a while those playing the parts might feel ready to speak in role. In psychodrama we call you *auxiliaries* and the one doing the work the *protagonist*.

At this point each triad took about twenty minutes for this exploration. Then they switched roles so another member of the triad could be the protagonist.

Okay, now we are back together are there any questions or comments?

Workshop member: What is the difference between psychodrama and role-play, because I have used a lot of role-play in my work and often I get lost in the role?
Peter: That is a very good question, because role-play and psychodrama are clearly very linked, but there is a difference. Often in role play we are working from the outside in – we are looking at the role and seeing how accurately we can

enact it. In psychodrama you are working from the inside out – finding the psychic essence and following its energy, letting it find its own voice and its natural movement. It is giving shape to psyche, not enacting a role. Some of the worst people at psychodrama are actors, because they work from the concept. If they are asked to play someone's father who is a vicar, they go into their stereotyped vicar number. I am not interested in play-acting, but in following the smoke to find the fire of what is true and authentic.

Workshop member: But the people can not be tabula rasa. They are bound to bring their own material into the parts they play.

Peter: Yes, that is true, but they are often picked because of their connection to the part they are asked to play. We must not underestimate tele. I was once in a workshop with over fifty people. A woman was working on how her father had run off to sea when she was two, and she chose an unknown man from this large group to play her father. After a little while the psychodramatist asked the man playing the role what feelings it was bringing up for him, as he had tears running down his cheeks. He told how he had left his own daughter when she had been two and went and joined the Merchant Navy. This kind of thing happens a lot in psychodrama.

Okay let us take a break here and go and get some lunch.

Day one, afternoon

This afternoon I want to move onto the second stage of research psychodrama. This morning we all got involved in the action in the warm-up phase. This afternoon we will move on to a fuller research psychodrama using the whole group.

Helen has asked to explore her research, so where would you like to start?

Helen: Well my research is working with families in which both partners have careers and the dynamics that this creates. This afternoon I would particularly like to explore one family that I have been meeting with for some time as I am particularly concerned about my relationship with them. I feel somehow 'stuck' with them.

Peter: Where would you set this family? If you think about them where do you picture them?

Helen: I normally meet them in their living room, so perhaps we could use that.

Peter: Can you create their living room as you imagine it using the furniture here. It doesn't have to be physically accurate.

Helen, with the help of the group, shifts the furniture until she is happy with what she has re-created.

Peter: Now I want you to choose members of the group to play members of the family. I don't want you just to make rational choices based on similarity of age and looks, but to go with your instinct of who has the feel of this person for you. When you have chosen them I want you to place them in a sculpted position in this room you have created and then to double them as a way of introducing them to the group. That is I want you to put your hand on their shoulder and speak as if you were them.

Helen chooses the members of the group to play the parts and is already surprised by one or two of the people she picks and what that makes her realize about how she sees this family member. She places them in the sculpt and doubles for them.

Peter: I would like you to come back to the front of the stage and have a look at this scene you have created. Remember this isn't the real family, but a representation of the family image you have inside your own head. What would you like to say to this family or what would you like to ask them.

Helen spends some time looking at the family and then wandering around inside the scene. She begins, at first tentatively and then with more conviction, addressing the family members. Each time I ask her to role reverse with the family member she has addressed and respond to herself from the other role. After a while those playing the roles begin to feel their way into the parts and start to speak in role, which further enlivens the drama. Once or twice I check with Helen that they are speaking true to the dynamic as she perceives it. One time she says no that isn't how the Mum would respond, so I once again ask her to role reverse with the person playing Mum and speak as she thinks Mum would.

Gradually the issue emerges that Helen is being seduced away from her initial contract with the family to do the research into becoming a quasi-counsellor to the two parents on the stuckness in their relationship. There is also a hint that there is some covert sexual seduction towards her from the father in the family.

Peter: We seemed to have discovered some of the nature of this stuckness that you began this session referring to, both the stuckness in the couple relationship and your stuckness in deciding what role you want to be in relation to them. Let us stay with the focus on you; what are your options for your role?

Helen: Well I could stop doing the research with them and become their marriage counsellor. I could confront what I think is happening and say that isn't part of the role I agreed with you. Or I could finish the meetings and tell them that I need to move on.

Peter: Would you like to do a forward projection and try out these different propositions?

Helen: No, I know from the drama that has already happened that I want to finish, but I have always tried to work co-operatively with my research families and I don't want to make a unilateral exit.

At this stage I could have challenged her eagerness to choose the third option, and explored what she might be avoiding in the situation, but instead I choose to follow her direction.

Peter: Okay let's set up this option. This scene is your next visit to the family and you have decided that you want to terminate the research with them.

Helen tries out telling the family what she thinks is happening and that she wants to finish, but those in role are very successful at wearing down her conviction and resolve, and trying to get her to stay on in some facilitative role.

Peter: You seem to be stuck again. How about coming out into the audience and let us have someone else play Helen, so she can see how she gets stuck.

Someone else plays Helen while she watches. She both laughs and grimaces in recognition of how she gets seduced.

Peter: How did that seem?

Helen: It felt very accurate, but I still do not know how to be any different.

Peter: Well, let's use the resources of the group and have two or three people try out how they would confront this issue.

The scene is replayed three times with different people playing the role of researcher while Helen watches.

Helen: I really liked the way Mary was clear and direct with the family. She did not beat about the bush, but she was also caring and concerned to listen to the family's reaction without getting swayed by it. But I still do not think I could manage that. Perhaps I should just send Mary along to the next session!

Peter: Let us use Mary to help you now. We can re-do the scene with you back playing yourself, but this time you have the added resources of having seen others play the part. Also I am going to ask Mary to be your double. She will go into the scene with you and if you get stuck she can speak what she senses you are feeling and not saying. If she senses right then repeat it in your words, if it is not right say what is true for you.

With Mary's support and encouragement of the group Helen finds a way of terminating the research fieldwork and relationship with the role-played family in a way that feels finished and clear both for her and the family who give her feedback in role before deroling.

Peter: To get out of role I would like you each to say one way you are like the part you played, and three ways in which you are different. That includes you Helen so that you share with us how you also have many different aspects to you than the one you have shown us here today.

Peter: Having deroled I want to move into the final stage of the psychodrama process, for this morning we had the *warm-up*; this afternoon we have done an in-depth piece of *work* with Helen, and now we have the *sharing*. This gives us the opportunity to share with Helen our fellow-humanness. It is not the place to give her advice or good ideas. I invite you to share the feelings that you had either watching or being in the psychodrama, or what parallel experiences did it stir up for you?

Several members of the group share with Helen their feelings and experiences.

Peter: So Helen, how are you going to change your work with this family?

Helen: Well, after today I am quite clear that I want to finish the work with this family and I would like to thank the group for giving me the confidence and showing me some ways to tackle finishing. It isn't going to be easy but I have found my resolve.

The group then finishes the day with a closing circle of appreciations about the day and to Helen for sharing her vulnerability.

Workshop: day two

Welcome to day two of this workshop on using psychodrama as a form of phenomenological inquiry. Yesterday we all were involved in doing research psychodrama and becoming familiar with the terms and ways of working. We used psychodrama with Helen to explore both the structure of the family and the personal process of her as researcher, which is an essential part of the field that is being studied (see Reason and Marshall, 1987). Today I want to concentrate more on how we can use psychodrama phenomenologically.

Yesterday many of you experienced group sculpting for the first time. Today I want to share with you how these psychodramatic sculpts can be explored more deeply. When I was doing the research for my own Ph.D. (Peter Hawkins, 1986) I explored the learning environment of a large charity organization that works with the down-and-outs. I created a sculpt in the same way that Helen did yesterday, using sculpting, doubling, role reversal and spontaneous dialogue from those playing the parts. Like Helen I had several spontaneous insights from bringing this world alive. I was struck how I had chosen a woman to play one of the two male community leaders, and by what that told me about his role. There were also one or two significant 'Freudian slips' in my doubling, such as when I called someone by the wrong name. So far none of this is strictly phenomenological and could be more accurately called dramatic qualitative data analysis. But we then moved further in our exploring through what I term *psychodramatic reframing*.

In psychodramatic reframing I endeavour to explore the underlying patterns in the world that is being researched by means of making the familiar strange. This is done by looking at the situation as though it existed in a different context. Thus with the psychodrama of the down-and-out charity I did this by asking the question, 'if this organization was a family what sort of family would it be?' It is important that in this reframing you use frames or metaphors that fit. Thus when I was working with an architecture practice I asked them 'if they were a building, what sort of building they would be?'

When psychodramatically exploring the down-and-out charity we went on to reframe the sculpt through other metaphors. These further metaphors were chosen by the participants in the psychodrama volunteering the metaphors that the psychodrama suggested to them. There were a number of suggestions and from these we decided to explore the three which had the most resonance with the participating group. These were a playgroup, the early Christian church, and the period of adolescence. Each of these metaphors was worked through by recasting the same scene within this new frame. Thus the playgroup analogy arose because the down-and-out residents would mess up what they did not like, would break up the furniture, throw tantrums and seek attention. But what the psychodramatic reframing illuminated was how in this scene my role became that of 'Her Majesty's Inspector of Nursery Provision', which illuminated the fear of the charity workers concerning what I would write about them.

The early Christian church metaphor illuminated a quite different aspect of my role. For this drama centred on how the dead charismatic founder of the organization was like the dead Messiah, and how the workers and residents were still waiting for the resurrection or the second coming. They were at the stage of the disciples locked in the upper room or later in the catacombs; living with a sense of fear, persecution and the importance of staying true to the teachings of the dead leader, whose sayings are regularly read to the faithful. There was even a split within the organization similar to that between the Pauline church and the primitive church under Peter: one part of the organization had split away and now received government money and had paid staff, while the organization I worked with had stayed true to its fundamental beliefs and was determinedly independent of government agencies.

So in this drama what was my role? One member suggested I was the new Messiah, another the Holy Ghost, another the one who led the disciples to the right place at the right time to receive the Holy Spirit. Or was I Paul?

This exploration recalled to me how hungry the management committee had been first for a new charismatic leader and then for consultants, but how they had been anxious lest we preach a false doctrine. There was a danger that my colleague and I could be set up as the new Messiahs, with the risk that we would then be killed off as false prophets!

There is, of course, a danger of letting the metaphors carry you away into false grandiosity but the reframing does help to write large some of the underlying dynamics.

Phenomenology has a similar procedure which is called *fictive variations*. In both procedures the process is one of identifying what belongs to the underlying structure of the phenomena as presented. This underlying structure or form is like melody within music, which remains constant when transposed into a different octave or played on different instruments, because the notes remain in the same relationship to each other, or the listener immediately can hear the melody has changed (Valle and King, 1978, p. 16).

Workshop member: How would you have used reframing or fictive variations yesterday?

Peter: Well, we could have gone on with Helen to explore the underlying structure of the family, or more specifically the system that she and the family co-created. What sort of frames might we have used? I can only guess, as the best ones are those that emerge out of the psychodrama itself, but we might have looked at the family as a country or a business, and each of these would have thrown up interesting reflections on Helen's role and the boundary crossings involved. As when we use storytelling (see Chapter 4) we could have explored the drama through the frame of a suitable myth or fairy story. There are lots of possibilities, but what is most important is to try several so you can discover what is the unifying essence that echoes throughout the different fictive variations.

So we have looked at several aspects of the first level of phenomenological psychodrama: how you can use it to look at the assumptions you are carrying into your fieldwork; how you can explore your role and choices as researcher; how you can explore the many levels of data by sculpting the data, becoming it and exploring how various aspects of the data relate; finally, how through reframing you can illuminate the underlying structure from various angles.

Let me end this session by quoting a contemporary phenomenologist: 'Without thereby first disclosing the foundations of a phenomenon, no progress whatsover can be made concerning it, not even a first faltering step can be taken towards it, by science or by any kind of cognition' (Colaizzi, 1978).

After coffee we will look at using psychodrama to explore the second level of phenomenology.

The psychodrama of transcendental subjectivity
Before coffee we explored the use of psychodrama to carry out the first stage of phenomenology. Now we are going to turn to the much more difficult and subtle work of the second level of phenomenology and discover the psychodrama of transcendental subjectivity. To do this we must first be clear about the distinctions between the two phenomenological epochés.

The first epoché of phenomenological method is the attempt to see what is there more fully than we normally do when we are using 'common sense' and a 'natural scientific attitude'. To do this Husserl suggests that we 'bracket' our preconceptions, our expectations and conceptual frameworks which we normally bring to an encounter, which cause us to see an amalgam of what we expect to see and what is there. It is a process akin to the mystical traditions of opening the senses and suspending not just disbelief, but also belief and analytical conceptualizing.

There is a time for leaving the world of thought and to begin seeing as does a little child, by 'tarrying alongside' with the attitude of 'astonishment' (Heidegger). It is only by this open submission of oneself to receiving the world of the other that Husserl believes one can truly encounter the 'whatness' of the first order of transcendence, that is transcend the division between 'inside of me' and 'outside of me'.

However, at this stage phenomenology does not simply return to oneself with the acquisition of new pure data to develop what Hampden-Turner (1970) calls 'mental matrices of developing complexity'; instead it moves into the second epoché, and turns its attention to the second order of transcendence. In the second epoché the 'whatness' discovered in the first epoché must also be bracketed or held in abeyance, so that the 'howness' of their coming-into-being within our consciousness can be contemplated.

To do this Husserl infers that we need to develop a meta-level of study, although he does not use those post-Husserlian terms. He introduces the idea of a 'transcendental ego' that can apprehend and witness the functioning of our naive ego, that is the part of ourself that has been involved in doing the research. In this workshop I do not want to go into the philosophical subtleties of this phenomenological process, but if you want to know more you can read it in my Ph.D. (Peter Hawkins, 1986). What is important to grasp here, is that this epoché is concerned with developing a perspective within us from where we can see *the rest of ourself as part of the field we are researching*.

If we now turn to psychodrama we can look at how psychodrama can perform these two phenomenological epochés with a delightful simplicity that combines clarity and depth. Let me describe a psychodrama I once directed. A woman, in her early twenties, whom I will call Janet, was working on how, in her relationship to her boyfriend and other adult peers, she seemed to react in one of two ways. Either she would be very childlike and dependent, or very rigid and emotionally cut off and judgmental. A Freudian using the 'scientific attitude' might interpret a weak ego structure, a regressive id in conflict with an introjected parental super-ego. A transactional analyst may use more everyday terms and talk about her internalized child and parent states.

Using the first-level phenomenological epoché, the psychodrama director would bracket off any interpretations they were tempted to make and would invite the protagonist to bring their 'life-world' into the here-and-now on stage. This is how I proceeded, asking Janet to sculpt both sides of her self as she experienced them. Like the sculpting we did yesterday, I asked her to use her spontaneous creativity to sculpt two members of the group as if they were clay, to use her hands and not her words to get them into the position that felt that it accurately echoed her feeling of being in that role. In phenomenological terms we are engaging the protagonist's 'prereflective thinking' and in Bateson's terms we are encouraging analogic mapping rather than digital explanation (Bateson, 1972).

When the sculpt was finished I asked Janet to become each of the parts portrayed – taking up the positions she had sculpted and giving expression to that part of her. Once again this move from talking about (what Perls (1969) calls 'aboutism') to 'becoming' in the 'here-and-now' is a parallel process to the phenomenological 'bracketing' of the 'scientific or natural attitude' and directly moving into the world of the 'Lebenswelt'.

Janet, having become both the parts, was able then to dialogue between the two sub-personalities (Assagioli, 1965), role reversing from one to the other. At this stage (or on this stage) we have replicated in the therapeutic theatre what the woman describes as happening in the external world, namely the coming-into-being of the two sub-personalities. But there is a difference between this coming-into-being and those of the everyday world as this time they have been produced 'at will' – the protagonist with the support from the director has brought them into being.

This fundamental difference allows the next important psychodramatic move to take place. I asked Janet to step out of her drama and watch while the two group members (auxiliary egos in psychodramatic terminology) played out the scene she had created. In the external world she had experienced her self or her 'I' as the victim of this process, but here in the therapeutic theatre it was her creative 'I' that was directing the drama, and was now able to stand back and become witness to it.

Her play having finished, I said that I would now like to talk not to the two Janets on stage but the third Janet, the third 'I' she had brought to the group. At first she was understandably nonplussed until I explained that I meant the Janet who had done the sculpting, the role playing and witnessing. This was the creative Janet within whom the drama was 'coming into consciousness' and through whom the consciousness was becoming expressed and psychodramatically manifest. This was the creative Janet for whom the possibilities for change could start.

In this dialogue we were now 'bracketing' the particular aspect of the Lebenswelt we had encountered, to reflectively turn our attention on the 'I' in whom and through whom the Lebenswelt came-into-being. The Lebenswelt was clearly bracketed because there it was in frozen tableau on our psychodramatic stage.

When asked what she, the third Janet, wanted to do about this scenario, the therapeutic insight was not in the answer, but in what Perls calls the 'Aha', the sudden awareness that there was a third Janet who could answer, who could become conscious of her sub-personalities in their coming-into-being within her, both within the therapeutic theatre and then, hopefully, back in her outside life.

What I am suggessting is that this simple but effective therapeutic shift is parallel to the second epoché of Husserl's phenomenological method, and that the move from 'naive ego' to 'transcendental ego' can be simplified when spatially and dramatically enacted.

Let us break for lunch and renew our strength before embarking on using psychodrama to explore this second-level phenomenology.

Day two, afternoon

This afternoon we are going to engage in doing what I talked about this morning. To do this we are going to divide up into fours and work in a similar way to how we worked yesterday morning. If you remember we developed a dialogue between you and an aspect of your research. To do this we used the psychodramatic techniques of sculpting, doubling, and role reversal (becoming your research).

Psychodrama of epoché 2 exercise

Step 1. This time I would like the person who is the protagonist to choose another aspect of their research, preferably something in your research that you feel has engaged your inner self in some way, and to use one of your colleagues to be sculpted and doubled in that role. Then I would like you to sculpt another member of your quartet as the you that researches this aspect of your study, your fieldwork and encounter researcher part. Is this part of you close or distant from that which it is researching? Are you confronting the aspect of study, hiding from it or creeping up on it? Try and feel your way into portraying the relationship between you as researcher and the researched. Feel your way back into your feelings when relating to this bit of the research and let the feeling come out through your hands into the sculpt.

Step 2. Now you have two statues in some form of relationship to each other, I want you to have the chance to bring them to life. You can either develop the dialogue by alternatively doubling one and then the other statue; or you can alternatively role reverse with each of them. As it develops those playing the parts might feel ready to speak in role. The job of the fourth member is to be the *director* of this psychodrama, (see Figure 3.1).

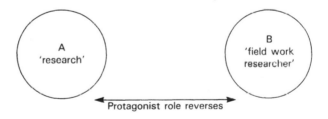

Figure 3.1 *Step 2*

Step 3. Now I want to have a word with the directors. I want you to get the protagonist as involved as possible in creating this enacted dialogue drama, and when it is in full swing I want you to take the protagonist out of the drama so that he can watch his research relationship be enacted by the two auxiliaries. This is similar to how I described working with Janet this morning (see Figure 3.2).

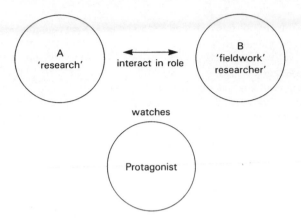

Figure 3.2 *Step 3*

Step 4. Now comes the interesting part. I want you as directors to facilitate an encounter between the reflective researcher who has been watching their own research drama and the part of them which is being played on stage; that is their fieldwork researcher. Use role reversal, so that they can play both sides of this internal dialogue between the active and reflective parts of themselves (see Figure 3.3). Then have them take your colleague who was in the research role and put them into the role of reflective researcher (see Figure 3.4).

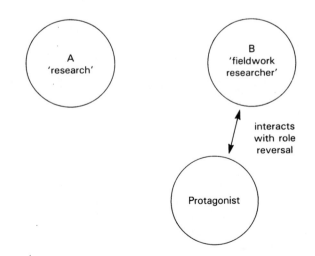

Figure 3.3 *Step 4a*

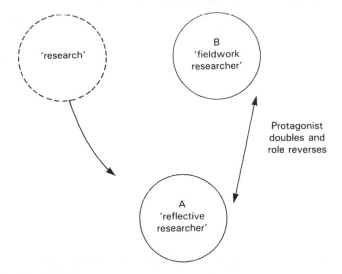

Figure 3.4 *Step 4b*

Step 5. So far neither of these *sub-personalities* is a transcendental ego in Husserl's terms, both are naive egos. So when you have this second dialogue under way psychodramatically, I want you once again to remove the protagonist from the drama and have them watch the two other members of the group enact for them their internal dialogue between their active and reflective research sub-personalities (see Figure 3.5).

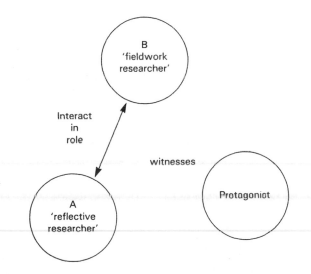

Figure 3.5 *Step 5*

This time ask them to watch as witnesses of their own coming-to-know. By this time I mean not to get carried away with the content of the action, but to focus on the *process* of their coming-to-know about that which they are studying. Help them write down or record what they become aware of when watching this process, including their sensations, feelings, images or surprising thoughts.

You will need thirty minutes for each drama and ten minutes for sharing before swapping around roles. In order for you all to have a chance to do this and get a tea break we will come back together in three hours time.

In this last session are there any questions about psychodrama as a form of research, its application and limitations.

Workshop member: You have mainly concentrated on using psychodrama in the reflection phase of the research. Can you say a bit more about using psycho-drama before meeting the people with whom you are going to do the research?

Peter: Psychodrama is a useful mode for looking at your assumptions, expectations and researcher counter-transference (see Chapter 2) prior to encountering your research group. When I went to work with the down-and-out charity I had all sorts of expectations and stereotypes concerning the people they worked with. These were going to block me meeting the situation openly. I could have used psychodrama to discover these attitudes so that I could 'bracket' them and put them aside, or at least be aware of their existence.

I would have done this by sculpting my image of a down-and-out and of those that work with them; then dialogue and role reverse with my imaginal figures. This way I would also discover more about my own subconscious motivations in working with this group, and the nature of my identifications and projections on to down-and-outs and those that work with them.

Workshop member: Can you also say more about using psychodrama in the co-operative encounter stage of research?

Peter: I mentioned earlier in the workshop how I asked the architecture practice to sculpt themselves. This I find an excellent method for actively accessing the underlying dynamics of a group with which I am working.

I start this process by asking the group to clear a space in the room of furniture, and then place in the middle some objects that symbolically represent the centre of their group, in whatever way they see it. I then ask them to stand up and walk around and place themselves as near or far away from the centre as they feel themselves to be; to place themselves near to those they feel most connected to, and away from those they feel distant from; then to adopt a pose that characterizes how they typically are as part of the group. This whole process takes some time, as while you are trying to find your place the people you feel close to are also moving.

When everybody is in position I ask each person to make a statement – 'In this position in the group I feel...'. After this round I invite people to share 'In this position what I need or want is...'; or 'How I need to move is...'.

This can lead on to members of the group experimenting with changing their position and exploring what repercussions and reception it has in the group. Only then would I invite the group to explore looking at their own dynamics by reframing the sculpt; for example if this architecture practice was a building what sort of building would it be?

Workshop member: What have you found to be the limitations of this research approach?

Peter: Well, for a start, every time you use it with a group you are researching you have to spend time teaching them about psychodrama and warming them up to using it, just as we had to do in this workshop. Psychodrama increases people's creativity, spontaneity and ability to share their analogic and right brain awareness, but it takes some time before they feel warmed up and familiarized enough to play around with the methodology. Up until that time the use of psychodrama increases my expert role as researcher and psychodramatist. This runs contrary to attempts to achieve more equality in participative and co-operative research.

The complexity and sophistication of the methodology also make it difficult to explain to those you have been psychodramatizing in their absence, what you have been up to and how you came upon your new insights. I have been talking with Helen about whether she is going to tell the family about the psychodrama. This brings up all sorts of ethical and professional, as well as research issues. I try and share as much as I am able of my reflective process, with those I have been reflecting on, but I also need to have private space to explore what the research process is doing to me. Thus I am entitled to some private space with my research colleagues and supervisors. It is important to decide which parts of the psychodrama process belong to each of these categories.

Finally psychodrama is also difficult to do on your own. I have done psychodrama in the context of a one-to-one consultancy and supervision sessions. We have used pieces of furniture and objects of the room to represent various elements of their research situation. However, psychodramatic research is best done with consenting colleagues, and sometimes they need convincing and help with their fears that they are going to have to 'act'. My experience has been that once colleagues get over their initial fears and scepticism, they get deeply involved and gain a lot from the experience, even when they are not focusing on their own research.

We must stop here as we are almost at an end of this workshop. I want to take just a few minutes to review where we have been. I have introduced you both to phenomenology and psychodrama, and we have all been engaged in some very interesting dramas and encounters.

In psychodrama you have met Moreno and been introduced to the three stages of warm-up, work and sharing. We have explored the key concepts of tele, sculpting, doubling, role reversal and reframing, and have learnt what are protagonists, auxiliaries, and directors.

In phenomenology we have explored the two epochés of Husserl's methodology and have followed Heidegger down the 'Holzwege' or firebreak to the 'Lichtung' or clearing.

But most important, we have developed together ways of bringing alive our research data and experience, so that we can walk around it, become it and begin to see how the parts relate to each other and what pattern or form is at their essence. Also we began to explore the relationship between our active and reflective research sub-personalities and witness our coming to know.

Thank you for your hard work in exploring with me this complex but exciting field of research and I wish you well with all your future explorations.

4

Storytelling as Inquiry

Peter Reason and Peter Hawkins

> The Master gave his teaching in parables and stories which his disciples listened to with pleasure – and occasional frustration, for they longed for something deeper.
>
> The Master was unmoved. To all their objections he would say, 'You have yet to understand, my dears, that the shortest distance between a human being and Truth is a story'. (Antony de Mello, SJ, *One Minute Wisdom*)

One day, in a graduate research seminar in Bath, a group of researchers were exploring how to use qualitative research methods within the context of co-operative inquiry. Several of them became bored and dissatisfied with categorizing the 'data' from their experience and developing grounded theories from this (Glaser and Strauss, 1967; Glaser, 1978). They wanted an approach which would express more the liveliness, the involvement, and even the passion of their experiences. So they started to tell the stories of their lives and of their inquiries. This chapter tells how, from this beginning, we continued to explore how stories and storytelling might be part of an emergent paradigm of inquiry.

This emergent paradigm of inquiry appears to us to be multidimensional (Reason, 1986). It tends to be co-operative rather than unilateral; to be qualitative rather than quantitative; to be holistic rather than reductionist; to work in natural settings rather than in artificial laboratories. When we start to see storytelling as an aspect of inquiry we discover an important new dimension: inquiry can work either to explain or to express; to analyse or to understand. This is part of the realm of presentational knowing (Heron, 1981a) – knowing expressed in art, in poetry, in dance, and here in the telling of stories.

Explanation and expression: two paths of inquiry

We see *explanation* and *expression* as two basic modes of reflecting on and processing experience.

Explanation is the mode of classifying, conceptualizing, and building theories from experience. Here the inquirer 'stands back', analyses, discovers or invents concepts, and relates these in a theoretical model. There are two classic approaches to this: first, the approach of observation and description – as for example in botany, astronomy, and anthropology. In this the inquirer senses the world either directly or through instruments, and endeavours to describe and then map out that which is experienced. This is essentially an analytical approach: dividing holistic experience into manageable components. The parts into which the whole is divided may either be physical boundaries – such as bones, planets, or tribes – or conceptual boundaries – such as stages of economic development, character patterns, etc. As Bateson (1972) points out, all these boundaries are arbitrary, and it is a matter of choice where the inquirer applies the 'scissors': the distinctions are necessary and useful, but have no objective existence. The second classic approach is experimentation, in which the inquirer attempts to manipulate the experimental field in order to test a theory. Experimentation depends on some prior descriptive inquiry. In the social sciences these two modes of inquiry are exemplified by anthropology and qualitative sociology on the one hand, and experimental academic psychology on the other. Orthodox science is an exercise in explanation, endeavouring to answer questions of *what* and *why*?

Expression is the mode of allowing the meaning of experience to become manifest. It requires the inquirer to partake deeply of experience, rather than stand back in order to analyse. Meaning is part and parcel of all experience, although it may be so interwoven with that experience that it is hidden: it needs to be discovered, created, or made manifest, and communicated. We work with the meaning of experience when we tell stories, write and act in plays, write poems, meditate, create pictures, enter psychotherapy, etc. When we partake of life we create meaning; the purpose of life is making meaning. Here we follow James Hillman (1975), who argues that 'my soul is not the result of objective facts that require explanation; rather it reflects subjective experiences that require understanding' (p. 15). Indeed, Hillman has developed his own rich archetypal epistemology 'of the heart', based on loving and personifying as a way of knowing, which is one of the influences on our thinking.

We are arguing that the expression of experience, and thus inquiry into meaning, is an important aspect of research which has been almost ignored by orthodox science. In the tradition of C.P. Snow's notion of 'two cultures' it is seen as belonging only to the realm of the 'creative arts', which are classified (sic) as being an entirely different world from the scientific pursuit of knowledge. One field in which the question of meaning has arisen, and in which there has been some marriage between 'scientific' inquiry and meaning-making, has been the development of psychotherapy, which although growing in part out of the scientific medical tradition, had very soon to incorporate storytelling (which developed into the therapeutic case study) and later turned to myth, imagery, metaphor, and religion. Very early on Freud, while trying to analyse his neurotic patients, adopted the classical Greek myth of Oedipus in order to *illuminate* and make meaning of his patient's story, and in the Jungian tradition religious myth is frequently used as one way of deepening the meaning of experience.

Since much of our professional practice has been in fields related to psychotherapy, as well as in academic behavioural science, and since we have long been dissatisfied with orthodox approaches to human inquiry, it is not surprising that we should have focused on the creation of meaning as an important and overlooked aspect of research:

> Academic psychology, in its eagerness to be as scientific as physics, has devoted all its energies not to understand but to *explain* the soul (psyche) from the view-point of natural sciences. In this way the soul has been exorcised from the only field which is traditionally dedicated to its study: it has been explained away, reductivised. (Avens, 1980, p. 32)

What Avens says about psychology may also be said of sociology and of the other anthropological sciences. In this chapter we have drawn primarily on psychological and psychotherapeutic sources for our ideas and inspirations, since this is our base discipline. We invite readers from other disciplines to make their own contribution to inquiry into meanings.

To make meaning manifest through expression requires the use of a creative medium through which the meaning can take form. This is not to be confused with a conceptual grid which divides up experience, it is rather the creation of an 'empty space', a Lichtung or clearing, as Heidegger describes it, which becomes a vessel in which meaning can take shape. There are many languages in which meaning can be created and communicated: the languages of words which lead to stories and poetry; the languages of action which lead to mime, gesture, and drama; the languages of colour and shape that lead to painting and sculpture; the languages of silence and stillness which are part of meditation. The languages are analogical and symbolic; they do not point out meaning directly; they demonstrate it by re-creating pattern in metaphorical shape and form. 'Image and meaning are identical; and as the first takes shape, so the latter becomes clear. Actually the pattern needs no interpretation; it portrays its own meaning' (Jung, *CW* vol. 8).

The medium and the meaning are essentially interpenetrating: it is foolish to ask the meaning of a story or painting as separate from the work in itself. And sometimes the meaning is released and made manifest by the medium, as expressed by Michaelangelo in his statement that he did not create his sculptures, only release them from the stone. Here we touch on an issue we must return to: is meaning created by and through individual life, or is it lying there in some 'collective unconscious' awaiting to be brought into the light?

Creative expression is often relegated to the production of the beautiful or the entertaining. We see it also as a mode of inquiry, a form of meaning-making, and a way of knowing. So what is needed is a *methodology of meaning-making as part of human inquiry.* We have chosen as our methodological vessel to explore and develop story and storytelling, as this is the most universal of all expressive media, and one we were familiar with in our professional experience in the worlds of therapy, education, and organization research.

In this argument we parallel Eckhartsberg (1981), who makes a similar distinction to that between explanation and expression when he contrasts denotative and connotative thinking.

> denotative thinking and theorising contains all scientific thinking. . .
>
> *Connotative thinking and aesthetic experience* is concerned with the domains of the Arts and the capacity of the human individual to create worlds and objects of polyvalent meanings: metaphors and symbols. . . . Symbolic thinking is connotative thinking, allowing multiple readings and interpretations of the given. . .
>
> Whereas denotative thinking can be said to be a modulation of clear and distinct perception, connotative thinking can be understood as the elaboration of feeling and emotional imagery and intuition into created form and expression. (1981, pp. 82–3)

He goes on to point out that connotative thinking is carried out through 'hermeneutical experience and activity'. Wilber defines hermeneutics as

> the science of interpretation, or the determination of the meaning of mental productions (e.g. what is the meaning of Macbeth? of last night's dream? of your life?). As such it is a transempirical discipline, for no amount of analytic–empirical–scientific data, no matter how complete, can totally establish meaning . . . . Rather, meaning is established, not by sensory data, but by unrestrained communicative inquiry and interpretation. (Wilber, 1981a, p. 32)

Eckhartsberg sees storytelling as central to the hermeneutical process:

> Human meaning making rests in stories. Life making calls for accounts, for story, for sharing. To be human is 'to be entangled in stories' (1981, p. 90)

Another stimulus to this quest of ours was Ian Mitroff's notion of the varieties of social science experience. In describing the inquiry style he calls the conceptual humanist (CH), he concludes:

> According to C. West Churchman (1971, p. 178), 'The Hegelian inquirer is a storyteller, and Hegel's Thesis is that the best inquiry is the inquiry that produces stories. The underlying life of a story is its drama, not its "accuracy". . . . But is storytelling science? Does a system designed to tell stories well also produce knowledge?' In summarizing the CH view of science, we repeat Churchman's question: 'Is story-telling science?' For the CH the answer is 'yes'.
>   This does not mean that any story qualifies as science but that science consists of taking stories seriously. Stories can be used in a variety of ways: as amusement or as devices with which to peer into human desires, wishes, hopes and

fears. In this sense, stories form an essential ingredient of the CH's method because they provide the 'hardest' body of evidence and the best method of problem definition.

The best stories are those which stir people's minds, hearts and souls and by doing so give them new insights into themselves, their problems, and their human condition. The challenge is to develop a human science that more fully serves this aim. The question then is not, 'Is storytelling science' but 'Can science learn to tell good stories?' (1978, pp. 92–3)

In answer to this question, our answer is an emphatic yes! But we are novices in knowing *how* to use stories as inquiry, how to engage with stories as 'unrestrained communicative inquiry' (Wilber, 1981a). Our questions are 'How do we use stories as inquiry? how do we draw forth meaning through storytelling? and what are the stages in the process of meaning creation in and through stories?'

Explanation and expression in an overall model

Before we develop the storytelling notion in more detail, let us return again to our distinction between explanation and expression and see how these two modes can be related in an overall model of inquiry. For we see explanation and expression not as competing modes but as poles of a dialectic: any complete model must eventually show how these two complement each other. A simple model, which illustrates in part this relationship, is shown in Figure 4.1. All modes of inquiry start with experience: it has been well argued earlier that any form of inquiry that does not rest in experiential knowing is quite inadequate (Heron, 1981a). This experience is held or contained firstly in sensory experience and memory, and then collected as 'data' in record or account. It is at this juncture that the paths of explanation and expression divide.

Looking first at the path of explanation, we have adapted the general description developed by Diesing (1972) in his account of holistic inquiry, which seems to us to be a most adequate overview of the descriptive mode of explanatory inquiry. Diesing describes how social scientists, once they have entered a field situation, proceed by gathering information, and identifying themes; how they weave these themes into a descriptive case study, which contains within it a 'pattern model' of explanation; how they then compare and contrast case studies, and maybe seek new cases to fill out the categories, so they can develop a typology; and how the 'mid-range' theory of typology leads on to the development of a general theory. We would argue that all this usually takes place within an overall paradigm (Kuhn, 1962).

If we now turn to the path of expression, we posit a similar progression through levels, or stages of development, from account through metaphor to archetype, which Hillman (1975) describes as 'the deepest patterns of

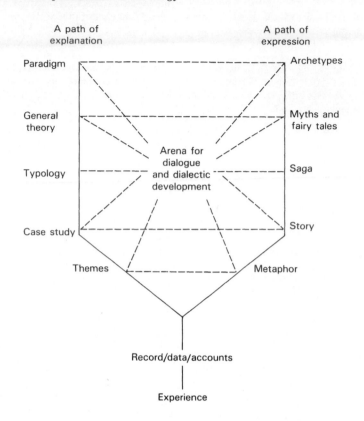

Figure 4.1   *Explanation and expression. Note:* We are grateful to
Tish Feilden and Tony Greenall who contributed to the development
of the original version of the model. See also Greenall (1982)

psychic functioning, the roots of the soul governing the perspectives we
have of ourselves and the world'. This path is less well explicated and
with fewer signposts left by previous travellers, but is nevertheless there:
the signposts we have adopted have come from a number of sources,
including our own experience, and the writing particularly of James
Hillman and Marie-Louise von Franz.

Hillman draws on Vico to show how metaphor is 'a fable in brief'
because it 'gives sense and pattern to insensate things'. Thus metaphors
are 'more than ways of speaking; they are ways of perceiving, feeling,
and existing' (Hillman, 1975, p. 32).

Von Franz (1982) has developed through her study of fairy tales a theory
of how personal stories become 'sagas' through entering the local collective
folklore; and how sagas become fairy tales or myths when their archetypal

patterns and relationships become increasingly divorced from their original content. The path of the inquirer may be from experience through metaphor and story towards myth and archetype; but von Franz, Hillman, and others point out also how meaning can 'break through' from the archetypal level into individual lives and stories.

Thus we have two paths of inquiry: from experience through explanation to general theory; and from experience through expression to myth and archetype. Thus we create between them a space for dialogue and for dialectical development, so that a theme may be illuminated by a story, or a theory may clarify a myth. Indeed, some of the most illuminating researchers have used both paths: we have already referred to Freud's use of the Oedipal myth; another example is Ruth Benedict's (1935) use of the Apollonian and Dionisian archetypes to illuminate and express different cultural patterns; and modern physicists have turned to the metaphors of wave and particle to illuminate and express their mathematical formulations of matter and energy.

Launching into storytelling

The initial ideas about stories as inquiry came from a number of discussions with colleagues: we found, for example, that when we wanted to share our practice with each other the best way was to tell each other stories. We also noted how we used stories for a variety of purposes in teaching, when working in groups and in therapy. The model of explanation and expression emerged as part of a research seminar in which we were exploring different means of working with qualitative data. So we decided to pick up this theme of storytelling as inquiry more carefully and creatively, and we started by writing stories about simple aspects of our lives for each other, sharing these, and then taking time to work with the story, recording both what happened to the story, and also the method and approaches we had used in our exploration.

The first story we looked at was written by Peter R. as a memory of the family summer holiday:

> We sailed out from Hope Cove in the afternoon. The wind was onshore and quite light, and sea was grey. We had to watch for underwater rocks as we went out. And then we set out along the coast on a reach, and with some trepidation, set the mackerel line; a little boat, two small boys, and a mackerel line – feels like a lot to keep an eye on. Matthew, holding line, says it is tugging. Into the wind, heave to (having gone right round onto the other tack, that is not necessary). Pull in the line and find the mackerel. Quick, bat it on the head with the cricket stump, mind the hooks, blood on the boat, let the line out. (And I think that that fish was the biggest

alive thing I have intentionally killed) (so much is happening). Off
we go again, Ben holds the line. And it gets caught on the buoy.
And we free it (and there's another fish). And off we go. And the
line gets caught on the bottom. And off we go. And lose the line.
And pick it up – brill man overboard drill (but it could be better,
really must practise).

Pause to mop out the boat, and then in my excitement throw the
sponge over the side. And off we go. And I catch two fish (Matthew
is at the helm, smart lad that one, keeps his attention on the sails
and steers a good course). And so home, tired and with fish to Dad
and Anna.

We found it helpful to start with the author reading his story aloud, thus
adding tone and feeling to the simple words and recalling some of the
feel of the experience itself. Moving on, we found that if the listener then
took the story and read it back, with *his* style and intonation, the original
story would begin to take more of a separate life of its own (moving, in
a sense, to the beginnings of the level of saga). When the listener read
the story back, the storyteller could hear his story in a new way, which
we found both validating (Did I really write that?), and helping to develop
a wider perspective. In a sense, when the story is distanced in this way,
it can be seen not only as part of me, not my product to fret over whether
it is 'good enough', and can be enjoyed more for its own sake. So one
way of expressing meaning is to play around with who is the *storyteller*,
and who is the *audience*; and also with the variety of *voices*, *roles*, and
dramatic style which the storyteller can adopt.

When we had done this, we found that each story contained many stories
interwoven within it. We found that the task of expression was to open
up the story more fully, rather than tie it down to one tale or simply identify
the 'sub-plots'. So if we 'walk around' the story, and view it through
different perspective windows, then like a prism, it appears differently.
Each different view will awaken a different state of consciousness in the
storyteller and the audience.

So, we can see this story as a simple tale of family adventure; as a moden
version of male initiation (Bly and Thompson, 1985); as reflecting two
small boys (Peter and Peter) launching into storytelling; as a version of
the classic Hero's Quest; as a journey from safe land into the unknown
waters of the unconscious to return with fish, the traditional symbol of
gifts from unconscious depths (Jung, *CW*, 9, p. 237). These different
stories-within-the-story carry different meanings for the storyteller, reflecting different aspects of the current life position. The meaning of each of
these interwoven aspects of the story arises out of the interaction of the
story, the storyteller, and the audience. The stories should not be seen
as separate states or levels, but rather as interpenetrating reflections of

how the present drama of the storyteller's life is reflected in the drama of the story. At a communal level we would assume that the stories told within a community reflect the processes of the community. Levels reflect levels; outside reflects inside; the individual reflects the collective; and the past reflects the present.

After wandering around the story we wandered inside. First of all, using our experience of the humanistic therapies (particularly psychodrama and gestalt) we could relive the story, becoming each or any of the characters or objects to which we became attracted, speaking in the present active tense and in the first person, thus personifying and giving them voice: 'I am a boat. I am small, and blue, and I feel small and tipsy in this great grey water. It is good to be away from the rocks, and I feel confident, although scared to be out here in the deep seas . . .' and so on. By becoming the parts, we found we could express that which could not be pinned down, holding the nuances of meaning in dramatic suspense (Hawkins, 1980). An extension of this approach is to talk directly to a chosen part of the story, and indeed to carry on a dialogue. Thus the fish could be asked how they feel about being 'killed', how they feel about leaving the under-waters and coming ashore.

And we can, by wandering inside the story, 'dream the dream on', as Jung put it. So we found that the boat, when given a voice, had other journeys it wished to make: one of these was to take Peter, Elizabeth, and the two boys to a golden island of beach and sunshine, which was then expressed in a poem by Peter H:

To Peter the Boatman

The boat that grips your legs and body
and sets your magical I free.
The boat that is your legs and body
and carries you through this dangerous sea.

Where shall I take you – I ask the magical king
To enchanted Island, deserted of others
Save my wife, my sons and me.

What will you do there? – I ask the magical traveller
Play with shells and sand and pebbles
and lie in the shade of the banyan tree.
There we will float in peaceful suspension
weaved in a golden blue hue.

What is the voice of this enchanted island
And what is the voice of the golden blue hue
What is the voice of the boat body poem
And where will this boat take us to?

It was here that we first discovered the richness of having the listener reflect or echo back the story in their own words and in their own style, an approach we used more fully later in a storytelling workshop (see below). The approach is to respond to a story *with a story*, or with another expressive mode such as a poem or a picture. To do this marks a major break with the path of explanation, with its interpretation, classification, and theorizing; and is a way in which the expression of meaning can be significantly deepened. Bound up in this example is another important way in which the story may be loosened from its pragmatic holds, which is to transfer it to another medium of expression, as, for example, we have here transferred a spoken story into written prose and later into a poem contained within a very simple set of 'rules' – three lines of five, seven, and five syllables each:

> Sailing sea naked
> cockleshell boat and two boys
> brought the fish back home.

Putting the story into this kind of simple form may help to identify the *rhythm* of the story: this story of a fishing trip has the rhythm of the orgasmic cycle (Randall and Southgate, 1980) and of the Hero's Quest. This is a rhythm of preparation; of going out and building energy through confronting dangers and crisis; of a peak, a vision, an accomplishment; and of a return to ground. We hypothesize that all stories have rhythms, maybe more complex, which are an essential aspect of their meaning – a sense of direction and completion. Another way in which the rhythm could be expressed would be by changing into the medium of music and melody, or even of drumbeat. (Compare the use of psychodrama in Chapter 3 as another means of freeing experience from its literal content in order to identify an underlying form.)

Moving yet another level, away from the experience and the account and towards the archetypal, is to transpose the story into a *mythic form*, to rewrite the story 'as if' it took place on Mount Olympus, or within the realm of the Brothers Grimm. We can play with our story more fully if we allow our fantasy to wander, and to take the story into a magical dimension through imagery and our conscious and semi-conscious aware-ness of collective myth and archetype:

> Once upon a time, a fisherman and his two sons went out to catch magical fish. They had all the normal food they needed, but thought it would be fun to catch something special. And so they went out to a particular place with their boat, launched out through all kinds of dangers, and set their lines. The fisherman was concerned at the danger they were facing, but he knew his boat was sound, and his

sons were skilled and clear. And they had many adventures and many dangers, nearly losing their line several times. The fish were beautiful and clearly magical, so the fisherman was doubtful about killing them. But they were clearly giving themselves to him, and so they fished till they had just what they needed, and sailed home safely.

Another way of entering this realm is to *story-associate*; to ask the question, 'What stories and myths does this tale bring to mind?', and thus to discover the *story relatives* of the original tale. Our fishing story reminds us of *Sinbad the Sailor, Parsifal, Ulysses,* and *Swallows and Amazons.* By bringing these stories alongside each other it is possible to 'sense' the underlying essence which they share.

We followed this exploration of the fishing trip by looking at another story, written by Peter H., about an afternoon's walk in the rain with a friend. In using the same kind of approaches with a very different story, we were led to different meanings reflected in different myths and different rhythms.

Men, women, and storytelling: a two-day workshop

Following our explorations as a pair, we wanted to take the storytelling as inquiry theme further, and to see how the process worked in a group. Since a number of our colleagues and friends, both within the research community at the University of Bath and in our personal development programmes, were also interested both in the themes of storytelling, and also in understanding more fully relationships between men and women, we decided to take the plunge and set up a workshop based on these twin themes. (We would like to acknowledge the contribution of the participants on this workshop, and especially Judi Marshall who worked with us as co-facilitator.)

We met for two days, fourteen people, roughly equal men and women. In the spirit of co-operative inquiry (Reason and Rowan, 1981a), we invited the group to explore together our experience of gender, using storytelling as a vehicle. As initiating facilitators we drew the distinction between explanation and expression, but chose not to offer the methods we had already developed as a pair, rather allowing space for the group to evolve its own approach and method. Through this workshop we learned a lot, both about how groups may be helped to use the storytelling method, and also about the one particular method this group evolved for itself.

We found at the beginning of the workshop there was almost a 'hunger' for stories; and yet people saw themselves much more as listeners than as storytellers. We kept being asked, 'But what do you mean by a story?'; and we kept responding that any event retold from life which appeared to carry some meaning, however small, is a story. But we found that once the first story was told, it was much easier for others to join in. As the workshop unfolded we were all amazed at the creativity that the group developed, as people discovered their ability to recount stories from their lives, to respond to others' stories in poetry or prose, to reflect a variety of shades of meaning from an original tale. What is needed is the development of easy, concrete ways to start the storytelling off, to create an inviting space that may then be filled.

The method the group evolved for exploring stories was both quite different from and similar to the approaches we had used as a pair. We did not, as we had expected, enter the stories through gestalt and psychodrama; nor did we consciously pose questions to 'complete' the stories, or to move them towards a mythic level. After quite a long period of forming and tentatively discovering our own way of being with stories, the main approach we used was to respond to story with stories. Typically, one person would tell a story from their own lives which carried some meaning about male and female; the rest of the group would listen, and then privately compose some kind of response – another story, a poem, or a re-telling of the original story. This was a short, immediate process, taking about ten minutes, so there was no time to worry about perfecting a work of art, but enough time to give form to the response which the story had triggered within them. And then we quite simply took it in turns to read our own response back to the original storyteller and the group.

Following the workshop, we collected together four 'families' of stories – that is to say, the original tale and the various responses. Looking over these afterwards, we can classify these responses into four types, which we have termed *replies, echoes, re-creations,* and *reflections.* In doing this we are using the path of explanation, and in particular the creation of an empirical typology, to clarify our progress along the path of expression.

To illustrate these four types of response, we will use Don's story, which was responded to only by the men of the group:

Don's Story

I must have been about four, when my brothers and I were at Miss Pulford's school in her front room on the main road. One day, we went to Dawn Brodie's party. Dawn Brodie! A name that stands in my memory like a monument. She was a Mabel Lucy Attwell kind of girl, all blonde curls and bows and ankle socks. What we did at the party I can't remember, my eldest brother, who was backward, my other brother and I. I suppose there were jellies and cream cakes, and we must have played Postman's Knock or something, because when I got home, my mother was informed that 'Don's been kissing the girls'.

A *reply* is 'my reaction to your story': an expressive way of giving shape to the feelings and ideas arising while listening to the story. Thus Peter R's reply to Don:

> How can we be with them?
> Silly little girls.
> What do we say to them?
> Silly little girls.
> With their bows and their curls.
> Silly little girls.
> With their ankle socks and their patent black shoes –
> Silly little girls.
> With their frills and their giggles,
> Their cream cakes and fancy jellies –
> Silly little girls.
> How can we be with them?
>
> And when we do find a way,
> We're betrayed by our brothers:
> 'Don's been kissing the girls'!

An *echo* or sharing response is 'your theme in my story': here the listeners tell their own stories on the same theme. So Don's memory of his early relationship with girls is echoed by Philip's story about his son:

> 'Don's been kissing the girls!
> Don kissed Dawn Brodie.'
> Don remembers – REMEMBERS.
>
> Dick loves Shirley Read.
> Dick spend sixty pee on sweets for Shirley's birthday
> Dick loves
> cooee
> sexee
>
> Dick calls loud from the tree,
> 'Dad, to have me
> Did you put your penis into Mummy's vagina?'
> Embarrassed laughter.
> 'Come down from the tree
> Let's talk about it more quietly.'
>
> Will Dick REMEMBER?
> I was into sex up to here
> And all Dad did was laugh, and say,
> 'Don't shout about it.'

And the women
and the men
eye each other uneasily.

A *re-creation* 'your story as re-created by me': here the listeners take the story and re-shape it into another form, finding their own way of telling the tale. This could be a poem, a fairy tale, or some other kind of story; it may stay at the same 'level' as the original, or move toward the archetypal level, as does Peter H.'s retelling.

The King had three sons, who were sent out into a foreign country where there lived a beautiful princess, with blonde curls and golden treasures.

The King said to his sons as they left home 'Be ware' but as they rode off they could not hear of what they should 'be ware' and were too frightened to ask each other.
  At first the youngest two sons spent their time taking care of their eldest brother who was backward – for it might have been to that, their Father had warned them.

The middle brother also took no chances and put on a coat of proper armour, refusing food in case it was poisoned.

But the youngest who was Don grew impatient with protecting his eldest brother's foolishness and his middle brother's proper armour and followed his eyes that alighted on cream cakes, blonde curls and golden treasures.

Only two brothers returned home, for the youngest was destined never to know the end of this Father's sentence, and his brothers were destined never to know the taste of cream cakes, blonde curls and golden treasures.

Finally, a *reflection* is 'my story about your story': essentially the reflection involves standing further back, it is more 'about-ist', pondering the story. Thus Don's reflection on his own story:

What did *he* do at the party, I wonder? Standing, looking sheepish, his neck sticking out of his collar, dressed neatly like me, 'a refined child', as some priest once described us, to my mingled delight and disgust. These are random images that float in from different stages of my childhood. These small children we once were – 'little Donny' – I don't really feel you small. I feel me, as you, stubby and tough and yet primly dressed and quite soft really, a lovable child, wanting to break out of this web of timidity they threw around you – 'they' meaning, I suppose, my mother (my ineffectual though physically powerful father remaining somewhere in the background) – my mother, so timid in some things, so strong and fearless in others.

As we told stories and listened to responses we became aware how quickly a story seemed to move from belonging to an individual to becoming part of the collective; Sarah's story about her mother coming for Christmas evoked, particularly with the women, a generalized experience of mother–daughter relationships, both from the mother's and the daughter's perspective ('Mother that I am/Mother that I have', as Pat put it in her story). The responses were both intensely personal, and at the same time put alongside each other evoked the archetypal aspects of their relationship. At these points we felt that we moved on to, and evoked, a higher or deeper level of expression, that there was 'something in the air' in the shared consciousness of the group, that we could feel but not yet touch, we could experience but not tie down. In later storytelling we have tried to find ways to express this collective story in the air, and found it almost palpable and at the same time elusive.

So our experience of what we got out of the workshop was profound yet not easily spoken. As Anne put it at the end:

> I'm very confused. I don't know what I have found/discovered/learned. But I think we went further than in a debate or discussion. By not intellectualizing there was much more depth to it.

A clear example of this was in the final stages of the workshop. Someone remarked that we didn't seem to have told a classic man's story. In response to this, Timothy told of his plans for a tour of Singapore and the Malaysian Peninsula, just three men, with no women to complicate the party or to disapprove. When asked what they were going to do of which women might disapprove he casually remarked, 'Oh, a little bit of rape and a little bit of pillage!'. This comment shocked and infuriated some of those present, and in response, a heated, bitter, and polarizing debate quickly caught fire. The quality of listening rapidly deteriorated as stances were taken and personal hurts restimulated. In the midst of this, one of us firmly cut through the onslaught, saying 'Wait!! Let us stop right now, and do with this story what we have done with the others.' And we did, taking our own private time to compose a reply, and then reading these aloud. In this way some of those who had felt deeply hurt were allowed space to speak and be heard; and some others composed replies which spoke from both sides of the polarized positions. We could see that this simple story could contain within it the expressions of a wide range of anger, hurt, misunderstanding, mistrust, and envy, all of which can characterize relationships between men and women. The expression through the stories had provided for us a firebreak, to use Heidegger's image, which gave us clear space to experience the depth of this hot and tangled forest.

We offer here as illustration two of the responses to Timothy's story. First of all Christine's 'reply', which we feel conveys some of the depth of women's rage towards men with a quite startling degree of emotional expression.

From the Voice of Rage

I chickened out.
You didn't get the knife in the throat
Your hair ripped off your head
Your prick flung like a limp sausage
To the floor.
I didn't even tip you off the chair
Where you sat
Cock sure
Soft irish brogue still lilting
With your tale of travelling
Your man's story
A so-called hero's journey
Into pus poverty.
Here you get your slick badge
Cheap with 'different' women
More easy going
Loosely uninhibited lithesome
Childwhores
Serving, starving, conned and tricked
By tradition.
Soft sister
I didn't act
But you may strip the sham
Of European privileged aftershaven
Warriors
And swallow his raping pillaging soul
Along with the spunk.

Do not jest thou pallid man
Beware of wounded women.

There is no way that orthodox forms of inquiry which concentrate on explanation alone could convey this depth of feeling. Our point is that any human research worthy of the name needs to be able to express the intensity of conflict between men and women emotionally as well as analytically.

Our second example is Philip's 're-creation' of Timothy's story and the fury which followed it, in which he 'dreams on' toward a possible resolution. We feel that he tentatively feels the way forward towards a synthesis without artificially creating a compromise, or explaining away the differences.

> Three men set out on a great adventure through an unknown land. Each day they decided just what they wanted to do, and then they went right ahead and did it. If they disagreed among themselves, they fought, and the strongest got his way. They were like brothers by the end of the journey, with a lusty confidence and love and hate for each other. Behind them they left the shattered ruins of their passage.
>
> Three women watched from a hilltop. They despised those three men and turned their backs on them. Together they tilled the soil, brought forth fruits and flowers in abundance, and shared the wisdom of the years. Long were the silences between them, and their tears and their laughter flowed as one. No man wrote their history, for there was nothing to write.
>
> In a world that is yet to be, these men and women meet, and choose each other's company. Together they make love, and children are born to them – yes, boys the sons of women and girls the daughters of men. Sometimes they till the land and share the wisdom, and they journey through fearful and dangerous lands. In each other's eyes they recognize the light of their own, and the recognition is fearful, but they know the answer though they had not known the name of the question. And there is no end to the stories which are told.

Again, returning to Anne's comments:

> The concept of the story turned out to be a device which freed us from argumentation, discussion on abstract levels and moralizing and theorizing and provided quite a different means of communication which is rare but led to a depth of communication we should value.

Questions we carried forward

We were left, at the end of a year's thinking and inquiry, knowing we were onto something important and creative which is not yet fully formed. We had three questions to carry forward.

Dialectics of expression

We can describe what we are doing as creating a *dialectic of expression*: this is quite different from the debate or dialectic between opposing explanations. Within this dialectic there are two levels of relationship or dialogue: first between the original story and each separate response, as we we had in our work in a pair. In addition to this is a dialectic between the different responses that were elicited by the stories shared in the group, each catching and contributing different aspects of the whole, so that the range, multiplicity, and interpenetration of meanings contained in the original story may be expressed. Again, the next phase of work is to find ways of working with what emerges from this dialectic in a way that holds this multiple kaleidoscopic meaning and expresses it as a whole. This is in contrast to a way which would find a neatly unified interpretation.

Dialectic between expression and explanation
In addition to the dialectics within expression is the dialectic we mentioned earlier: that between explanation and expression, in which the expression may illuminate the explanation, and the explanation may clarify the expression. It is probable that as one moves along the path of expression one may need to call on the clarity of explanation in order to see the available choices: otherwise one may become swamped in the collective psyches' unquenchable ability to create expression. Similarly as one moves along the path of explanation one needs to call on forms of expression to give meaning to what may otherwise become arid and ungrounded concepts.

> Internally, philosophical rationality must balance itself between two needs, *clarity* and *depth*. There are 'two requirements of philosophical thought – clarity and depth, a sense for distinction and a sense for covert bonds [which] must constantly confront each other' (Paul Ricouer). A clarity without depth is empty so far as it is capable of shedding any ultimate light upon the mystery of human existence; but a suggestion of depth without rational clarity is merely romanticism. (Ihde, 1971)

Our argument is that a full human inquiry will also be able to develop this dialectic of clarity and depth; so that what we know and can explain we can also fully express.

Meaning: creation or discovery?
Expressive inquiry also raises questions about the nature of meaning. When we tell stories, are we *creating* meaning or *discovering* it? We had noticed that when we took a story from our lives and 'worked' on it in the way we have described, the original event held more 'power' for us, or spoke to us more fully: Thus Peter R. will not now forget his fishing trip; nor are we likely to forget Don's four-year-old birthday party. It is clear that we have chosen the events to recount because we have a sense that they are infused with meaning in a way that is elusive – sensed but not seen, touched but un-holdable, not grasped. But was the meaning already there lying dormant and unseen, ready to be woken to the light of day by the

storytelling; or did the act of storymaking and storytelling create the meaning that we now recognize? We sensed that we needed a 'theology' of storytelling, and indeed of meaning creation, and our speculations take us in three directions.

From the perspective of archetypal psychology the fundamental patterns of human experience lie beyond the individual in the collective psyche and are expressed through archetypes. This is what Jung meant when he called the collective unconscious the *objective psyche* (Jung, *CW*). Here we also follow Avens' argument that 'Imagination is Reality'. Psyche, or soul

> has an objective or collective aspect which shows itself in our capacity to conceive, imagine, behave, and be moved according to fundamental patterns called 'archetypes'. (1980, p. 31)

> The Jungian psyche is no longer based on matter or the brain or on mind, intellect or metaphysics, but on soul – *esse in anima* as a third reality between *esse in intellectu* (the mind, the idea) and *esse in re* (the matter, the thing). *In the psyche idea and thing come together and are held together and are held in balance* (our emphasis). (1980, p. 33)

From this perspective the objective reality of psyche or soul images us and through us and thus 'the psyche creates reality every day'. This psychic reality is the

> creative realm of emotions, fantasies, moods, visions and dreams and its language is that of images, metaphors, and symbols. (1980, p. 33)

To say all this is to take a major step epistemologically, and to move beyond our earlier position of radical subjectivity (Reason and Rowan, 1981a). We need to find a way to acknowledge both the independent meaning-making of the authentically autonomous human being and the universal patterns to which we all belong. John Heron's latest writing (1987), in which he explores the possibility that we inhabit two worlds, offers one challenging view of this.

A second way of looking at meaning-making is to borrow Ken Wilber's three-fold epistemology (1981b). Wilber distinguishes between the empirical/analytical (something like we have called explanation) which is appropriate for the study of the material world; the hermeneutic/phenomenological (something like we have called expression) which is appropriate for the study of the mental and social world; and what he calls the paradoxical/mandalic, which is appropriate for the study of spirit. While the primary task to this chapter has been to put forward storytelling as a hermeneutic method of inquiry, once we begin to inquire into the origins of meaning we begin to enter the paradoxical realms of trans-personal and spiritual knowing.

In a holistic view of knowing, matter, mind, and spirit interpenetrate: we have moved beyond the unreformed materialism of orthodox inquiry, and we need now to integrate a knowing from spirit (psyche, soul) with our existential human inquiry. A science of persons is inadequate without a knowing from soul.

Thirdly, we can turn to the world-view of David Bohm (1980), who sees the explicit order of the world as constantly unfolding and refolding in and out of an implicate order:

> Bohm's theory proposes that, in general, there are three major realms of existence: the explicate order, the implicate order, and a source-ground beyond both. The explicate order is the world of separate and isolated thing-events extended in space and time. The implicate order is the realm in which all things-events are enfolded in a total wholeness, a wholeness and unity that, as it were, 'underlies' the explicate world of separate things and events. The 'source-ground'...is radically unqualifiable and totally beyond thought-symbols. (editorial, *Revision*, Fall 1981)

We recognize that in drawing these comparisons we are entering a complex and difficult field – that of the relationship between the material world, consciousness, and realms manifested in religion, imagination, and psyche. This field is being explored by many contemporary thinkers in a very wide range of disciplines, for example Bohm and Capra from the world of high-energy physics; Sheldrake in biology; Wilber in philosophy; Valle and Eckhartsberg and others in psychology; Hillman and the archetypal Jungians in the field of psychotherapy; and probably many others in fields with which we are not familiar. Maybe we can say that at a strictly material level we discover meaning – certainly we discover form. Existentially we create our own meanings from events, in Sartre's terms 'we are our choices'. Adding to this a perspective from soul we have to hold the paradoxical notion that our meaning is simultaneously created by us and manifested through us.

A word of caution

Having discovered stories and storytelling, and seen how they may contribute to an expressive inquiry process, we must be careful also to ask the cautious and the devil's advocate questions. For surely stories can distort meaning as much as they can uncover and create authentic meaning? And what are criteria of 'validity' for stories and storytelling?

Early on we realized that while stories are created from experience by what we have termed 'loosening the bonds' of the original event and *selective emphasis*, so propaganda may be developed by *selective distortion*. Martin Buber (1958) sees propaganda as an inevitable outcome of the failure to maintain dialogue. We may suggest that storytelling becomes propaganda when the story is treated as It rather than Thou, in Buber's terms, and we seek to impose a meaning onto it, rather than allow its meanings for us to become manifest through dialogical relation.

To treat a story as It means we treat the truth of the story as being of the same nature as the truth that pertains to the level of matter (Wilber) or personal ego-reality (Jung). To do this perverts the truth, collapsing levels of meaning and multiple meanings to support one world-view. Thus Hitler used the Aryan myth in a way that pretended it had something to do with genetics. To treat a story as Thou is to personify rather than to objectify it. There is also a danger of subjugating the world of story and expression to the colonization by the analytic ego of explanation; erecting a world where stories are merely raided for insights and become base material for intellectual understanding.

This is similar to David Miller's (1981) warning about over-enthusiasm for the story:

> The danger I see lies...in how one views a story or how a story is used. Narrative form is no better than abstraction if it is used ideologically, that is, for ego-security. (p. 17)

Miller points out how stories may be used to 'shore up ego against its ruin' (p. 18) and in psychotherapy as 'a way of defending against depth and deepening' (p. 18). Clearly storytelling can also, in a cultural setting, be used both for creative and oppressive socialization. One mark of a liberating process is to help people critically tell their own stories (Freire, 1970). We need to do a lot more thinking about authentic and alienating uses of storytelling.

This final word of caution may point to some important qualities of the scientific tradition to which we would like to hold: ideally, science has always been critical and open to amendment, and scientific inquiry at its best has been a blend of careful, cautious, and bold, creative knowing. We hope to develop storytelling as inquiry in this spirit.

The continuing story

Since we finished the original work on storytelling, the approach has been used in a variety of ways and settings. Peter H. (1986) invited members of a community to collectively tell the story of each individual's involvement in that community as part of a co-operative inquiry into community learning. After listening silently to their story as told by their colleagues, each individual had a chance to add their own version. Then the group searched for an image to express the essence of the members being in the community. They also experimented with telling the story of the community, as a way of giving the whole organization a voice.

In a similar vein, our colleagues have used storytelling within organizations to explore and exemplify the organizational culture (McLean and Marshall, 1988); one particular technique is to invite people to tell stories of those who are seen as the organization's heroes, villains, and fools.

We have also used storytelling to explore specific aspects of personal life. At a conference on Jungian psychotherapy and creative expression built round the myth of Narcissus we both used storytelling to explore how this myth resonated in individual lives. We explored the route from individual account through multiple echoes and retelling of stories, to see if the myth could find new form in our collective expression.

How to incorporate storytelling in co-operative inquiry

We have found that our interest in storytelling has changed our approach to our work in many ways. It changes how we ask questions, how we explore sense-making, and how we tell what we know. One obvious application of storytelling is to the co-operative inquiry process.

In establishing a co-operative inquiry group it becomes important that right from the outset a culture is set which honours expression as well as explanation. As well as inviting the group to define its area of exploration we must also invite them to find images that envision it and stories that give it expression. People are grabbed by stories, and group members will create deeper links to the area of research if these grow out of their own expressed stories.

Stories can also change how experience is gathered. Instead of asking 'Tell me about. . .', which leads to an explanatory account, one can ask, 'Tell me the story. . .', which invites more expression. Thus an inquiry group may provide a forum in which members' stories of their experience can emerge.

It may then be important not to jump immediately to analysing members' stories, but to take time to deepen them, and thus the experience they contain, using some of the approaches in this chapter. Also the group can move from the individual stories to discover the collective patterns of the whole group by responding to story with story (replies, echoes, re-creations, and reflections).

Storytelling can then be used for the phase of making sense of the experience of the inquiry. One outcome of making sense is an explanatory theory. But as many writers are pointing out, all theories rely on root metaphors and images (Lakoff and Johnston, 1980; Reason, 1988). Story-telling, and in particular the method of story response, is one way in which root metaphors may be discovered and given form.

And finally, stories are a powerful way of communicating the findings of inquiry to other people. The outcome of a co-operative inquiry is often deeply personal and practical, as well as theoretical. The theory and the practice can often be well grounded and expressed in the personal or collective story, and an inquiry group may wish to spend time developing different stories in different voices for different audiences.

Thus science can learn to tell good stories, and then explanation and expression become married, and the progeny are theories born of story, and stories born of theory.

'And there is no end to the stories which are told...'.

PART TWO

VENTURES IN CO-OPERATIVE INQUIRY

5

Whole Person Medical Practice

edited by Peter Reason

This research project grew out of the educative work of the British Postgraduate Medical Federation at the University of London. John Heron, Assistant Director of BPMF and in charge of its education department, had since 1977 run an annual programme of workshops focusing on communication, interpersonal skills, and educational, philosophical, and personal development for doctors. In 1981 there had been the first official encounter of a co-operative kind involving dialogue between conventional medicine and various practitioners of complementary medicine at a conference organized by BPMF; and at the same time significant numbers of medical practitioners were concerned to relate conventional medicine practice to the principles of holism. It seemed therefore by early 1982 that the time was ripe for a direct exploration of the practice of holistic medicine, and the project was initiated by John Heron with these ideas in mind. He invited Peter Reason to join him as initiating facilitator.

In initial discussions it was decided that the best way to pursue this exploration was to invite medical practitioners to join a co-operative inquiry group which would explore systematically the theory and practice of holistic medicine. A letter of invitation was sent out to all general practitioners on the BPMF mailing list outlining the project, and inviting attendance at an introductory meeting. At this meeting, which was attended by about 34 GPs, the initiating facilitators outlined their ideas for the inquiry, gave a thorough account of the co-operative inquiry process, and offered some suggestions as to the structure for the programme. The meeting discussed these issues thoroughly and agreed an overall plan for the project.

An important part of the meeting was the evolution of criteria for membership of the project. After discussion it was agreed that those joining

This chapter reports the work of the Holistic Medicine Co-operative Inquiry Group, and is based on the original report of that inquiry (Heron and Reason, 1985). A draft of this chapter was circulated to all members of the inquiry group, and many of their comments incorporated.

the project should have a medical degree; some acquaintance with complementary medicine; some experience of personal growth processes and a willingness to explore emotional and interpersonal issues that might be stirred up in the inquiry process; access to patients; commitment to the project in terms of time and energy. It was agreed that participants would self-assess their suitability for the project in the light of these criteria.

While a lot of basic groundwork was covered in this first meeting, much remained unresolved, so a second introductory meeting was arranged for those who were committed to join the project. At this second meeting detailed arrangements for the project were worked out.

Participants

There were nineteen participants in the project, with an age range of 28–60. Sixteen were medical doctors, the other three being John Heron and Peter Reason, who were initiating facilitators, and Elva Macklin, who was secretary to the project. Of the sixteen doctors, fourteen were in general practice within the British National Health Service, four were trainers in the GP vocational training scheme, two were trainees in this scheme, two had university appointments in Departments of General Practice, one was a member of a radical practice based fully on co-operative principles, one had a hospital appointment and one was exclusively in private practice. Four of the doctors were female, and of the total group two were Asian, the rest Caucasian.

We were disappointed that recruitment had failed to achieve a balance of the sexes, and we reluctantly accepted the balance we had. The participants varied greatly in their experience of personal development work, from those who had been involved in it for many years to those who had just opened the door. There were five trained co-counsellors in the group, several who had participated in Balint Groups (Balint and Norell, 1973), and several who had experience of meditation and transpersonal methods. All were interested in complementary therapies, and a small number included acupuncture as part of their practice.

The motivation for joining varied with each participant, but most wanted to develop new perspectives and skills. Some considered themselves well-versed in holistic medicine, others thought of themselves as enthusiastic novices. Some were dissatisfied with the status quo as they saw it, others were relatively content but keen to try new ways. There was a common underlying desire to provide a better service to patients and to increased personal satisfaction in their work. Most knew that they would have to make efforts in time and money, and many experienced resistance from colleagues in their practices who did not accept the value of the project. There were the expected variations of personality, and often clashes of temperament and ideology, but there was an overall commitment to the central focus of the inquiry and to the way of working with its implications of co-operation and creative conflict resolution.

Research design and rationale
The broad design for the programme was outlined in advance by John and Peter, and adopted at the first planning meeting. There were to be six cycles of inquiry made up of a two-day workshop for thinking and planning and six weeks of application on-the-job in the surgery. The inquiry ended with a four-day workshop for final discussion and processing of the experience.

Co-operative inquiry moves several times around the cycle from reflection to action and back again, and it is important to choose an appropriate amount of time for each part of the cycle, and an appropriate rhythm of action and reflection. The two-day meetings were time for concentrated reflection, the six-week intervening period was time for extended action. An important part of the reflection, which became progressively built into the two-day meetings, was a range of different validity procedures, including the development of a genuinely co-operative inquiry group. These validity procedures and their use are described by John Heron in Chapter 2 of this volume.

Luminaries
The idea of inviting visiting speakers was mooted in the original invitation letter and discussed at the first meeting. It was thought that if we invited individuals whose work is clearly innovative in their field this would stimulate our own thinking and practice. Accordingly at the preparatory meeting a list of possible luminaries was developed by brainstorming, from which list five were chosen.

The luminaries were invited to provide a three-hour presentation at one of the two-day meetings of the project on any aspect of holistic medicine that was currently of interest to them. They were also invited to participate as co-researchers during the rest of the meeting time, joining the group in whatever way they felt appropriate, contributing to the group's own activities. Our experience of this arrangement varied. We found that while some were able to join the group in creative ways, for others participation was problematic. Some were able to dialogue with the group in an exchange of perspectives, while others seemed able to do no more than reiterate their own viewpoint. Again, some visitors could contribute actively and relevantly to the group's activities, while one could only interrupt and interfere. The group for its part would readily confront those visitors who seemed to be insensitive to its ethos, but sometimes the confrontation became confused with scapegoating the visitor for the group's internal difficulties. We shocked one, were experienced as rude by another, and occasionally wondered if we were giving enough care to receiving our guests. Nevertheless, the luminaries did fulfil the purposes for which they were invited: to inject new perspectives, refresh our thinking, contribute to our programme design, and challenge the limitations of our inquiry. Our favourite comment on the group was from one visitor to the effect that he had been forced by the group to be 'stark naked and fast on his feet' with us, which we took as a complement. We are grateful to all of them for their time, interest, and involvement.

The progress of the group
The inquiry proper started with a two-day residential meeting at a retreat centre. We gathered one Friday evening, had dinner together and met for a session of getting acquainted. In the morning we discussed in some detail the model of co-operative inquiry, and decided as a first step to develop a model of holistic medical practice as the group currently understood it.

We made the assumption that each member had some degree of holistic medical experience. So we decided to start by working in pairs, reviewing this experience in order to glean from it the major conceptual features of such a practice. Following this pairs discussion we met in small groups to compare notes, and finally met as a whole group. From this discussion we evolved the five-part model of holistic medical practice which is discussed below. This model formed the starting point for all our future work.

After we had developed the model we developed strategies for applying the model in the surgery. Taking each aspect of the model in turn, we brainstormed long lists of possible strategies and discussed these in detail. Finally, after discussion in small groups, group members developed their own personal plans and contracts for putting the model (or some part of it) into practice over the next six weeks. It was decided that these application plans should be idiosyncratic, at least in the first instance, so that individual participants could choose those strategies most relevant to themselves and their own practice, and so that the group as a whole would develop a range of diverse ideas and practices.

The group also discussed and agreed ways of recording their experience of putting these contracts into practice. The most common form of data recording was diaries, although some video and audio recording of sessions with patients was done, and some group members visited and observed others at work.

At the end of the first day of work on the model of holistic medicine we met for an evening session as an encounter group. As initiating facilitators John and Peter were aware of the personal and interpersonal tensions that could arise in inquiry groups, were committed to providing an arena in which such issues could be aired and explored. At this first session some simple ground-rules were suggested – speak in the first person, speak directly to the person you are addressing, make statements rather than ask questions, and so on – and the group members were invited to engage with each other openly and directly.

A range of issues were addressed that evening. Many concerned membership of the group, with people exploring whether they really belonged in the group, and working out which other members were similar and dissimilar to themselves. One man was strongly confronted about what others felt to be his dominating behaviour. A sub-group of men explored their growing affection and intimacy, along with their delight in discovering professional peers who shared their values; this intimacy caused some jealousy around the group. There were tears and laughter, intimacy and distance, clarity and bewilderment and on the whole this encounter session provided a lively start to this aspect of the inquiry and contributed to the development of a genuinely co-operative group.

The work of the group continued through the year in similar fashion. We did our best to make sure that our meetings were holistic, attending to body, mind, emotions, and spirit. Thus we included:

Body: linked hands, hugs, dance, somersaults;
Mind: discussions of concepts, model building, brainstorming, data collection, progress reports, business;
Emotions: here-and-now encounter sessions, co-counselling, catharsis, interpersonal feedback both positive and negative;
Spirit: meditation, silence, blessing, invocations.

Typically a two-day workshop would commence with some improvised ritual of re-joining, following which we would spend time in open discussion of personal experiences since our last meeting, this serving to bring the group together after the break. We would then proceed to share the outcomes of the previous six-week cycle of application work, this usually starting in small groups and continuing in open discussion of the whole group, with conceptual discussion reviewing and revising the model of holistic medicine. Each meeting would include an encounter session at which interpersonal difficulties would be explored and resolved, and often we also took time for an exploration of emotional issues stirred up by the project. Other activities during the workshops were a range of 'holistic' practices including meditation, yoga, and sharing and exploring dreams. Towards the end of the workshop group members would revise their personal plans in the light of their discussions and reflections, and write a formal contract for the next application period. And finally we said goodbye for another six weeks.

Development of the research strategy

At the first workshop, having developed the five-part model of holistic medicine, we agreed that it would be best for participants to pursue their own idiosyncratic line of research, and this continued for the first two inquiry cycles. However, by the third session it was felt that a clearer convergent focus was needed for our work together, and after discussion it was agreed that two sub-groups be formed, one of which studied power relations between doctor and patient, while the other explored the place of spiritual interventions in holistic practice. These two issues were proving to be important foci of interest among the group members.

In the inquiry cycles which followed, individual members pursued a combination of their own personal interests and whatever experimental action was agreed within these two sub-groups, which met for intensive discussion of their topic at each subsequent meeting.

Development of the inquiry group
The life of the group started with enormous hope and enthusiasm: energy was high, people joined in and felt optimistic; plans were made; and friendship bonds forged. There was something of a downturn in morale by the second meeting, as the enormity of what we had taken on became evident, and as some of the different attitudes and approaches in the group became evident. But the energy level rose again at the third meeting with the formation of the power and spirit groups, since these seemed to provide a clear focus for what we were up to, and thus a new impetus to move forward. This energy was sustained through a lively and conflictful fourth meeting until at the fifth meeting a series of unresolved differences within the group, and strained relations with the visiting luminary, combined with external difficulties in members' lives, served to give a very depressing and debilitating meeting. The sixth meeting provided a way out of these doldrums as the group responded to both exhortation from within and encouragement and stimulus from the visitors to that session, so we were able to finish with some clarity about both success and failure. At the final meeting the group was energized by a deep and satisfying sense of achievement, together with a sense of excitement about writing up the inquiry.

We regularly met for encounter sessions during the whole inquiry, dealing with issues such as uneven contribution levels, the domination of the group by particular vocal men, personal attractions and antipathies, and so on. Similarly we took time in pairs and small groups to explore the personal distress that was restimulated by the inquiry process. Group members discovered, for example, that they hated both doctors and doctoring; that they had been grievously hurt and their aspirations to do good work crushed by their experience of medical school; that they had lost their way professionally and personally. The changes in practice brought about through membership of the project stimulated some violent disagreements with both professional and personal partners. And group members found the challenge of new ways of practice deeply disturbing.

For some group members the significance of the learning which emerged from these personal confrontations was far more important than the formal research findings reported below.

The model of holistic medicine

The model of holistic practice we developed at our first meeting contained five elements (see Figure 5.1), minimally conceptualized as follows:

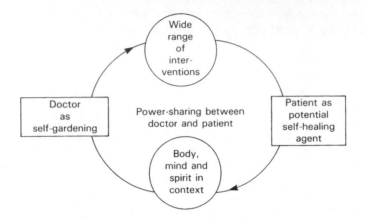

Figure 5.1   *One way of illustrating the five-part model*

Concern for the patient as being of body, mind, and spirit seen in historical, social, and political contexts.   The person as a being of body, mind, and spirit is a classic view which we invoked but did not at this point elaborate in any detail. Nor did we specify any definitions of mind or spirit, except to indicate that by mind we certainly included feelings, and will, as well as intellect. We also saw the wider context of the patient as of fundamental importance. There was some vague invocation of a systems account of the personal necessarily being understood in the context of their personal history, wider cultural history, and the prevailing social and political structures. For some members this social and political context was primary; for others the person over against their context was primary.

A major aspect of the inquiry was the sub-group which explored spiritual aspects of holistic practice, whose work is reported in detail below.

The patient as a potential self-healing agent.   The self-healing powers of the body are well recognized. At the level of everyday human observation there is the self-healing of wounds and the unaided recovery from viral infection for which orthodox medical science has found no specific treatment. We all have evidence of complete recovery, leaving no trace of illness and also the repair processes that leave their mark as scars. And our everyday human observation also tells us that there are limits to this self-healing capacity of the body: common sense shows us that a person who loses a limb does not grow another one, and medical science shows us that a severed spinal cord does not regenerate. Injuries, poisons, cancers sometimes kill.

But by self-healing we implied much more than this, including also the more radical principle that each person as a mental and spiritual being has the potential capacity consciously and intentionally to facilitate healing in their body by a variety of internal and external actions. It is clear from our discussions that we do not know the range of such potentials, but we assumed that human beings have far greater powers of intentional self-healing than is usually recognized by either patients or doctors; and also that a major part of holistic practice is to enable this human potential to be actualized.

While we did not explicitly focus our explorations on this part of the model, individual members were concerned with it in their own personal action. Various doctors encouraged intentional self-healing as part of their orthodox practice, through their manner and style inviting patients to see they could contribute to their own healing. Other doctors used education, teaching their patients positive health methods. Some facilitated self-healing in their patients through a variety of forms of counselling, set up self-help groups, and taught specific self-healing skills such as relaxation, meditation, visualization, and life-style management.

Power-sharing between doctor and patient. By this we meant shared responsibility for diagnosis and treatment. In diagnosis, while the doctor has the medical view, the patient has a personal view, and can understand and give meaning to their illness in terms of their total life situation. In treatment, the doctor may have medicines, surgery, and other interventions to offer, and the patient can take responsibility for devising and practising internal and external behaviour that facilitate recovery. This is co-operative problem-solving. There is a continuum of power in doctor–patient relationships: at one end all power is exercised by the doctor and at the other end all power exercised by the patient. The notion of power-sharing sits in the middle of this continuum, each part of which has its valid use depending on the patient, the doctor, and the circumstances.

Again, one sub-group explored power-sharing in depth, and an account of their deliberations is included below.

Ability to offer a wide range of interventions. This principle includes at least three dimensions. First, having a wide range of interactive skills, for example being able to move along the continuum of power as above. Second, being able to intervene appropriately in relation to body, mind, and spirit, and historical, social, and political contexts. And third, having competence in some aspects of alternative therapy – physical, emotional, and spiritual – as well as in conventional medicine. We did not systematic-ally explore this aspect of the model, but clearly this principle in practice starts to define the holistic practitioner; and of course holism as defined in this bundle of skills transcends any individual's competence.

The doctor as self-gardening.   Self-gardening was our term for the care and attention the holistic practitioner gives to his or her own personal process – again physically, mentally, and spiritually. The practitioner of holistic medicine needs to be mindful of behaviour, relationships and life-style, and to be consciously involved in the process of holistic self-development and social awareness.

It was suggested early on in the inquiry that medical practitioners are conditioned by their training and by the whole medical culture to use their role defensively, and this view was generally accepted. This means that the way medicine is practised is often a defensive denial of certain anxieties and distresses within the doctor, so that a good deal of denied distress is acted out in ostensibly legitimate therapy. As one member wrote, 'In order to understand and act humanely with others, it is necessary to feel sympathy with oneself. Otherwise the healer will inevitably foist his or her own "unaware projections" upon the patient, and attempt, unwittingly, to attack the patient, or to solve the patient's problems in his or her own terms.'

Our view is that professionalism is in part both a defence and a projec-tion. This is not only true of medicine, but is symptomatic of our culture as a whole because we lack any model of emotional and spiritual education which would help professionals understand themselves in relation to their role. Precisely because the medical profession has such high status in our culture, its members are caught in an invidious double-bind predicament: as the most senior helpers in our society they are not supposed to have any problems, and therefore cannot admit to themselves or others the very real problems they do have both individually and collectively. It has thus proved very difficult for doctors to seek psychological help and to practise in any depth and insight the ancient precept, 'Physician, heal thyself'.

The emergence of innovative humanistic psychotherapies over the past few decades has been important in enabling some medical practitioners to break out of their professional defensiveness. In particular, it is the realization that psychotherapy is better construed as emotional education, desirable and available for all adults, which gives permission for doctors to step out of the shadows of repression.

From the beginning of our inquiry, some of our members considered that self-gardening was really the hub of the model, on which all the other four parts depended; other members considered it was on a par with the other principles. What is of major importance is the experience reported by several members that it was by attending to their own self-gardening that they developed the confidence and competence to apply other parts of the model, and also to stand against the expectations of partners and patients in practising in new ways.

It was certainly widely held that self-gardening was essentially interdependent with the principle of the patient as a potentially self-healing agent. In order to be sensitive to the cues for encouraging the autonomy and growth of the patient, the doctors need to be familiar with and able to work with the same sorts of cues in their own growth and development.

We all espoused the view that self-gardening could occur at different levels of being – the bodily, the intellectual, the emotional, and the spiritual; and also in the context of personal, professional, and political relationships. We did not take any view as to which level of self-gardening was or was not most primary: it was rather considered that each member was the proper judge of whether jogging, meditation, co-counselling, or influencing and changing social relationships was most important at that time in their lives.

It is clear from the personal accounts that the experience of participating in the inquiry was in itself a fundamental self-gardening experience. Co-operative inquiry has a particular combination of activities, including reflection on professional activities integrated with personal and interpersonal development, and this in the context of a warm, supportive and confronting community of peers. Indeed, one of our members lovingly caricatured the researched group as a personal growth group for doctors, and for some it did seem that over some cycles their preoccupation with self-gardening distracted them from the content of the inquiry. In the reverse direction, however, the intensity of some members' commitment to self-gardening also made them deeply committed to the inquiry process, and to making fundamental changes in their practice of medicine.

For some, the emotional and spiritual opening involved in the self-gardening component of our meetings had powerful effects on relationships within their families and their medical partners. One member discovered the energy to confront issues within his family which had lain dormant for years. Another worked through longstanding differences with his senior partner. A third discovered deep resentment at the way his medical education had alienated him from his working-class roots, and agonized over whether to move away from his comfortable middle-class practice into a radical co-operative in a city centre.

This five-part model was the basis of our inquiry through six cycles of action and reflection. Since a large amount of time and energy, and indeed most of the joint systematic inquiry, was centred on the explorations of the power and spirit groups, it is appropriate to report on their work in more detail. The following two sections are edited extracts of their reports.

Power-sharing

One member recorded the following experience:

> I was aware in the next minute after this refusal to change his tablets
> that he was probably going to attack me if I persisted. I remember
> thinking, 'Well, at least this is going to be interesting!...' He
> grabbed me by the collar saying he was going to fucking kill me,
> that all doctors were the same. They'd done this to him to begin
> with and now they just treated him like a little kid....He let go of
> me and began to cry. I gave him a 'scrip and phoned the psychiatrist.
> Later I cried too – a mixture of shakiness, fear and melodramatic
> exhilaration.

Issues concerning power are present in every consultation. They may not
be as starkly visible as in the above example, but patients and doctors
still part disgruntled or satisfied, their objectives agreed or frustrated. There
is no neutral position on these issues since we are already operating on
certain assumptions about power, although it is rare for these to be made
explicit. Doctors often see the problem as one of control, usually with
the implicit assumption that they are the ones rightfully 'in control'. Patients
more often simply find it difficult to get what they want, and all too often
experience a loss of personal power inherent in their illness compounded
by a sense of helplessness when facing the overbearing authority of their
doctors.

For any holistic approach the issue of power is vital. The five-part model
touches in issues of power at every turn:

> What does 'power-sharing' mean in practice? why bother with it?
> is it any more than an irrelevant ideal?

> If patients are seen as the main agents of their own healing, what
> implications does this have for the way our institutions are run?

> Use of alternative therapies involves issues about the monopolistic
> power of the medical profession as well as the personal assertiveness
> of patients to get access to them.

> Medicine not only has an important spiritual aspect; it just as clearly
> has political implications which affect its outcome.

Dilemmas.   Sharing power is a paradoxical notion. Implicit both in the
five-part model and in our discussions is the assumption not only that power
should be shared appropriately between doctor and patient but also that
at present the balance of this sharing is swung heavily and wrongly against
the patient. Yet are not attempts on the doctors' part to correct this balance

themselves an exercise of power? Is not the desire to be dependent a valid choice for patients and who are to say that our 'power-should-be-shared' viewpoint should prevail? After all, is not the power to make decisions, with its attendant responsibilies, what doctors are paid so much to do? Patients who are given a choice often say, 'Well, you are the doctor, you decide'. Is this a reflection of a culture-wide passivity or a legitimate request of a professional adviser? Maybe expecting people to make decisions when all they feel like is being looked after and dependent is an imposition of an ideology just as dogmatic and cruel as the view that sees the abrogation of all power to the doctor as good and just.

At the heart of these dilemmas lie several questions: Is it possible to 'give away' power, especially to those who apparently do not want it? Is it correct to do so? Are there any times when it is inappropriate? And how are these 'inappropriate' circumstances defined in such a way that they do not constitute an endless 'cop-out' clause for doctors acclimatized and socialized to the exercise of power?

The rhetoric of liberation implies that power can *not* be given away, it can only be seized by those who are oppressed, and any attempts to give it away through the liberal use of one's position are either doomed to failure or irrelevant since they will never be repeated by others. Happily this perspective on power is limited: the successful relinquishing of power is quite a common experience, and it seems very likely that power as it relates to doctors and patients is neither intrinsically oppressive nor a zero sum game in which my gain in power is by definition your loss.

The paradoxes and the complexities of these issues took up a great deal of our time initially, but at the same time we agreed to try out practical changes in our exercise of power in the action phases of the inquiry. At the time it felt as though our frustrating theoretical discussion had only a limited connection with these strategies, and that in turn the experience of experimenting and the insights we gained only rarely helped to clarify our conceptual difficulties. However, it is clear in retrospect that working out practical alternatives to our orthodox ways of practising and actually carrying these out did help us clarify the conceptual problems. The repeated reflection–action–assessment cycles of the co-operative inquiry transformed what might have been a sterile talking shop into something that has both changed our personal practices and restructured out theoretical understandings.

Our practical work focused on three significant areas:

1 The roots of doctors power, and strategies that attempt to change these.
2 Efforts to systematically increase the number of feedback loops to and from patients as a means of increasing people's autonomy.
3 The problem of assessment – what we were doing and how our patients felt about it.

The roots of power – levelling and demystifying strategies. The sources
of power that doctors hold are legion, including differences in class, age,
sex, race and education; inequality of income; particular knowledge and
skills; control over drugs etc; and the power to define what the 'real'
problem is. There is little the individual doctor can do about these givens,
except live with sensitivity to one's cultural- and gender-determined
blindspots while avoiding retreat into familiar but inappropriate guilt.
Cultivating such sensitivity is of course vitally related to self-gardening.

It is self-evident that the politics of society and the distribution of power
within society have an enormous effect on the way medicine is practised
and on people's health. We fully acknowledged these fundamental political
constraints, and in our small ways did try to influence attitudes toward
them. But clearly we were not going to be able to change the world.

In a sense the whole of the rest of the power group's work was precisely
about trying to find ways round these external political inequalities. At the
individual level, how we do something is just as important as what we
do. So what can we do within a consultation to balance the overwhelming
initial inequalities which systematically distort our interaction with patients?

The following strategies can be seen as attempts to level out some of
these initial differences.

1 *Skill-sharing.* One root of our power is obviously our diagnostic skills.
   People by and large are intensely interested in how practitioners come
   to think they have a particular diagnosis and seem delighted to be shown
   the evidence behind an opinion. We tried offering the chance to learn
   such skills by, for example, encouraging people to take their own blood
   pressure, or look at their toddler's infected red ear drum. People can
   never, of course, become fully their own doctors, and this was not
   the aim. They can, however, become more skilled in listening to signals
   of health or disease emanating from their bodies. Skill-sharing, and
   simply explaining what is being done, can also dramatically demystify
   for patients the medicine that is being applied to them.
2 *Changing the environment.* Many things about doctors and their
   surgeries positively underlie for patients that they are the ones expected
   to be passive. We tried to change such signals by dressing less formally
   and having more everyday furniture in the consulting room. We also
   considered the manner in which the patient was greeted, invited into
   the consulting, and bade farewell.
3 *Being personal.* In a similar vein several people deliberately started
   talking about their personal lives. One member of the group got married
   and another had a baby during the year of the inquiry. Patients often
   knew of these events and were delighted to be able to ask the normal
   sorts of questions about them. By doing so the distance between doctors
   and patients was inevitably reduced, our foibles and feet of clay became

more visible, and patients thus better able to judge our power and capabilities.

4 *Change of seats role-play.* On a variable number of occasions we all tried swapping roles with patients; the aim of this was to try to make *both* players more aware of the constraints under which they were working. In practice we tried this with people who knew us well and with whom there seemed to be some difficulty getting to the heart of the problem. The results were very varied: sometimes there was bewilderment on behalf of the patient and embarrassed retreat from the doctor; sometimes there were very positive changes. Typically it seemed to work best if we could get over our inhibitions and actually change seats and role-play each other. Perhaps the most dramatic example came when one young man moved into the doctor's chair and briskly said, 'Well, young man, I think you're just worried about drinking too much and becoming an alcoholic.' Here a matter that had been discussed before and judged (wrongly) to be unproblematic was reopened and the patient's worries brought to the fore.

Other advantages are that the patient can experience the relative powerlessness of being the doctor and not having a pill for every ill. It can also be much more fun than yet another circuit of the question-and-answer roundabout. Finally, just a little gentle and ironic overplaying can do wonders both for patient and doctor in understanding how they are seen by the other.

Increasing autonomy – access to feedback loops. In our discussions we came to realize that many of the dilemmas of power-sharing can be side-stepped by aiming instead at increased autonomy. As one member put it, 'Patients should always go out more autonomous than they came in.' Autonomy in this sense means being in charge of oneself and one's affairs. My autonomy as a patient depends in the first instance of knowing what is going on. By systematically increasing the information available to patients we hoped to shift the balance toward greater autonomy for them.

As one strategy, we tried dictating all referral letters whilst the patient was still present. The advantages of doing this are legion:

1 The patients know what their doctor is telling the hospital about them and also the doctor's view of their problems.
2 They can then go to the consultant uncluttered by all the common fantasies about what the doctor might have written, or the terrible diagnostic possibilities that we did not speak of but they dread.
3 The doctor can check out details there and then.
4 The patient can give consent to what has been dictated.
5 It is a simple procedure which actually saves time.
6 Because of all these things the patient feels included, and active participation is legitimized and desired.

It is apparently rare for doctors to write referral letters with their patients. Some of the reasons given (which we also initially felt) are that it is sometimes necessary to include opinions about the patient's personality, or diagnostic possibilities as yet undiscussed with the patient. While these objections are occasionally valid, we felt that the real reason for our reluctance was our fantasy that such a joint referral letter might diminish our control. As it turned out, such fears were unfounded: we discovered that power is not a zero-sum affair, patients obviously appreciated their increase in influence, and our work become easier and more enjoyable.

We tried a number of other similar strategies, such as routinely showing people letters and lab. reports from hospital (this not always appreciated by consultants), and encouraging them to read their notes if they wished. Reaction to these innovations was almost universally one of interest and approval. For ourselves, our initial experimental moves to share information were followed by bolder moves as the experience proved positive.

Evaluation.   Focusing on autonomy rather than on power as such helps to make the issues more accessible but does not deal with all the problems. There will still be times when there is a clash of viewpoint between doctor and patient. Obviously to explore this fully would need a co-operative inquiry involving patients as well as doctors, and this was beyond the scope of the present project.

However, we evolved several strategies to try to get more information about the patient side of the story. Some members of the group devised questionnaires, while other either contacted particular patients and asked for feedback about their experiences, or videoed consultations and then reviewed these with the patients involved. All members of the group agreed to set up open meetings with patients to try to find out how they felt about the practice.

These exercises felt very risky to most group members, especially those that involved personal contact. They seemed completely outside the normal communication between doctor and patient. They brought about an acute sense of being vulnerable, which was for some of us the touchstone for knowing whether we were indeed sharing power in any meaningful way. While these attempts to involve patients in assessing what we were doing were by and large failures, they were the riskiest things we tried out, and probably the ones that came closest to genuine power-sharing. In retrospect this was our biggest area of failing, perhaps not surprisingly in view of the hesitancy and insecurity that all our projects raised for us, but nevertheless significant and regrettable.

Spirit

The spirit group formed partly because it was felt unsatisfactory to profess a commitment to holistic practice, with concern for the patient as a being of mind body and spirit, if we could not give some account of the meaning of spirit for us, and of how we might work with a spiritual dimension. We were also stimulated by Murray Korngold, our second visitor to the project, and his strong affirmation of the spiritual dimension of practice, especially his uncompromising use of spiritual invocations to directly and dramatically ask higher powers for healing.

The group started by discussing intellectually the meaning of spirit. This was less fruitful than exploring our current work and behaviour in the surgery, looking for ways in which spiritual intention and practice might lay latent. We explored how we prepared ourselves for a consultation; how we clear our mind and centre ourselves, maybe having only just finished a previous encounter where we have been deeply involved or emotionally effected; how we meet and greet a patient; how we conducted ourselves in difficult consultations; how we close the consultation and part. We asked if the processes we used were akin to meditation or prayer.

We found that quite often 'spiritual' approaches were used. Members of the group would from time to time silently pray during consultations, and at the end of a consultation might say, 'God Bless you', or 'Peace be with you', as if invoking some higher force or power.

So we found, by studying our everyday work, that at least at times both prayer and invocation were used, and so concluded that perhaps the spirit is always present in medicine, though usually unobserved and uncultivated.

After these reflections on current practice we agreed on a set of activities for our surgery practice that would help us explore these matters. We contracted

1   To have the *intention* – as a mental act – to raise the spiritual dimension in work with patients.
2   To practise explicit invocations at different levels from the implicitly spiritual (for example 'Have a good day!') to the explicit and direct ('May you be whole in spirit!'). We thought of an invocation as a direct petition or summoning of a higher power for assistance through some form of prayer.
3   To practise asking spiritual questions of patients; for example, 'Do you pray?', or 'Are any particular beliefs important to you?'
4   To cultivate our own spiritual practice through prayer, meditation, or some similar discipline.

The work of the spirit group proceeded from this initial discussion through three cycles of application and reflection.

We winnowed out a number of principles for spiritual practice – these were points and distinctions which we believed had some modest pragmatic justification and helped to make sense of the practice of spiritual intervention, and experimented with a range of spiritual interventions. Some of the more important points were as follows.

We distinguished early on between the *psychic and the spiritual*, and following this between psychic and spiritual healing practices. The psychic refers to the domain of extrasensory perception, of subtle energies beyond the immediate range of ordinary consciousness and sense perception; the spiritual refers to the divine spirit that moves through creation, the ultimate creative presence out of which both psychic and spiritual become manifest. Thus human response to the psychic dimension, and human activity within it, need not necessarily involve awareness of or intentional relationship with the spiritual.

Following from this, psychic healing is entirely lawful and within the range of voluntary choice and effort, involving mental action to direct subtle energies for physical benefit. The mental action may be visualization, concentration, meditation, invocation, and so on. On the other hand, spiritual healing is a function of the evident presence of divine spirit or unknown presence in the practitioner–client relationship, is not lawful in the same sense as psychic healing, and is thus outside direct human control. Spiritual healing may come unbidden, as an unpremeditated and unsought act of grace; or it may occur following prayer, aspiration, or invocation.

These concepts are helpful in distinguishing between interventions that are non-physical – such as visualization – and which require an act of will on the part of practitioner and patient; and those which, while equally non-physical, involve an act of faith: one may invoke the intervention of spiritual power, and then one must just wait. One member of the group put forward a classification of invocations which usefully shows the range of possible ways of inviting spiritual intervention in both tacit and explicit ways (see Table 5.1).

Table 5.1

A: Tacit invocations
Ordinary greetings, farewells, pleasantries, validations of personal qualities or deeds, said with charismatic intent and tone, or with additional silent prayer.

B: Explicit invocations

    B.1 Benedictions (implicitly spiritual): May you be whole (implying whole in spirit).

    B.2 Benedictions (explicitly spiritual): May the spirit make you whole.

    B.3 Commands (implicitly spiritual): Be whole (implying be whole in spirit).

    B.3 Commands (explicitly spiritual): Be whole in spirit.

    B.4 Affirmations (implicitly spiritual): You are whole (implying whole in spirit).

    B.5 Affirmations (explicitly spiritual): You are whole in spirit.

We discussed the *paradox of preparation and spontaneity* at some length. Clearly spiritual interventions cannot be forced: they are essentially spontaneous movements of the spirit within the practitioner. Yet spiritual training and preparation are both possible through the regular cultivation of spiritually oriented states of mind and attention. We likened this to the preparation of a musician, who practises formally and rigorously so that the actual performance may include a spontaneous element, and accepted that some form of spiritual discipline is appropriate for the holistic practitioner.

In all the complexity of the issues involved, we felt that simple *permission-giving* was not to be overlooked. By this we meant anything said or done that enabled clients to identify, own, and talk about the spiritual dimensions of their life. Such permission-giving counteracts the widespread taboo in our secular culture, and within secular medicine, against the affirmation and exploration of spiritual realities.

In doing this we found the metaphor of *spiritual spaces* helpful. This is the notion that there are gaps or openings in the interaction with clients in which the psychic and/or spiritual were latently or tacitly present, and could be made explicit through some kind of intervention. Another way of looking at this is in terms of openings between two worlds, the world of ordinary sense-perception and social interaction, and the extra-sensory psychic/spiritual world 'beyond' or 'within' (for a later exploration of this, see Heron, 1987). Such openings could be created by ceremony, invocation, sound, gesture, appropriate questions and statements, or they could be noted when they occurred spontaneously and then used to empower appropriate spiritual interventions. We concluded that such 'spaces' are very much more common than a secular viewpoint assumes, and that practitioners could usefully train themselves to notice and to use them.

Finally, we found the *spiritual psychology of the Huna* – the old model of the human being from Polynesia – a useful working model and guide to practice. In this model the Low Self is the unconscious mind, the seat of emotions, the store of memory and feeling, and the store of mana or vital force or energy. The Middle Self is the conscious mind, the seat of free will and reasoning, the teacher and guide to the Lower Self. The High Self is the seat of the superconscious mind, the connecting link with Creation, which transcends memory and reason, while guiding and protecting the free will of the Middle Self. Interestingly it is the Low Self that is in direct contact with the High Self in this model. If healing or treatment is needed, the Middle Self can request the Low Self to send its vital energy to the High Self to empower the prayer of the Middle Self. Importantly, the Low Self has the character of a small child, and can be beset with compulsive guilt; so the Middle Self needs to forgive the Low Self, and help it lift this burden of guilt. One appeal of this Huna system is that it presents a working model for spiritual interventions free from doctrinal bias within European spiritual traditions (Long, 1948; Hoffman, 1976).

Turning now to actual psychic and spiritual interventions we tried, we have already mentioned having the intention to raise the spiritual dimension with patients, practising spoken invocations, asking spiritual questions, and cultivating the spirit as part of 'self-gardening'. We also explored self-preparation before the surgery, using various forms of meditation, mind cleansing, centring, and prayer to get ready to be appropriately present for the next person. We explored using touch, being present with patients empathically, silent and spoken prayer, and spiritual quotations.

Maybe an example of blessing the surgery can give a feeling for the simplicity yet significance of some of these activities:

I close the door. I place my pipe on the window ledge, out of reach. . . . Starting from the left-hand side of the surgery, I slowly move across and around, touching and re-adjusting like an obsessional housewife the arrangements of the place. The wastepaper basket, my trainee's chair, the desk with my stethoscope, auroscope, prescription pad, notepaper, certificate block, the patients' records for the coming surgery (carefully not looking at the name of the first patient). . . . I move to the instrument trays on a bench down the right-hand side of the room and touch them and straighten them: the sink, the soap, the examination room, the pillow, the sheet and the couch – all is straightened and made good. . . . I move back to the sink and run cold water over my hands in a formal lustration, and dry my hands on one, then two, paper towels, thrown formally into the waste-bin under the sink. As I move back to my chair I take off my watch, sit down comfortably and watch the second hand progress twice round with my mind blank and breathing in a proper abdominal manner. I replace the watch and move to the door, which I open and say, "We are off."

It is difficult to give an assessment of the impact of this study group. Whatever 'findings' we can report are inevitably tentative and hesitant, as were our experimental actions in this difficult realm. We found the whole idea of spiritual interventions elusive, yet simple, and at time disturbingly powerful.

The outcome of this part of inquiry is a tentative set of principles and a modest set of practices, and probably most importantly a deep conviction in every member of the group that there is a central place for the spirit in holistic medicine, which can be felt and expressed, but not grasped and defined, as one member wrote at the end of the inquiry:

I have thought extensively about the spiritual element of consultation which I now believe to be very important although not usually acknowledged. The spiritual element acts where ordinary forces cannot act. For instance, there is an important spiritual element in the will to fight illness and to survive in spite of overwhelming odds. It is present when hands are held to express comfort or reassurance, or give permission to grieve, or when the seriously ill patient is touched and prayer is made to help give them strength in their suffering. The ability to help is enhanced by the two minutes of silence, contemplation and prayer, for instance for patience and skill before surgeries at the start of each day. This enables a centring upon the surgeries which are to be performed. I sense that it exists and is more important than anything that actually happens in the consultation, and it is something outside us all which can be incorporated to give additional help. I very clearly witness it leaving people when they die. I do not know where the spirit goes.

Personal accounts

In some ways the essence of this project lies in the personal experiences of members and the changes in personal and professional practice they initiated. It is here that the fundamental issues of validity of the project lie, in the experiential and practical knowing of participants.

Roger

I am a forty-year-old white male doctor. My background is working class and I had the misfortune to go to a London teaching hospital. The traditional medical education I received was my first introduction to the profession. Initially it was frightening and disturbing, but I learned to adapt and, on qualifying, the workload left little time for questioning what I was doing. Following several years in hospital I became a general practitioner firmly entrenched in the traditional doctor mould and out of touch with my working-class background.

I practice in a semi-rural environment from a purpose-built health centre with five other partners. We are a teaching practice for the local medical school, and offer a high standard of medical care.

Several years ago I began to feel ill-equipped to deal with the problems presented to me. My medical training seemed inadequate and inappropriate. Many consultations had a 'warlike' quality about them, a battle between the person trying to convince me they were ill and myself trying to slot them into rigid categories, giving advice and talking too much. I began to look around for a different model on which to base my medical practice, and after some experience of humanistic psychology I joined the co-operative inquiry into holistic medicine.

I became aware of a growing anger towards doctors based on their attitude towards their patients. How angry were my patients when they came to see me? They had come, they were ill – how did I use my power? I began to look critically at myself in a three-piece suit giving an air of confidence; if not actually behind my desk, then across the corner from it. I was surrounded by my instruments, stethoscope often around my neck. I was fully dressed and the patient often undressed. I kept control, dispensing knowledge, advice, and prescriptions. Was this showing power?

I then found that if I listened carefully to the person's account of their symptoms, in the majority of cases all I needed to know was contained in this account. I did not have to go through the catechism of diagnostic questions, I simply had to give attention, provide a safe atmosphere, give space and time. This was extremely difficult to do; I was no longer in control.

The first practical step was to do away with my desk and suit, but it was so difficult. Gradually I was beginning to trust and gain confidence in the other people in the co-operative inquiry. We met every six weeks and for me this was a recharging of energy, realizing I was not so isolated. Now I was allowed to express those feelings; I was listened to, other people had similar doubts and fears about the profession and the medical model. This served as a great source of strength; my desk went, my suit remained in the wardrobe and what happened? My partners became uneasy; the staff laughed to hide their feelings, and my patients made no comment. They accepted these changes and gradually over the months seemed to be much more relaxed, history-taking became easier, diagnosis did not seem so central to the consultations, and treatment came to consist more of joint planning.

Roger continues his account to tell of struggles with other local practitioners, and his worries and doubts about whether the changes he has made really make any difference, and how to change the medical profession as a whole.

I have continued to change, initially in superficial ways but slowly at a much deeper level. Where this will lead I do not know. I think medicine has got to change, the balance has got to be altered, but the force to change it is going to come from the consumers, not, unfortunately from the doctors – I may be wrong.

Diana

After mentioning her initial difficulties with the inquiry project, and how to fit all the ideas into a busy practice, Diana continues

It was not until the inquiry split into two groups, one studying power-sharing, and the other the place of spirit in consultations, that I discovered that by allotting a few minutes of quiet prayer to be more patient and understanding and to know what people were saying it was possible to be more fully present for people and to be more receptive to their needs both spoken and unspoken. I learned about the importance of touch and how helpful it was for me when faced with an untreatable problem to touch the person and pray that they be helped by powers outside my own. This use of prayer to help people gave me another tool to use. I am not sure how the recipients experience it. I had not dared to ask them.

I began to feel more able to intervene in other ways when I visited a dying patient one morning. She told me that she had dreamed that she was falling into a pit and her husband had pulled her back. I said it must have seemed as if the pit was death and she said, 'Yes, I wish he (my husband) would let me go. I am so tired of living.' That evening there was an urgent call from the husband, and as I drew up to the house I heard the teenage daughter crying for someone to help save her mother. I went to the bed to find the husband cradling his wife in his arms but this time I called the teenage daughter to the bedside and the four of us formed a close circle while we watched the mother slip away. The girl had time to kiss her mother goodbye and tell her how much she loved her. It was all so quiet that the sleeping toddler in the room did not wake even when the family came in later to kiss the woman goodbye.

Use of validity procedures

The validity procedures described in Chapter 2 were evolved in part during this inquiry. They were introduced to the group progressively through the project. In the early stages Peter and John took sole responsibility for keeping an eye on the issues, keeping track of their use, and raising validity issues in the group. As the project progressed there was increasing internalization of both the ideas and the procedures by group members, so that they were raising issues for themselves. A full review of our use of each of the validity procedures may be found in Heron and Reason, 1985.

Research cycling, divergence and convergence. The six cycles of the inquiry, the initial divergence, and the convergence with the power and spirit groups has been described above. This felt adequate, although of course far more cycles would be needed to do full justice to the topic.

The notion of recycling implies that data gathering in one cycle will be used to inform plans for the next cycle: this can be done consciously, so that there is some explicit, rational, and deliberate decision; or on the other hand through a tacit process in which the transfer is more subliminal and unconscious. Both these processes occurred. In the power and spirit groups the cycling was more deliberate; in the rest of the project usually more tacit. It could be argued that we needed a more conscious balance between these two, and that more purposive strategies of recycling would have been helpful. However, it does seem inevitable, in a wide-ranging project of this complexity, that a considerable amount of recycling would be tacit.

Authentic collaboration.   Some of the issues of leadership and collaboration have been discussed above. In our view we did fairly well: the work was sufficiently collaborative to mean that the findings were an authentic product of the group. However, we were by no means satisfied, and are aware that much remained to be done.

Falsification.   We did not really use the devil's advocate procedure systematically. While it was effectively used from time to time by individual members to challenge particular assumptions and collusions, we did not set up a full procedure in which major portions of our thinking and practice could be thoroughly challenged and either thoroughly defended or abandoned. It could be argued that we were prematurely persuaded by the soundness of our model, and that we then colluded to avoid thorough use of falsification procedures throughout the inquiry. This is the severest critique of this project's validity which we wish to make.

Countertransference.   As described above, we worked quite hard to identify sources of distress in our work. In a variety of sessions, deep-seated rage towards oppressive medical teachers was expressed and abreacted, along with anger towards fellow-practitioners. Also anger and grief towards parents who had channelled development into the profession, conditioning the child to continue to be a 'good boy' by becoming a doctor.

We believe we addressed these issues modestly, but maybe not enough to liberate members to make the kind of innovative changes in practice that their work situations would have tolerated. We wonder if there was an underlying fear about the amount the project could challenge established ways of medical practice which was inadequately dealt with. Maybe this was why we failed to use the falsification procedures adequately?

On the other hand the gap between professed ideal and actual practice was bridged in many ways. Much was accomplished that was truly innovative.

Open and closed boundaries.   The project affected spouses, professional partners, co-professionals, and above all patients. From time to time the group agreed to find ways to integrate their views, but these were in no instance thoroughly carried through. This does seem to be a major limitation on the inquiry's claim to validity. On the other hand, members collected an enormous amount of experiential data from face-to-face interaction, which was thoroughly integrated in feedback sessions in the group.

Chaos. Although the project was coherent it clearly was not overly ordered; several of the members went through a good deal of personal upheaval and disorder. However, actual chaos – of the kind that will bring about new levels of order – was minimal. On the one hand it can be argued that the degree of chaos was inadequate for true creativity; on the other that the project was so complex and carried so many inter-related strands that it was as disorderly as it could be without completely falling apart.

By way of summary

Overall, we would argue that the project has some claims to validity in terms of research cycling, the management of convergence and divergence, and the degree of authentic collaboration; but that its validity could seriously be held in question with respect to falsification procedures, of countertransference, and of feedback at the open boundary.

In our view the inquiry was a primitive and modest beginning to a journey along a most promising road. For a group of doctors to take on board what for them was an entirely new way of doing research; to apply this at the frontiers of medical practice in the British National Health Service; to relate broad holistic notions to actual and feasible medical practice; all this was a major challenge. We therefore make no claim to have provided all the answers to the theory and practice of holistic medicine. At most we claim to offer some pointers about such theory and practice; pointers which are, however, well grounded in a searching inquiry through action.

While acknowledging the limitations of our inquiry, we hope it will provide an inspiration and a challenge both to medical practitioners and to researchers. Our experience tells us that it is possible to apply holistic principles to medical practice in the NHS; it is possible to share power with patients in a variety of ways; it is possible to affirm the reality of spiritual life of patients and how this affects their well-being; it is possible for doctors to pay attention to their own personal development, and to share their vulnerabilities and their secret aspirations with colleagues and patients.

And we hope also to inspire those interested in medical and social research. Again, it is possible to inquire systematically and rigorously into a complex field of human action, and do justice to its wholeness without distorting or fragmenting it; it is possible to link inquiry and action in fruitful and illuminating ways; it is possible to co-opt busy practitioners into committed inquiry into their own professional and personal processes; it is possible for co-researchers to descend into the confusion of chaos and order that is real life without the protective clothing of questionnaires, experimental designs, and other forms of defensive armour, and to emerge with worthwhile understandings.

Several members of the inquiry responded to the draft of this chapter that was circulated. One wrote:

It would be fascinating to meet again in our group five or ten years later to see where we all are and what has changed. I would guess that all of us will have quietly (or not so quietly) catalysed dramatic changes in our families, partners, practices, patients, and in all those with whom we come into contact.

We have a new purpose-built centre with six partners now. We have four complementary therapists working with us. I have two spiritual healers who sit in with me during surgery alternate weeks. We have a very active Patient Participation group. . . .

Life is amazing. . . .

6

Participatory Inquiry as an Instrument of Grass-roots Development

Marja-Liisa Swantz and Arja Vainio-Mattila

Introduction

It seems contradictory to speak about participatory inquiry in the context of an irrigation scheme launched under the auspices of the World Bank, and which in its basic initial stages was implemented by a prestigious international enterprise (Sir Malcolm MacDonald and Partners, UK). The Bura Irrigation and Settlement Scheme, Eastern Kenya, is yet another example of how development aid reflects the capitalist world order, so that outside investors exert control over planning, decision-making and, consequently, resources, and thus exclude local-level actors. The account that follows argues that people do not have to passively accept what is thrust upon them: participatory inquiry may become an important channel for people's action and reaction. It offers one way to escape from the prevailing state, at times enforced by misleading information or inappropriate technology, of being merely acted upon.

The Scheme was established for growing export-quality cotton to contribute to the national economy by increasing foreign currency reserves. For the main subsistence crop the tenants grow maize in rotation with the cotton.

The combination of a fast population growth and the fact that only one-fifth of Kenya's land area is medium- or high-potential agricultural land (Gustafsson and Ouma, 1979) underlie most policy development in Kenya today. Consequently, in addition to the primary purpose of cotton growing, the Scheme was seen to increase the utilization of semi-arid areas through irrigation, and expediting the settlement of landless people from the high potential agricultural areas of Central and Western Kenya.

In short, the planned irrigation scheme in Bura was to solve land, food, employment and other social problems, all at one go. Eyes were closed to factors which gave early warnings to both internal and external decision-makers about hardships the would-be settlers were likely to face. According to stories recounted by Bura tenants they had been attracted to the irrigation scheme with false promises. They came with the illusion that they would eventually become independent farmers on their own plots of lands. They have remained as tenants and have faced numerous hardships. They have suffered from lack of water and domestic fuel, poor-quality housing, a poorly operated irrigation system, lack of transport, failing crops, and delayed or reduced payments for cotton due to operational problems in financial administration, or to increased overhead costs incurred and charged to the tenants.

There were precedent schemes in Kenya for the launching of a new project. Some of them had been initiated already in the colonial period, when people suspected of collaborating with the Mau Mau movement had been settled on such schemes. One of them is situated just 50 km south of the present Bura Scheme, in Hola. There were experiences also from other large-scale irrigation projects funded by the World Bank elsewhere in Africa (for example Nigeria and Chad) which could have been scrutinized before initiating another one. Important lessons could have been learned from other previous projects in both Africa, even in Kenya, and Asia, which were enormously capital-intensive, relied on subsistence-level wages, and had often left tenant families on declining incomes, at times without funds to cover daily household needs (Vainio-Mattila, 1987: 36; Saha, 1982: 273–6; Chambers and Morris, 1973).

In assessing the Bura Scheme plans Saha (1982) came to the conclusion that at a development cost of US$16,716 per hectare, the project was likely to be one of the world's most capital-intensive irrigation schemes. The plan was initially to settle 5150 tenant families on 6700 hectares of irrigated land. For that purpose twice as much land was cleared than was needed for the first phase, with the consequence that in 1987, when 2700 hectares were under cotton, thousands of hectares remain bush-cleared and erosion-prone.

One of the serious problems was that the sharp increase in population of the area meant a parallel increase in the pressure on the environment for household fuel. The consequent shortage of firewood was the reason for the engagement of FINNIDA (Finnish International Development Agency) in the Bura project. The socio-economic research which utilized a participatory approach was in turn an aspect of the fuelwood project, as will be described below.

Saha, in assessing the planning of the Bura Scheme in 1982, suggested that it was one of the many cases in which engineering and agronomic aspects of irrigation development were considered, but the social dimension was neglected. From the planning point of view irrigation should involve a combination of material and social means of production with a given set of social objectives. An understanding of these interactive relationships between the material, technical and social aspects is an essential prerequisite for an effective irrigation policy (1982: 261–2).

Prior to the final decision to go ahead with the Bura Scheme, a consultant to the Office of Environmental and Health Affairs of the World Bank had spelled out many of the likely problems which the Scheme, and particularly the tenants, would eventually face should the plans be implemented unchanged. The consultant, a woman anthropologist, called for further clarification of several points which nevertheless failed to attract attention. In her words:

> We should also be aware of the fact that these settlers will be tenant farmers in a scheme which will produce about 70 per cent of Kenya's cotton for export, along with corn, ground nuts and other food crops. In order for Bura to be a human settlement with basic social amenities and not just a 'factory in the field' with minimum living quarters, a myriad of socio-cultural factors must be taken into consideration. (Elmendorf, 1976)

Other examples could be quoted of the conflicts between those concerned with the social and human aspects of the Scheme, and the agents with different interests in mind. In a consultancy report a recommendation was made (ILACO study, Part II, Netherlands, 1975) that tenants be men of a certain age group, while another report prepared by officials of the Ministry of Housing and Social Services of Kenya recommended strongly that selection of tenants should not be based on gender since about one-third of the rural households in Kenya were headed by women and 75 per cent of the agricultural work was undertaken by women (Elmendorf, 1976). The implementing consultant ended up adopting as one of the criteria, 'He [the head of the household] and his family had to be physically fit to undertake farm work' (Sir M. MacDonald and Partners, 1977).

These examples indicate also that the human and social issues concerning the people whom development projects affect, are not always appreciated only after the mistakes have been made. Conscious disregard of such factors is often part of the planning and implementing process, and as such reveals the rationale for political and economic decision-making and use of power. This has implications for the role that PAR (participatory action research) could play in the implementation of a project, in this case a large irrigation scheme. In PAR proper the concern *for* people turns to a concern *of* the people themselves.

There is no need to elaborate here the stages through which the planning and implementation of Bura settlement has progressed; it suffices to concentrate on aspects pertinent to the topic of participation in action research by Bura tenants. First the prerequisites for participatory action research are discussed, then the way the research itself was planned and carried out will be sketched. This is followed by a discussion on the effects of the research project on the people concerned, particularly on women. In the end, broader implications are analysed.

Prerequisites for participatory action research

Participation is an ambiguous concept. It is frequently used in development discussion by all parties concerned. In the vocabulary of the development agents and funders it is often equated with the agents' desire to secure the co-operation of the people who form the target group for the particular programme or project. For a government it means making the people participate in planned programmes, preferably out of their own free will and motivation, thereby supposedly demonstrating their consent and agreement with the plans. Participatory action research as an approach, on the other hand, starts from the concerns of the people, and because of this it is often considered inappropriate to refer to it in top-down situations, such as the Bura Irrigation Scheme clearly is.

In an earlier study Swantz has suggested four different degrees of participation by the 'target group' in the research process itself, following Cornista and Escueta's classification (Cornista and Esqueta, 1982; Swantz, 1984: 13); these depend on the extent to which the people participate in the different phases of programmes, from planning and initiating ideas to the actual carrying out of the plans. The crucial criterion is not the degree of participation but whether the planning and action accompanying the research emancipates the people involved, and gives especially peripheral groups more room for action, or whether the ultimate result is to incorporate the people in plans made from above and to build on people's sentiments of obedience to the authorities. The plans can have been made with good intentions and yet turn against the people whom they intend to serve.

PAR can be used for different purposes and with varied political intent. In this study it is conceived as a kind of trajectory in a struggle of people who are peripheral to decision-making for greater 'space', room for manoeuvre, and power to determine the direction of their lives and the values on which they are built. It is applied in a specific historical situation in which people from different educational levels and classes of wealth are in conflict over the control of the same resources in a development aid context. There is a tendency for this situation that those with higher education and more control adopt patronizing attitudes towards the less educated, whom they also deem to be incapable of taking care of their own affairs. Development planning becomes that of planning *for* instead of planning *with* the people with less education and control.

Even in countries which have started from high ideals of sharing resources equally, the gap between different levels of society widens rather than narrows. The hierarchical positions of control become more established, and policies of gradual transformation of a society to a harmonious one in which people's interests converge become more and more utopian. In such situations PAR can serve as a tool for emancipation; the growth of self-esteem of individuals and groups in the periphery of decision-making, the increased consciousness of the limits of their power and their potential to extend them, and the creation of more 'space' for their own action and struggle for their rights. When perceived this way, any situation can offer liberating elements, not only those which politically build on 'people's power' or ideals of equality.

According to McCall, people's participation in local level development can be used

1   as a means to facilitate and lubricate outside interventions and policies, or
2   as mediation, that is, as a means to modify, guide or redirect interventions, and
3   for empowerment of the weakest groups, in which case it becomes emancipating and liberating. (McCall, 1987: 1)

In the case of Bura, instead of becoming a means for facilitation for the project administration, PAR had a chance of becoming a tenants' tool for uplifting their life situation to a small measure, perhaps more than the actual physical results would have permitted one to anticipate. Of course, the tenants' satisfaction also benefits ultimately those who run the Scheme for primary interests other than the tenants' welfare; it can therefore be argued that in this sense PAR becomes a facilitating device in any case in the long run. The crux of the issue is whether the people can maintain their struggle for their own rights. In the present research phase this may be too early to determine. It would also cage the authenticity of the effort in the first place.

Participatory inquiry in action

Research context
The Bura Scheme is situated in semi-arid landscape with sparse bushland surrounding it. With the arrival of some 1900 tenant families since 1981, and the emergence of additional semi-official settlements in and around the Scheme, the total population has grown to some 20,000. As a consequence the environment has come under increasing pressure for provision of woodfuel, on which all households in the area depend for domestic energy.

Presently woodfuels are obtained from three sources. Immediately surrounding the Scheme is light–medium scrub; beyond this there is dense–medium. Finally there is the riverine forest, forming a belt of up to 1 km wide along the River Tana. All of these sources are rapidly deteriorating, and this is also reflected in increasing distances for firewood collection (Vainio-Mattila, 1987).

Some attention was paid to the woodfuel situation in the original Scheme plans, with suggestions made for possible alternative sources, but the shortage of woodfuel was not regarded in any way a priority, as it did not directly contribute to the agricultural productivity of the Scheme. By 1981 it was clear that there would not be a sufficient woodfuel supply from the immediate environment, and that already the ecologically precious nearby riverine forest was coming under high pressure.

In late 1981 the woodfuel supply was identified as a project for Technical Co-operation Programme between Kenya and Finland. However, the process which took place involved prolonged planning of substantial changes.

This meant long delays in starting the establishment of irrigated forestry. In fact, the first 100 ha were planted in 1987, and the first harvest cannot be expected before 1993.

On the other hand, some positive changes also took place. At least on paper the Fuelwood Project shifted its focus so that it was no longer simply concerned with producing a certain amount of fuelwood in a set time, but also aimed to develop self-sufficiency in woodfuels within the Bura Scheme. In addition, two separate research projects were established which would be able to influence the implementation of the Project.

The Silvicultural Research Programme was to determine appropriate species for growing in Bura, and to study the changing environment around the Scheme. The Social and Economic Research Programme (SERP) was established to serve the interests of the Forestry Project. SERP was expected to provide a social and economic analysis of present fuel production, distribution and consumption patterns. It was to determine means of reducing woodfuel consumption to an acceptable level and to identify alternatives for woodfuels, and finally, it was to provide an analysis of existing social structures and organization so that there could be tenant participation in the Forestry Project, and as a basis of planning the administration of the fuelwood plantation at the village level.

One aspect that quickly came to dominate the research process was the co-called stove programme. The idea of testing improved stoves to reduce firewood consumption was suggested by the Project planners in terms of building a few trial stoves; but the initiative to build stoves that then developed into the stove programme came from the women who had immigrated to Bura from areas where such stoves were used. The stove in question was derived from the Lorena stove developed in Central America, and is made of sand, clay, water and cowdung/ash. It very quickly became part of a process where alternative solutions to the domestic shortage of woodfuels were identified by the women. This process was based on resources which were controlled by the women themselves. The stoves also became an important window into many issues not previously perceived as linked to domestic fuel. For example, while Project Planners still regard the stoves purely in terms of fuelwood consumption, for the women they mean in addition – and at times more importantly – a reduced fire hazard in the houses, greater safety for children, and a cleaner, healthier (smokeless) working environment.

While expectations the Project had of SERP are documented in various plans and reports, the expectations of the tenants concerning the research are not. These expectations were raised as SERP became better known in Bura. It is fair to say these expectations varied through different stages of the research, and according to the degree the people were involved.

Research process

A mixture of research techniques was used. To some extent traditional tools of anthropological field research were used, including formal and informal interviews, free communication, and observation, both participant and direct. However, we would regard as the most important tool that of *networking*. By networking we mean dialogue that has been born within and between groups that have formed temporarily or permanently around a common problem. In the context of PAR the research team is an active partaker in the dialogue, and at times initiates it.

Before describing the networking process further it is necessary to say that in the field the research team consisted of three people; the 'resident anthropologist' (Vainio-Mattila) and two research assistants, who were both Kenyan women living in Bura, and who had formerly been employed in casual employment and had no 'academic' background. One of the long-term aims of the research process was that it would be the research assistants who would carry out most of the extension work in the villages even after the SERP had come to an end. This was reflected in our interview strategy so that the main purpose of the semistructured interviews in the villages was that the research assistants would get to know, and to become known in, the villages they were to carry out extension in.

Networking took place mainly at three levels: in the villages, with others involved in research and extension, and with administration at different levels. Through the dialogue within this network it was possible to incorporate different kinds of information and expertise into the research process.

In the villages a group of people (5–15) became a nucleus in motivating discussion and action among the rest of the villagers. Such discussions took place informally in small groups, or at stove workshops (attended by about 20), or in village meetings attended by 20–70.

There are now 10 villages on the Scheme with 140–250 tenant households in each. The population of each village consists of a mix of at least 10 Kenyan nationalities. This meant that the villages were quite different in character; for example some villages were predominantly Christian, others Muslim; in most villages tenants came from sedentary agriculturalist backgrounds, but in others most came from a nomadic background.

In the first two or three villages the initial approach varied slightly, but then a procedure was arrived at which was carried out in all the other villages. This procedure involved the following steps: (1) Introductory phase, (2) stove workshop, (3) stove programme. The stove building became a central activity because it was experienced as a partial solution to the fuel shortage, and it easily fitted within the forestry framework. On the other hand women building the stoves had control themselves over the materials needed and the procedure adopted.

In the introductory phase the research team spent six weeks to two months in each village getting to know the villagers and the village. In practice this meant that the research assistant to whom the village had been assigned, and the anthropologist, carried out semistructured interviews, organized and attended meetings with village chairmen, village committee, and women's groups. In short, the time was used for mutual introduction.

One of the aims of this introductory period was to identify the priority issues in each village. Firewood was always regarded as a major problem, but seldom the most important one, by the villagers. The priority problems varied from housing and crop failures to nutrition and health. In general these could be grouped within two categories. The first included things where a lack of information was seen as the problem, such as what to plant in the small (0.05 ha) vegetable plot in order to produce a more balanced diet. The other category involved things where direct action was needed. For example, despite promises, very little was being done about collapsing houses by the Bura Scheme landlords.

One of the reasons for the meetings in the introductory phase was to determine who would be attending the stove workshop. The stove workshop took place over a week, during which the first improved stove of the village was built. The numbers of participants were restricted because the tenant houses in which building took place were small. The people to attend were always chosen by villagers, usually on the basis of who were regarded as good teachers to pass on the skill they would learn, but also according to positions of influence and leadership. This procedure in itself was usually very enlightening as regards the decision-making processes in the village.

The only criterion set by the research team was that the numbers should not exceed 20, and that the group should comprise roughly half men and women. This last we found necessary after we had in one village targeted the stove development solely at women, thinking that men would not even be interested in something so specifically belonging to the women's sphere. However, we found that even if this was true in the long term, in the short term women needed the approval of the men to carry out stove building as a group activity. So even if nominal, their participation was desirable.

Apart from becoming a tool in passing on stove-building skills, the workshop functioned as a stage for networking in two other distinct ways.

In the process of building the stove there are two days in the week when nothing can be done to the stove. This is when the wet mixture of sand/clay/water/cowdung dries. One of these days was used for a village workshop. This could be attended by anybody and usually took place in one of the village nurseries established by the Scheme forester. The forester usually took the opportunity to teach about nursery establishment and tree planting, and was available for questions. This workshop was also an opportunity to discuss the priority issues in a larger forum. Usually relevant professional staff were invited to answer questions on issues outside the administration of the forester, for example home economists on vegetable gardening or irrigation officers on irrigation. At times it was difficult to get the appropriate officer to attend the meeting, and it could be that other kind of action was suggested by the meeting. On one occasion it was suggested that the research team would draft a letter to the Scheme Manager including the questions the tenants had. It was seen that whereas this was not particularly difficult for the researchers to do, similar action by an individual or a group of tenants was feared to revoke censure by the Scheme administration.

The other free day was used for a visit by the workshop to a village where the stoves were already in use. This opened the possibility of discussion between users and potential users, but usually it also opened a discussion on a wide range of issues concerning village development. On the question of stoves it was obvious to all that whereas the people organizing the workshop (the research team) did have some technical knowledge on the stoves to combine with the tenants' knowledge on the materials used, none of us were actually using the stoves. So even if we could answer questions on expected firewood consumption we could not really know how differently the stove cooked chapati (a type of bread) from the open fire.

The villages are arranged in pairs, and the distances between the pairs vary from a couple of kilometres to some 20 kilometres. There is no transport arranged for moving from one village to another, and the only way to visit another village is if that village is on the way to the rural centre, or to walk. As group visits between the villages were previously unheard of, the discussion was lively, covering topics from comparison of crops to what kind of projects were being funded in the villages by the various organizations and ministries.

After the workshop the stove programme would really start. The research team was never directly involved in building the first of the stoves in each village, but one of the assistants would always be present for advice. The building was organized by the villagers, and took place usually in groups of about five people. The group would together build the stoves for each household. Apart from the stove building the research assistant would continue to monitor changes in issues regarded as problems in the village. She would at times become the village's link to other parts of the administration.

As a research team we also took part in regular fortnightly meetings between the women involved in extension work on the Scheme. Although these meetings were initiated by the research team, they were still continuing a year after the end of the research component in the field, as was confirmed during a visit to Bura. Apart from the research team these involved the two or three Home Economists stationed in Bura by Ministry of Agriculture, the Nutritionist from the Ministry of Health, representatives from the American Maryknoll Sisters who had a mission house in two of the villages, and any women on the Scheme staff involved with work in the villages. (During 1985–1987 this in practice meant the officer in charge of crop research.)

The need for these meetings was twofold. To an extent they were to ensure that limited resources were not being wasted through unco-ordinated efforts resulting in overlapping, and more importantly to share the available resources, often in very practical terms such as transport. Even though there were Home Economists in Bura to do specifically extension work, they did not have a fuel allocation and thus were often immobile. The benefit to the research team was the regularly shared perceptions on the problems and possible solutions by professional women involved in extension. Also it was possible to raise discussion on issues of fuelwood, and to take part in a continuous dialogue on development of the women's situation in Bura.

Networking with senior staff and administration (at Scheme, Local and District levels) was of necessity more formal, and took place mainly at prearranged interviews and workshops.

From the research point of view we would regard a networking situation participatory if all participants in the situation had some control over what took place. For example in the stove seminar, apart from the building the one stove, the rest of the agenda was really up to those participating from the village. In the same way the agenda for meetings with the other extension staff was decided in each meeting on the basis of what everyone most wanted/needed to discuss.

It could be argued that the networking in a village, and with other extension staff, was generally participatory, in terms of control of the dialogue situation, and decisions on activities and topics. Networking with the administration was largely non-participatory. The dialogue was often restricted by expectations regarding information obtained, and fear of consequence resulting from something said.

Research conclusions
In the field the research was constantly going through a three-stage cycle of problem identification, solution-seeking and solution implementation. At any one time several such processes could be ongoing. Through the networking it was possible for any villagers interested to take an active part in this process.

Because of the nature of PAR, there are continuously situations in which the interest group and the researchers share common experiences, but to what extent is there actual participation in the research? Do we call research participatory if the community in which it takes place can influence the research by suggestion, or is research participatory only when they don the role of an anthropologist?

In the case of Bura there were at least two occasions where it could be said that the interest groups were involved in research in a very traditional way.

On one occasion women in a village initiated research of their own. This was the first village we had approached, and so no stoves had been built yet in other villages. In fact it was largely these women who initiated the process of stove building in Bura. The problem was that, although the women felt that the improved stoves would be a very good idea, they also felt that they would need some means of persuading their husbands that the time invested in stove building would be worth it. They suggested that if they could prove that the time and money presently spent on fetching and buying fuelwood was already substantial, this might be enough to convince the men. The research team then prepared exercise books in which 20 women, chosen by the other women, for two months marked, by ticking the appropriate column, the time and money saved. The results, which were compiled by the research team, may not be statistically significant to prove anything about fuelwood consumption in general, but they were a clear indication that time and money was spent. The results were presented on a large poster which was then used by women leaders in meetings with the village committee.

Another similar, but repeated, activity took place during the identification of materials for the stoves in the vicinity of the village. This required some knowledge of the soils and their durability in a building mass.

On the other hand there were research situations where the technique used could hardly in itself be called participatory, for example, analysis of maps and aerial photographs, and even the semi-structured interviews, because although the collection of statistically valid data was not their aim, they were introduced to collect information relevant to planning forestry strategies, and to collect information on existent structures and ongoing processes.

We would argue that in participatory research two kinds of different expertise – one based on knowledge from living in specific circumstances, the other on knowledge that has essentially been taught – always exist side by side. This is especially so where research is carried out within development aid framework, because in that specific context the research takes on particularly strongly the role of communicator between the community and the project.

At the same time we would argue that PAR can be a tool of empowerment within the aid context. In the case of Bura the networking situations were often the only opportunities for tenants to identify problems and solutions together with Project personnel. The research facilitated the process of tenants taking control over those partial solutions to the fuelwood shortage that were possible with the resources they had available to them; stove building, food and fuel preparation techniques, alternative fuels and so on.

One frustration concerned the follow-up of the priority issues identified in the villages. Because the terms of reference of the research programme were restricted by the interests of the Forestry Project, it was not always possible to carry out the suggestions made by tenants regarding different situations. We could only go as far as to prompt the relevant authorities. The fact that development aid is commonly perceived, and thus planned and implemented, in terms of narrow sector expertise is a difficulty for PAR, because the approach has such obvious potential for integrated approach, rather than the top-down framework of development aid.

The experience in Bura was that while problem identification and solution seeking were participatory, implementation of solutions was possible only if the resources needed were controlled by the villagers, or if the solution was regarded as relevant and appropriate by the Forestry Project. For example, suggestions regarding the use of agricultural waste as a substitute for expensive irrigated fuelwood have never been taken seriously into consideration. A closed cotton season is common practice in Bura, and presently the cotton stalks are burned in the fields. Elsewhere in the world (Ethiopia, Nicaragua) there are positive experiences from converting this waste material into domestic fuel. However, the use of agricultural wastes is not within the expertise of foresters, so it is not seen as a practicable solution.

On the other hand, if a solution is seen to be beneficial and available by some means to which the villagers had access, it would be applied. For example, despite it being forbidden, cotton stalks are continuously burned to supplement fuelwood and are also used as fencing in the kitchen garden.

Because of the constant interaction between the research team and the villagers, problems and solutions are identified as a part of the dynamics of the changing living environment. Consequently the research results become active agents of this change, accessible to all those concerned.

Ideally, with PAR it would be possible to influence the development of an aid project all the while it is being implemented. But as they are implemented to strict plans even small changes can cause problems. One obstacle is the presentation of 'results'. Waiting for the final report at the end of the research period restricts the PAR into forms of traditional research, and does away with its potential strength of information that reflects dynamics of ongoing processes in favour of static data.

Participatory inquiry in grass-roots development

Participatory inquiry and development practice
Participatory inquiry has been referred to in this article as participatory action research or PAR, in line with the practice adopted by the network

of PAR researchers globally (*EADI Bulletin*, 1987). It is apparent on the basis of the Bura case study that the approach is not without problems. One of the main difficulties is the potential misuse of this kind of research. People's participation can be used as a means to facilitate and lubricate outside intervention, and not principally in the interest of the grass-roots people. This issue requires further discussion here.

PAR claims to be an approach with less exploitative qualities than research which treats people as research material and as objects, such as ordinary surveys and especially research which uses people as test cases. When the people who are surveyed or interviewed are not informed about the purposes for which their answers or they as persons are being used, or they get only very superficial explanations about it, their answers can be used against their interests. Those conducting research may be ethically sensitive, but the research setting itself is instrumental.

PAR as an approach is not instrumental but it too can be misused. In fact, because of the closeness of the researchers to the people with whom they work, the eventual exploitation of the situation could be even worse. Thus even here the crux of the issue is in the integrity of the researcher.

The claim was made at the beginning of this chapter that PAR within the socio-economic study of the Bura project had a chance of becoming a tenants' tool for uplifting their life. The crucial question is whether the tenants could determine the way the research served them or not.

The tenants were not a homogeneous group. The study of the fuelwood economy of the Bura settlements conducted parallel to PAR by the Institute of Development Studies, University of Nairobi (Ruigu and Makanda, 1987), showed that there was an increasing disparity among the tenant incomes in Bura. Despite the increasing differentiation in incomes the resident tenants could be classified as being rich only in exceptional cases. The problems within the PAR were formulated by those who felt them sorely. The problems of delayed start of cotton growing because of maize planting as an alternating crop, and the shortage of irrigation water because of it, was felt by majority of the farmers. Similarly they all suffered from the lack of fuelwood and vegetable crops. Even those engaged in selling firewood faced the difficulty of transporting it from great distances. All were aware of the increasing threat of the fuel problem.

Thus by and large the problem formulation in PAR was widely shared by the tenant population. That men as well as women became interested in stove-building indicated that they too, not only women who traditionally were wood-carriers, shared the worry about availability and expense of fuel.

To what extent then did PAR become a tool for the tenant farmers themselves? It has already been indicated that there were occasions on which some of the tenants undertook parts of actual research tasks like that of weighing and recording the amounts of wood used by them. Those who did this volunteered for the task after realizing the significance of it. Also the stove model and the materials available for building the stoves were suggested by the women in Bura. These were important aspects for the success of the total action research. They served also as an evidence of the willingness of the research staff to act on the basis of the people's own initiatives. This had great significance since the irrigation project itself had otherwise no channels for heeding the pleas of the people under its authority. The knowledge and greater understanding of their own situation which the tenant farmers gained with the stove project created an inquiring environment and a sense of not being satisfied with everything that was given as an answer. This came out in informal group discussions as well as in individual encounters.

Further, the networking, and the opportunities it offered for the villagers to get into contact with other villages and with community workers and to discuss their problems openly in the seminars, became another empowering element within the social and economic research programme.

In more general terms PAR does not require an ideal initial, bottom-to-top setting. What is crucial is that there is sufficient room in the given situation for the people to strengthen their own active part in their life situation. PAR can play a part in clearing space for the people for their own action and for at least partial, sometimes only minimal, increase in control of their own affairs. Each situation determines how much room there is for the people involved to co-operate with outsiders. The role of the outsider may only be to spark off a process which then ideally takes its own course.

In the Bura situation PAR was used with the hope that it would start an ongoing process which would be continued by the people engaged in the common effort. Although the socio-economic research was a commissioned study there was room to make it a genuine PAR effort. The funders were not so much concerned about the unorthodox methodology as about the results. PAR did not only produce useful information and samples of stoves, as stated in the terms of reference. It had social and economic consequences which surpassed the expectations. However, the process needs to go on; it requires the return of the researcher to the place from time to time, but ideally the process goes on also without the continuing research presence because of the inbuilt networks among the women workers and tenants.

Orlando Fals-Borda (1987) gives as the focus of work which utilizes PAR 'people's counterveiling power defined as the capacity to exert vigilance and control over processes pertaining to community development, in relation to external and internal forces for change'. In the case of Bura there was no background of people's movements nor any precedent studies which would have alerted the tenant farmers to handling their problems with the instigation of outsiders. Also the results must be assessed accordingly.

Yet the experience was sufficiently substantial to give reason to present the Bura case as a positive practical experience in the exercise of PAR.

Participatory inquiry as a scientific approach

Some thoughts need to be added about participatory inquiry in general, and the PAR used in Bura case in particular, as a scientific approach.

According to Fals-Borda three elements are combined in the process of using PAR for radically transforming the social and economic milieu and for building people's power in rural areas. They are: scientific research, adult education and political action. In adopting a participatory action approach there is an underlying assumption that the existing social situation needs to change, and that people should be empowered to carry out their own development (Fals-Borda, 1987: 41).

This contradicts some of the generally accepted basic scientific postulates, those of objectivity and non-biased, non-political approach to subject-matter. Research becomes part of a social movement and as such a means of promoting it. In Stavenhagen's words, the researcher becomes a 'partisan' (Stavenhagen, 1971: 251–9).

In Bura there was no social movement to join in. The choice was between a study which would produce a report for the financiers and project planners and a study which would take its departure from the tenants. The latter had already gone through a multitude of hardships in the beginning stages of the irrigation project. They had been caused by lack of drinking water as well as irrigation water, food shortages and severe illnesses without organized health care, poor-quality housing which necessitated rebuilding and fortifying the poorly built structures. Many family members, especially children, had died. The catastrophe of decreasing supplies of domestic fuel also loomed ahead.

The task of the researcher was not to predetermine what to do in the given situation. It meant making the research tools and the personnel available for the people in need. In doing so the process became an educational situation. But in addition, whether those involved want it or not, research is a political action. There is no need to emphasize here that it is so regardless whether it consciously sets itself on the side of a specific group of people or not, so self-evident it is. A social scientist, any scientist for that matter, cannot separate his or her scientific self from being an ordinary citizen in a given situation.

There is, however, a difference between actively engaging in political action and coming to the situation as one who brings the tools for acquiring knowledge needed for action. There may be situations in which the research turns to active engagement in a struggle and the researchers join in it, no longer making a distinction between scientific research and popular research. In such a situation the question of whether research is scientific is no longer asked. Action and engagement in struggle have taken over.

Being a scientist has become secondary or even irrelevant. This is not the case here.

Another question concerns the kind of knowledge that has been produced. Clearly we are not talking about knowledge produced through orthodox scientific methods, tested in laboratory or by statistical means. Rather we argue that the project produces a form of knowledge whose most evincible validity is its practical workability. We are not attempting to show that building of a number of simple stoves by the tenant households in Bura was a proof of PAR being a successful scientific method. We rather argue, that through the use of PAR within the Bura project, there opened up an avenue of knowledge formation which would not have been there without it.

A further issue concerns the way that 'everyday knowledge' which the scholar makes use of is given recognition in his or her work. In conventional social science after the names of collaborators have been given they may be forgotten. In ethnographic and anthropological works they appear as informants. One can well ask whether this is the correct picture of how the knowledge was arrived at and formulated. With the explosion of scholarship it is impossible to keep check of ideas appearing in social or cultural scientific writings. It means that they can be 'stolen' from other sources without references, often even unconsciously relying on thoughts from others. The body of scholars, however, keep watch over other scholars so that indiscriminate borrowing is not done too boldly. But there is no such checking on ideas and knowledge formation which derives from contacts with people who are not recognized as being scientific in their thinking and background. This is even more so with illiterate people, who have no control over the written products of their knowledge.

It is at this point where the significance of PAR as used in the Bura project becomes evident. The people involved in inquiry for the purposes of their own action recognize their own contribution to that action, and to the store of knowledge required for the action. The common quest for greater understanding of the situation also increases the researcher's capacity towards greater awareness of the roots and elements of the produced knowledge.

Within conventional scientific practice scientists stay aloof from the people, not only because their method requires it, but because in most cases they belong to a different social class or milieu or ethnic or cultural background. While social scientists may argue that they need distance in order to better reflect on the issues at hand, it is also one significant reason for separation of theory from practice, because the knowledge produced by social science or culture study becomes separated from the way the ordinary people think and conceive life. An important role of participatory action research can be to seek to create common consciousness between the researchers and the common people, and thereby also build a basis for a common field of knowledge in which theory and practice come together.

It can be argued that basic contradiction between social classes cannot be overcome by creating a common field of consciousness. It may be true that through the dialogue and dialectics of different viewpoints, and the conflicts discovered, the researchers may not come to consensus with people holding differing views because of their different existential situation. However, the awareness thereby created of the differences is what is needed for the right understanding and for two-way communication of ideas as well as for needed action.

It is thus suggested here that participatory inquiry has potential, not only for creation of needed theoretical knowledge but also for social consciousness and action based on it, not only for the privileged researchers but the people whose knowledge and social as well as political action based on it otherwise remain largely hidden.

7

Managing to Learn:
Action Inquiry in City Hall

Robert Krim

On a bulletin board above her desk the Mayor's trade union liaison had tacked the newspaper headline 'Sharks are circling' over a poster of waves. Pinned to the poster was a toy shark with a small girl plastic doll in its mouth. The same official jokingly gave a 'victim of the week' award to the City Hall figure who had suffered the worst defeat in his or her daily swimming with sharks. It all fitted in with the message I got when I started work at City Hall.

'Don't trust anyone except for myself and my secretary', my boss told me on my first day as Assistant Director of Personnel for Human Resources Development of a major US city government. My job was to start a new labour–management co-operation programme based on employee participation in management decisions, working co-operatively with the City's management and unions in a new populist administration. Developing trust would be critical to what I wanted to accomplish, and yet I was being told at the outset to abandon trust at the door.

The opportunity: labour-management co-operation in City Hall

To develop a successful labour–management employee participation programme in the politicized City Hall environment was a major challenge. None of the first seven efforts to create a labour–management programme in smaller municipal governments in the same state had lasted two years. Most had failed due to the power politics in municipal governments. I was trying to do this in an organization which had become a national legend for its degree of power politics. The previous administration's infamous political 'machine' had operated out of the same Personnel Department which now housed myself and my new co-operative programme.

If I were to achieve anything in reconciling the political traditions embedded in the City Hall culture and the co-operative principles of the labour–management employee participation programme I needed a learning strategy which would enable me to swim safely around the treacherous reefs and sharks which had torn apart other municipal labour-management programmes. I hoped to lead City Hall towards a culture based on participation and labour–management co-operation using co-operative inquiry. I sought to apply a reflective action inquiry methodology as a practitioner myself, so that eventually City Hall, and those who I worked with, would be better prepared for co-operative forms of inquiry.

My project grew out my effort to create a new organizational culture – one which would be founded on collaboration and openly surfacing problems in order to resolve them – within the line departments of a major city government. The new Administration accepted my proposal to develop a new unit to do training and organizational development, of which the first part was the labour-management programme.

While I had only limited success in establishing an action inquiry approach within the labour–management programme, the effort provided an outstanding opportunity for me to both examine the barriers to the programme's success and to study myself and my own growth as a manager using a reflexive methodology. Many times practitioners of action inquiry work in organizations which are comparatively receptive to intervenors who wish to improve the operation of the organization. I chose the challenge of entering a particularly rough environment, consciously seeking to use collaborative processes to improve the organization, and to look simultaneously at improving my own effectiveness against this backdrop.

During my first two years (the period covered by this chapter), there was a clash between action inquiry and the norms of this organization where open sharing of information was viewed as dangerous and foolhardy. My experience in City Hall raises general questions for all who seek to practise inquiry collaboratively. Can a manager learn critical lessons that improve his or her on-the-job effectiveness through becoming, in Don Schon's terms, a 'reflective practitioner' (Schon, 1983)? What was the impact of all of this on me? Would I do it again? And, at a broader level, how are practitioners to operate in unsympathetic environments such as the one described in the US City Hall? Others who worked in organizations with 'power cultures' like the one in the US City Hall (Reason, 1984), have suggested that in such organizations we need to wait for change from the outside before we can establish successful organizational development efforts. From the beginning I posed the question: Do we have to keep to organizations that are ready for our skills, or can we find ways to act creatively in hostile environments?

Action inquiry

The methodology I used – action inquiry – is related to a wide variety of other action research techniques and approaches. I tried to create an organizational culture with a learning strategy following William Torbert's 'action inquiry' model (Torbert, 1987). It is founded on:

1   An understanding *and continual re-evaluation* of the question 'What
    are we trying to accomplish (in the unit, department, or government
    as a whole)?'
2   The setting up of regular systems to test whether the organization's
    strategies and operations in fact match its vision, and to test its effect
    on the environment.
3   The promotion of members' development towards their capacity for
    exercising 'action inquiry' (continuous learning from experience) –
    a true school for adults.

The essence of action inquiry is that practitioners – whether managers,
union employees, or programme staff – will become more effective by
continually seeking as consciously as possible to take actions and then to
reflect on them.

My action inquiry process

While I was unsuccessful in getting my staff to adopt an action inquiry model
in our day-to-day work, I sought to use it myself as a key learning strategy in
managing the unit and learning about my own management style. This was
part of my own managerial training in a unique joint MBA/PhD programme
in which I was studying while I worked for City Hall. My doctoral programme brought together Bill Torbert, the head of the graduate school
of management with his focus on developing reflective managers using
action inquiry, and a sociology department with its emphasis on grounded,
inductive field research. The processes I used ranged from the participant
observation of the sociologist to newer organizational development tools.
One might view this as a pyramid (see Figure 7.1) with the base the more
private, lower levels of recording and observing (qualitative data collection), and each higher level both more reflective, and pro-active with
increasing public testing and intensity. Through the use of this pyramid
of action inquiry tools I sought to learn how to lead and manage an effective
municipal quality of work life (QWL) programme.

At the most basic level I spent approximately an hour a day recording
the day's events and reflecting on them. Prior to work I would tape my
intentions on some of the day's scheduled meetings, at times brainstorming
on different approaches and rehearsing one or another. After work I would
make notes and/or tape on the day's meetings and conversations – using
the processes of the sociological field-work researcher. I kept a daily
appointment book which served to summarize all events and became an
index to the tapes. I taped during my drive to work and home; my requests
to tape meetings at work were turned down by both managers and union
leaders uncomfortable with how these might be used later.

While the daily notes and tapes provided the background, more important
for analysis and reflection were 'critical incidents' which I wrote up,

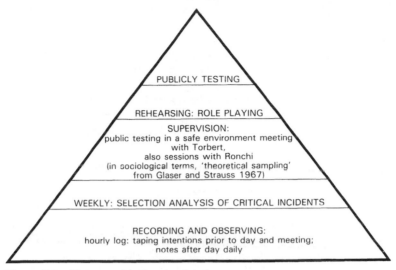

Figure 7.1   *The pyramid of action inquiry processes*

usually once per week. The most useful of these took the form of a several-page reconstruction of a difficult incident from the week. I listed my perceptions prior to the meeting or incident (taken from the morning tape), reconstructed the most difficult part of the dialogue (using meeting notes), and then sought to analyse the incident, looking at my own feelings and seeking ways that I could have taken a different approach which would have surfaced an issue or confronted a difficult person or situation.

The next level of my action inquiry pyramid was to open up my analyses of my own work and the direction of the programme – to 'publicly test' them – in a safe environment. I did this on a regular basis in two ways: meeting once every three weeks in a supervision with Bill Torbert, and talking once or twice a week by telephone with Don Ronchi. Torbert, a member of my dissertation committee and a leader in the field of action research and inquiry, had agreed prior to the project to give me a super-vision in management – both practical and academic. Don Ronchi, a social psychologist by training who had worked with Bruno Bettleheim and Jane Loevinger at the University of Chicago, had, as a professor at Ohio State University, helped to initiate labour–management employee participation programmes in the public sector in the mid-1970s. Although not as well known as Torbert, he has a broad background which combines psychology, organizational development, action research, and public sector experience with labour–management co-operation.

One of the techniques which Ronchi and Torbert used with me was to role-play a particular scenario (from a critical incident paper) as a way of rehearsing a difficult response. Rehearsals, whether live in a supervision or alone using tape, whether prior to or after an important incident, were an important technique for reflective learning. Much of the rehearsal might be viewed as a performance. By showing Torbert, Ronchi, and at times others the critical incidents I took the risk of learning something less than complimentary about myself.

At the highest level of the pyramid, action inquiry can be seen as a process of continual rehearsal and performance. Eventually the rehearsal should blend into the performance. According the Torbert: 'Ultimately the sense that one is simultaneously rehearsing and performing in action inquiry introduces the manager to a new quality of awareness – to a continuous, silent impartial observing of one's own performance amidst others' (Torbert, 1983: 22). [Note the parallels between Krim's use of rehearsal to develop impartial self-observation and the similar use of psychodrama in Chapter 3. Editor]

The environment
I needed an innovative learning strategy like action inquiry to survive and learn in City Hall. For several reasons it is a rough environment in which to manage, and a formidable place in which to initiate organizational change. First, City Hall is a fishbowl. The organization is covered by more news reporters for its size than any similar organization in the state. Any memo, any mistakes, could be on the TV evening news, or in the next day's headlines. Frequently memos in the Mayor's Office on sensitive issues are written without a 'to' or 'from' to keep reporters (who are known for reading papers on desks upside-down) from being able to pin down stories.

Second, there is a strong perception that nice people will get eaten up if they don't have 'street smarts'. The 'sharks are circling' poster and the 'don't-trust-anyone' advice were representative of the culture. Given this environment, there is often little commitment to purported work-related goals. 'Politics' – office politics and neighbourhood politics – carried on at a very advanced level predominate in many of the units of City Hall departments, though not all; programmatic goals simply have not existed in many units. Most key players in City Hall get there by taking risks and rising through the use of political skills from working-class neighbourhoods. Taking risks and fighting it out with others in the organization – known for both women and men as 'having balls' – is highly prized. The rewards for winning are increased support from the Mayor's Office, and with that more control over the currency – information and jobs – in use in City Hall.

The City Labour–Management Co-operation Programme
My employee participation programme – the City Labour–Management Co-operation Programme – has a three-tiered structure: worksite groups, labour–management departmental committees, and a Citywide Oversite

Committee'. The core of the programme is the worksite groups where employees and first-line supervisors can develop approaches to solving the worksite's problems. The departmental and citywide committees help the worksite groups to clarify and implement these initiatives. The departmental and citywide committees can also develop areas of concern which cut across broader levels than one worksite.

The programme has provided more facilitation staff and a greater amount of training in the early years of a department's participation than other municipal programmes have done. The staff has been composed of a programme director and two facilitators: one chosen by the union and one chosen by management. The facilitators have worked with the programme participants to help them develop proposals and learn on a continuing basis how to work effectively within the bureaucracy. While both facilitators are supposed to work with all participants in a particular department, the management facilitator is supposed to pay special attention to working with managers and supervisors on their managerial style, and the union facilitator to ensuring that the needs of the union and its shop stewards are protected. The programme hired Don Ronchi, because he is a leader in public sector employee participation, to be intensively involved in design, initial meetings, training of facilitators and the programme director, and working closely with union and management to facilitate overall programme problems.

It is important to note that the programme was successful in that it survived, grew, and continues nearly four years after its inception in contrast to the six other municipal labour–management programmes in the state. It has been a vehicle in three key City Hall departments for solving critical and incidental problems. In the police emergency phone service unit, where participants have worked on turnover and training issues, it has helped to improve the telephone operators' morale and their response time in life-and-death situations. For the City Pension Office it has led to significant decline in complaints. Growing out of the programme Pension Office management has changed the mission of the Office from re-active to pro-active: managers and employees now seek to work with potential retirees to help them to face issues of their own mortality as they relate to retirement, and applying for pensions. A number of individuals give credit to the programme for aiding them in improving their listening and their communication; this has helped them in promotions at work, and with their own families.

My personal learning through action inquiry: 'de-authorization'

As I will recount below, I learned much about my own blind spots and management style using action inquiry. One important area of learning was my ambivalence about power, leading to a tendency to 'de-authorize' myself – giving up degrees of authority or power in situations where I neither wanted to, nor needed to. This tendency led me to feel relatively powerless because I had given up authority to others (for example, my staff). In a culture where toughness is important the tendency to de-authorize oneself was a significant weakness. The issue created problems not only for myself but also for my staff, the union leadership, and the managers who needed to depend on my judgement.

This problem was noted by Ronchi and Torbert early in 1984. In addition, I attended a Tavistock Institute weekend conference in November 1985 on 'Authority, Leadership, and Organizational Life', in which the three dozen participants were given feedback by a staff of trained organizational development psychologists after two days of intense participation in a model organization. The organizational structure in the sessions – where the participant operated in a loosely shifting coalition of individuals and organizations – was close to the environment in which I worked in City Hall. At the Tavistock session I received positive feedback on the role I played in initiating and organizing in this sort of environment; at the same time the Tavistock Director pointed out that I tended to de-authorize myself by 'not going with your instincts'.

My commitment to labour–management employee participation grew out of a political interest in ending worker alienation, thereby improving the quality of life by creating a maximum of self-management. The most effective organizations, I concluded, were those where managers relinquished or shared power. However, as I came to see over a period of time, on another level my espoused theories reflected a personal ambivalence about power. Discussions with the Tavistock director, Torbert, and Ronchi as well, confirmed this analysis. I will examine how I uncovered this through interaction with others, and how I sought to develop new behaviour as a result of using the techniques of the action inquiry pyramid.

De-authorization in the selection of
the management facilitator
The first stage of uncovering my de-authorization dynamic came during a conflict over the staff selection procedure for the programme. I decided that the search for the management facilitator should also involve a key union leader (hereafter 'the union leader'). I felt that I was implementing a new model of how labour and management might relate when they agreed on long-term visions. We would leave the final choice of this facilitator up to the full Oversite Committee. My espoused theory on this was that I wanted both the administration and the union to genuinely 'own' the facilitator if problems were to emerge later.

However, when the choice of facilitator who would work with union members came up, the union leader did not invite my collaboration. She pushed for the union to have exclusive control over the choice. 'It is our choice, we need this to preserve ourselves', she said.

I had included the union leader in the selection of the management facilitator without ever investigating how the decision would be made on the union facilitator. She – the union leader – had not asked to be included on the management facilitator decision. Moreover, my strategy for choosing the management facilitator ran into a problem when our first-choice recommendation was not chosen by the Committee. I would later feel that I could not live with the Committee's selection. I had de-authorized myself on a key decision. The Committee did not have a large investment in who was chosen as facilitator, yet I had allowed them to override my clearly preferred choice. This selection of management facilitator, who I judged to be inadequate after our first staff meeting, would come back to haunt me eight months later, when I initiated a major crisis by trying to transfer her out of the programme. Furthermore, based on my espoused theory, I had singled out myself as the key actor who needed to collaborate more – rather than focusing on the lack of collaboration shown by the other key actors in the environment – the union leader and to a certain extent my boss.

Other situations followed the same course. Each time the union leader distrusted me – because I was management – and questioned my management style. In each of my decisions she would see a management strategy to weaken the union using an employee participation programme.

Based on analysing these and other cases I came to see that I was stuck in an unconstructive behaviour pattern relative to the union leader and to others. First there was a structural dispute concerning the reporting relationships of the union and management facilitators to me – their supervisor. Second, there were the union leader's problems with my personal style. These multi-tiered problems reinforced each other in a cycle:

1 The union leader's suspiciousness of management and employee participation (from both an ideological viewpoint and from a traditional union viewpoint) led her to take strong negotiating positions with me.
2 These led me to not assert what I felt was needed and so to be dissatisfied with the result of what was negotiated. When I pushed later for a reconsideration, this increased her suspiciousness.
3 The Director of Personnel (my boss), seeing my lack of strength in negotiating with the union leader, questioned both my negotiating ability and my management credentials (and loyalty). To him this indicated that I was 'too close to the union'.
4 Because I was not really convinced that I had won enough from the union leader, I agreed with the Director of Personnel when he later criticized my dealings with the union leader. Characteristically, I would then go back and try to get more from the union leader. She would ward me off me because of her suspiciousness.

A discussion at a meeting concerning each person's role in the programme led Ronchi to address the general problem. He defined the complexity of my role, and the importance of being 'democratic, yes. But everyone runs from the commitment which comes with their roles.' Increasingly, I was finding it tough to maintain the authority which was necessary to get things done in City Hall, while still holding to my democratic principles. It was easier for me to be democratic – and to set myself up for opposition from the union leader and others.

Six months into the programme, at my request, both Ronchi and Torbert met with me for a joint supervision. They presented me with feedback on my work. They confronted me with my behaviour with the union leader. Ronchi said that the union leader, the management facilitator, and others all felt I was not giving effective leadership. I sometimes came across as manipulative because my style was so self-effacing, and my verbal style often so halting when under pressure. Both said that they saw my instincts as being on the right track; I should follow them, and not suppress them when I was feeling pressured. I should allow myself to be more spontaneous. Torbert reiterated what he had observed at one of our evaluation sessions earlier in the fall about my passivity in the face of pressure. He suggested that I make up a set of working rules to help me to try new behaviour.

The meeting was one of the most powerful hour-long sessions of my life. I had never been part of a work-related session where I had received such direct, critical feedback shared in such a constructive mode by two people who I felt were trying to help me. A few days later I put together a set of working rules of thumb on new behaviour I wanted to develop. The working rules included:

1   Turn disappointment to anger.
2   State my view clearly, don't diminish it.
3   If another is strong, listen, see what I feel and respond challenging back.

I promised myself that in situations which were tense for me I would try to keep these rules in mind.

The session led to a different interaction. Soon after setting up the guidelines I met with the union leader. We had one of our most positive and useful meetings up to that point. I was clearer about my positions, and she doubted me less. In other meetings in the months following, I had begun to deal with the union leader and with others a bit differently.

Applying my learning from
action inquiry on de-authorization

Recognizing the pattern, devising rules of thumb to change it, and carrying out one good meeting with the union leader did not end the pattern. It set the stage for more rehearsals and experiments in new situations. An increasing controversy around the manager/worker relationship between myself and the management facilitator led to a number of instances where I needed to experiment. A number of the critical incidents which I summarized in writing, and the discussion on these in supervision sessions during 1985, concerned my tendency to de-authorize myself, especially under attack. In this context Ronchi helped both the management facilitator and myself to see how my tendency to de-authorize myself as boss, combined with her tendency to not share information, led to programme problems.

I had given the management facilitator copies of several of my critical incidents as part of my work on developing her facilitation skills. After the series of meetings with Ronchi, the facilitator and myself, in which we had worked at resolving the problems, she had commented that she did not want to have more meetings of that sort. Her facilitation with departments was not improving; key committees were suffering increasing problems which I felt could only be solved by active interventions.

The situation within the programme intensified when a manager in one of the departments which the programme served became angry at me, and called off the spring 1985 expansion which the oversite committee had approved the day before. When I returned to City Hall the union leader called me. She became furious when she heard what had happened at the meeting. She was angry at other decisions of mine as well. She ended up yelling and hanging up.

I felt that I was caught between the union leader's usual suspiciousness and management problems. This time the problems were very intense and fairly public. However, I had not de-authorized myself with her, although she was quite angry. I went into the Personnel Department in City Hall on two successive weekends and used the word-processor to explore critical incidents. On the first weekend I reflected on two issues in critical incidents: my dispute with the manager, and my pattern with the union president. The next weekend I explored my feelings that the management facilitator was 'underfunctioning' and that I was ineffective at changing it. The next work day I realized that I had inadvertently left the critical incident in the word-processing system 'library' after printing a hard copy; I deleted the file from the library several hours after I realized this.

I was later to learn that our former administrative assistant had gone into my word-processing files during those few hours, printed a copy of my 'critical incident' about the management facilitator, and sent it anonymously to the union leader with a note 'I thought you would be interested in seeing this.' (It must have taken considerable time for her to read through all my files that morning, realize that there was something important, and decide to print it.) The management facilitator had also somehow received a xeroxed copy of another of my recent critical incidents (not given to her) which included a recounting of the incident when the union leader had hung up and sworn at me. To make matters worse, the management facilitator had sent this to the union leader, who was suspicious and had queried her on whether I had given her any of my critical incidents. The union leader, I later learned, had asked the staff to see whether I had other damaging evidence lying on my desk or in the word-processor files.

The union leader asked to meet with me, telling me in advance that she was angry about my recent performance, but without specifying what this meant. She had prepared herself for a knock-down–drag-out battle with me. She had held meetings with the other leaders of the union on how to handle the situation. She had done considerable background work – reading worksite group minutes, etc. The union leader was angry with me for several reasons:

1 My notes referred to my 'tapes' of conversations. She assumed that I had illegally been taping conversations.
2 Convincing her of the illegal taping theory was the fact that the dialogue of the argument between myself and her appeared to be so close to the reality that she felt it was a transcript. The dialogue made her look so bad that she did not want anyone seeing data like that, which could be used against her or the union. Having this on paper was even worse – it violated the norms of working in City Hall.
3 Her reading of the management facilitator critical incident led her to believe that I had already decided to fire the management facilitator.
4 Moreover, her reading of the blurb in the notes on my meeting with Torbert led her to believe that he was controlling the programme from outside, so that 'someone on the outside who I have never met nor jointly hired is making the big decisions for this programme'.

She assumed that I would fire the management facilitator, and that Torbert had urged me to do it. The tapes she was concerned about were actually the tapes of my own musings on the drive home for work, not illegal tapes of the meetings.

During the face-to-face meeting I responded to the union leader's charges, diffusing them somewhat, and tried to turn the discussion towards the facilitation problems with the management facilitator. I assured her that I was doing nothing illegal. She responded saying that, while it might not be illegal, it was possibly unethical. I showed the connection of what I was doing to action inquiry, and pointed out that we had discussed this several previous times.

'What would the managers at City Hall say if they knew what you were doing?.... People are feeling manipulated by your writing things down', she argued.

I felt 'blown out of the water' by my meeting with the union leader. Despite the suspiciousness and the attack, however, I did not de-authorize myself as I might have six months earlier. I answered her criticisms of the research by trying to demonstrate (as I had with the management facilitator and union facilitator earlier) that the entire programme had been founded in trying to create co-operative inquiry – 'double-loop learning' from Chris Argyris' terminology (Argyris and Schon, 1974). We developed several structures called 'learning analysis groups' – one for the staff and key officials, and one within the union. She listened, but was not convinced. We agreed that she and the rest of the staff should meet Torbert.

In this instance at a time of great tension, I did respond more directly and less haltingly than previously. The experiments and rehearsals in the personal learning approach to action inquiry were having some effect. I did not absorb the whole attack, and did try to turn it towards a discussion of facilitation. Yet I also learned something else from the conversation: the union leader and others accepted the norms within City Hall against putting things in writing, or reflecting on them – norms which placed much of action inquiry beyond the pale.

From two key Mayor's Office staffers and from Ronchi, I received backing for my contention that the key problem was the management facilitator's actual job performance, not my personality nor my dissertation. However others – unconscious of my own work on de-authorization – still seemed to perceive a problem. The Mayor's trade union liaison – who sat on the oversite committee and had been involved in many programme meetings counselled me that I was not doing very well at handling my staff power differences: 'You don't know how to be a chief, and the management facilitator does not know how to be an Indian.' She added, '*you must be more shark-like*'. She gave me a copy of 'How to swim with sharks: a primer' (Cousteau, 1973: 525–8) and counselled me that 'the blood is in the water', and that other sharks would be circling. The article lays out six rules in order to be 'shark like' and to survive including:

Assume unidentified fish are sharks.
Counter any aggression promptly.
Use anticipatory retaliation.

While the thrust of the article was as uncollaborative as any I had ever seen, I took it quite seriously. It demonstrated that others continued to feel that I had a problem with de-authorization in the City Hall culture. It also gave me a benchmark of one strategy to use – which others perceived as successful – in responding personally to others within City Hall. I could see that, for others, whatever collaborative culture I sought to help develop would need to meet their needs as well as the 'swimming with sharks' solution did.

The union leader called frequently during the crisis. For example, on one day when she called and attacked me, I stood my ground. She hung up, only to call me back and apologize. She then discussed in a friendlier tone what she viewed to be my problem with authority, which in her opinion made me a difficult person to work with.

I agreed that I might be part of the problem – not being direct enough when I am angry – but that the central problem was the management facilitator's work. Later in the same day I met with my boss (a new one from the one mentioned in the incidents above). He told me that while he had given me autonomy up to this point, he was now going to intervene more. He said that he would back me up when I needed him, although he felt that I had mishandled the management facilitator situation. He was not interested in pursuing her problems with facilitation, nor pursuing the pilfering of notes from the office word-processing files.

I defended myself. I vowed not to be taken advantage of, by appearing too open. I was no longer de-authorizing myself; other were taking away my authority. The scenario Torbert had predicted was playing itself out. By the end of the day I *felt like* I did not want more feedback on my behaviour and personality *ever again*. I wrote in my notes that evening: 'If I am ever going to confront my problems with being in authority and dealing with people, today was the day.'

The crisis continued for nearly three weeks and eventually involved the City Council and several key department heads. Throughout, I continued to tape my intentions and feelings on the drive to work and the way home, to take notes, to write critical incidents, and to rehearse for the key meetings, as well as analysing them afterwards. The facilitation situation was at least temporarily resolved (by a discussion among the staff with the union leader, the Mayor's Office, and Torbert who came to the City Hall for the meeting). Torbert challenged the union leader to look both at her own learning strategies as well as some of her own activities. She declined, continuing to see 'action inquiry' as 'flaky'. On a more constructive note, the meeting led to agreements both on under-facilitation and action inquiry: the facilitator was to pursue several specific active interventions in her facilitation; action inquiry was permissible as long as there was a clear separation of my research/learning from the programme, and City Hall word-processing equipment was not used (for my own protection).

The management facilitator believed that I was psychoanalysing her. The union leader was much more suspicious of my alleged manipulation than before; I was more suspicious of her than before. I was conscious that I had survived, and very angry about how I had been treated by the union leader and others. On the positive side, I had not internalized her criticisms of me or becoming halting in talking with her and others.

Testing the new behaviour
Three months later I summarily removed the management facilitator from the programme due to her inability to facilitate groups in the activist manner which had been agreed to after the earlier crisis. My action and the union's

response created a second crisis of major proportions, which led to a several-month programme suspension and nearly caused the programme's termination. Paradoxically, it also led to confirmation of my own growth in the area of de-authorization, and an institutionalization of the programme which had seemed dubious prior to the crisis. For our purposes, what is important is that under enormous political pressure which eventually involved the White House and a union petition campaign against me, I grew beyond my previous fear of exercising leadership in a democratic programme without becoming autocratic. I grew both towards swimming with sharks more effectively, and staying on course in creating reflectivity for myself and others.

My decision to remove the management facilitator from the programme had been the result of my listening carefully to managers and researchers close to the programme. The key department head in whose department over half of the groups were located had urged me to fire the facilitator. To him, as well as to others, the programme was not generating the sort of results which I had promised; managers were being blamed for problems and saw the sessions as gripe sessions by union activists; problems were not getting solved, only aired; the facilitator did not know how to work *with* managers. I analysed this in my daily tapes and notes. I listened to what Ronchi and close friends said; I wrote up critical incidents on how to deal with the situation. I reached the conclusion that I could not delay moving without risking City funding in the next budget cycle, and the existence of the programme in the key department.

I began to prepare others for my decision, after a meeting with Ronchi and with the Mayor's trade union liaison. Critical was my approach to the union leader whose support I needed – due to the union's control of half of the Oversite Committee. An early-morning phone call to her to ask her to discuss the progress of the management facilitator's work led her to break a confidentiality agreement we had. She insisted that she would go that same day, before we could have our discussion, to tell the management facilitator that 'something was up'. I anticipated another political fight like the crisis three months before. I acted quickly, sought political support from the key powerbrokers in the few hours before the union leader would tell the facilitator, and then met with the facilitator. I pulled her off active facilitation, pending reassignment. I offered her another position in City Hall with equal stature to the facilitator position but outside of the programme.

The rest of the day, and the following day, was packed with fast-moving, pressured moves among the sharpest reefs of City Hall; the waters became clouded with my blood. Within a few minutes after my meeting with the management facilitator a counter-attack began. The union leader called an emergency union meeting to suspend the programme, and called for a full discussion of the matter at the Oversite Committee. Within hours the key powerbrokers in the Administration had called me to inform me that the facilitator was much better connected than I had understood – and was involved with the Administration's only contact in the White House. By the next morning those in the Administration who had seen the programme or myself as a threat had begun to join with the union leader, a member of the City Council, and the rank-and-file union activists who supported the facilitator.

I met with the union leader and with Ronchi that second morning of the crisis in a building outside of City Hall. In a very tense meeting I presented my case, received Ronchi's backing, and sought to answer the union leader's charges. There was only room for me to back off totally – to de-authorize myself – or to stick to a rigid position. The union leader started off by stating a strong disagreement with my action, personality, and the idea of employee participation. She finished by stating that she would recommend *at least* suspension of the programme until I took the facilitator back, and possibly termination of it: 'You seem to have some sort of hormonal problem that every few months you go crazy over the facilitator. I will think about this during my vacation next week, but I *want* to end our participation in this [programme].'

Arriving at City Hall in the mid-morning, I found the situation had gotten extreme. The Director of Labour Relations (a critic of me and the programme), was livid, and threatening to go directly to the Mayor (who luckily was out of town). A key manager in my department urged me to leave the building for my personal safety; she was worried from what she had heard that the head of Labour Relations would attack me physically. Rumours flew as well. The union leader believed erroneously that the administrative assistant who worked for me had resigned in protest.

The crisis had become a learning experience for me in taking responsiblity for an unpopular decision, not asking others for their support, becoming a manager who was a leader. During the next week the union leader pushed for my removal as effective leader of the programme, while the union facilitator organized a telephone campaign aimed at the Director of Personnel to reinstate the management facilitator. Later the union would organize a petition campaign to the Mayor geared to the Friday before Labor Day. The pressure on me was intense. I faced a meeting with a representative group of workers and the union leader. I was able to handle the situation without de-authorizing myself in a way that Ronchi felt as good as could be done with a group of angry employees. I came to feel that both my career with the City and the programme I had sought to build were at an end. I was ready to take a leave of absence rather than sit in a political 'do-nothing' job.

Some argue that under pressure we regress – that my gains around my tendency to de-authorize myself would be reversed as the stress of the political fight built up. I don't think I did regress in this situation.

I continued to tape-record my thoughts and feelings during the drive to work and back. I increased the intensity of my note-taking and my analysis of critical incidents (I also had a great deal more time with the programme suspended), as well as my rehearsals and public tests of new behaviour.

Emotionally, I felt like I was on a rollercoaster – though always on the downhill grade. I sought ways to release the stress and disappointment. My tapes of feelings on the ride home from this period are punctuated with screaming, crying, and 'Oh Gods'. Jogging, weight-lifting, and a catharsis-like end-of-day note-taking on the word-processor dominated the more 'up' points of the two-month fight. I reread several times Don Schon's *Reflective Practitioner* (1983) and the drafts of the chapters on personal experiments with action inquiry in Torbert's *Managing the Corporate Dream* (1986).

Both the Mayoral trade union liaison ('swimming with sharks') and Ronchi worked closely with me at this point. Ronchi felt – as he had pointed out eight months earlier – that I had a tendency to take on the full burden of the programme, not seeing that the Administration was failing to support me. If I did not give up this burden it would tempt me to de-authorize myself – to 'give away the store.' A proposed compromise by the union leader and the Director of Labour Relations which involved the management facilitator returning for six months was the same old problem of management not taking responsibility for the programme. Management was setting up a situation which could not possibly work, and then would leave me the burden of making it work, while the union leader pressed me and the management facilitator undermined me. Ronchi urged me to get top management 'to hold the burden', and to direct my anger at them if they would not. For me to carry through on this was new behaviour, and risky.

I was risking the programme and my career with the City by holding out in what became an intense internal management battle with my boss and several key administration officials allied with him through family connections – on the other side. With key managers I sought to use an action inquiry approach on a one-to-one basis in getting them to look at the situation (Krim, 1986: 275–81). I sought to be more direct and clear than I might have been before in dealing with the personal attack on me.

After two months, top management and the union leadership – both under pressure from rank-and-file employees who stated quite clearly that they liked the programme – agreed to my original action, and to transfer the management facilitator out of the programme. I had taken a very firm course, and survived a heavy attack during the last prolonged fight. For six months I was put on the 'seriously injured list' and privately voted the 'victim of the week' for several weeks running in the Mayor's Office. At first I was assigned a co-director (a friend) to help me to handle internal management. Yet the programme had survived, the management facilitator no longer worked for me, and I still had most of my job.

I voluntarily moved from being Programme Director to working as more of an in-house consultant on management development while holding the line position as Assistant Director of Personnel. My credibility as a manager in the high levels of the Administration had been seriously, though not irreparably, damaged. Within six months both the key managers who had opposed me in the internal battles over the management facilitator – the Director of Labour Relations and the Director of Personnel – had resigned, largely as a result of pressure from the Mayor's Office. (They were forced out over other issues, though their actions in the fight over the labour–management programme were viewed as revealing.) Within eighteen months I had recovered the power and status I had before the fight (and completed a doctoral dissertation on using action inquiry in City Hall), but was now seen as 'having balls' as well as an ability to 'move' innovative programmes in the City Hall environment. I arranged for a retreat for key departments heads with Torbert 'to learn from negative feedback in the midst of crisis' (one aspect of action inquiry). A new Director of Personnel sought consciously to retain me to develop and manage new programmes when I sought to leave.

Summary on personal learning and action inquiry

I had learned over a little more than a year a good deal about my tendency to 'de-authorize' myself, and had shown in several key high-pressured situations that I could learn new behaviour. My learning intensified as the process of action inquiry and the dissertation itself had became an issue. I had on some level learned how to swim in the City Hall environment. I had been able to turn around some top-level management situations, and to get the managers to own their decisions, rather than taking the full weight myself. These perceptions were confirmed by Ronchi, Torbert, and several other key participants in the events, who read over and commented upon an account of my de-authorization (Krim, 1986: 331–58). They were also confirmed by the new Director of Personnel (taking office after the events described in the de-authorization case) who commented to me in evaluating me that 'You are quite good at advocating for your positions and yourself'. I was given new programmes to manage, the right to choose my own staff, and increased responsibility and visibility.

While the considerable effort which I put into my daily action inquiry processes was well worth it on balance, there were paradoxical side-effects. First, my action inquiry processes tended to intensify the stress of meetings and daily incidents for me. Taping and writing were at once both cathartic and a reification of events and feelings – many quite uncomfortable. I might have been able to let go of some of the feelings and stress more easily if I had gone out for a beer after work, rather than taping my thoughts alone in a traffic jam. And second, the action inquiry led to a 'hot-house' effect on analysing programme problems. I tended to see problems long before others, because I was so focused on them. This helped me to target problems, but led to friction with the union leader and others who were more apt to see my insights as 'hormonal outbursts'. Only months later might she reach the same conclusion independently, as she did on many key points.

Neither Schon nor Torbert feel that managers who use a 'reflective practitioner' model will have an easy time of it – either from their organizations, or from their internal confrontation with their own problems. Schon outlines the difficulties the reflective manager will face:

> When a member of a bureaucracy embarks on a course of reflective practice, allowing himself to experience confusion and uncertainty, subjecting his frames and theories to conscious criticism and change, he may increase his capacity to contribute to significant organizational learning, but he also becomes, by the same token, a danger to the stable system of rules and procedures within which he is expected to deliver his technical expertise.
>
> Thus ordinary bureaucracies tend to resist a professional's attempt to move from technical expertise to reflective practice. And conversely, an organization suited to reflective practice would have features very different from those of familiar bureaucratic settings. (Schon, 1983: 328–9)

Unfortunately, the City bureaucracy was particularly unsuited to reflective practice. Yet the political view of myself and several top managers – the desire to make the public sector a model for the private sector – is what made this Administration an exciting opportunity to try employee participation and action inquiry. As I wrote in my notes two years after beginning the programme:

> From my perspective it has always been clear that the change in the organizational culture of the City could not happen without challenging existing 'games and norms', and so if City Hall were to change it could only come from individuals who have a commitment to reflective learning both for themselves and the organization.

Torbert describes the motivator which the reflective manager like myself using action inquiry feels:

> To be capable of working with the many levels of tension and negative feedback here described, the manager must feel a deep and clear calling or vocation emanating from a corporate dream or vision or mission. For negative feedback is bearable only to the degree that it serves a positive function – to help us correct course and increase our chances of making a dream come true.

He adds that action inquiry 'ultimately costs all one's illusions' (Torbert, 1986: 22–3).

One of the critical questions which I posed in a research proposal prior to beginning the programme and the job was whether a city manager could learn critical lessons that improved on-the-job effectiveness through using action inquiry processes. I did become more effective as a result of these efforts. And the theorists of this model are correct: the cost in illusions and pressure were high both because of the particular environment and the reflective process itself.

Working in unsympathetic environments like the US City Hall may lead those who would like to set up co-operative inquiry to turn inward at first. Yet the learning which we can do about ourselves and our own style can be significant if we are creative in developing processes which work in the particular environment. We do not need to wait for organizations to develop that are ready for our skills.

I believe I did become more effective as the result of my action inquiry effort. I also believe that through my efforts the employee participation programme has promoted a more co-operative form of working in City Hall.

8

Interactive Holistic Research:
Researching Self Managed Learning

Ian Cunningham

The research problem

In the mid-1960s I started to take an interest in what have been labelled 'learner-centred' or 'alternative' or 'self-directed' educational and training programmes. People like A. S. Neill and Carl Rogers were key influences (see Cunningham, 1984a). In the early 1970s I was involved in setting up the School for Independent Study at North East London Polytechnic, and it was there that the research problem started to crystallize. Specifically I became concerned that the success of the work we were doing rested heavily on the ability of staff to assist learners in their learning. However, staff who had been used to teaching found it difficult to adjust to a situation where learners wrote their own curriculum and took charge of their own learning process.

At this time I was also involved in management development work where it seemed that there were successful practitioners of action learning (Revans, 1971) and self-development (Burgoyne, Boydell and Pedler 1978), both approaches being clearly related to the independent study work in which I had been involved. I synthesized methods from independent study, action learning and self-development into an approach which I labelled 'self managed learning'.

In action learning there has evolved the format of using a small group of four to six managers as a support group (and more). This kind of group is labelled a 'set' and the developer who assists the set is called a 'set adviser'.

I introduced the 'set' idea into self-managed learning programmes and so one form of my concerns was 'what makes a good set adviser?' This hardened up into a key question for inquiry and I undertook systematic research in this field from the late 1970s until 1986. My earlier work was submitted for a PhD (Cunningham, 1984a). Other, more broadly based research has been involved in looking at the nature of learning and of managing (specifically during a stay as Senior Research Fellow at Ashridge Management College from 1985 to 1987).

A model for method

My approach to research is explained most fully elsewhere (Cunningham, 1984a) but it would be a reasonable generalization to say that it is largely consonant with the principles spelled out in Reason and Rowan (1981a) and in this volume. However, I do want to spell out some differences of emphasis or language. I also need to map out the components of my approach before detailing my research activity in studying management developers.

I call what I do *interactive holistic research*. It sounds pretentious, yet it's the best I have. It is based on the philosophy and principles I enunciated in my earlier discussion of methodology (Cunningham, 1984a); and it uses a number of methods to provide a holistic framework.

I want to spell out five interconnecting methods, and then to comment on the interconnections.

Collaborative research

The underlying principle here is that a group of people can together pursue an investigation of a topic, and that the initiating researcher should not dictate the process of research activity.

I distinguish between two kinds of collaborative research. Type I is consonant with co-operative inquiry modes where researchers study their own experience in the group of which they are all a part. Type II is where people come together to study experience that has occurred *outside* the group. They may, coincidentally, study the group's process and collective experiences. Both types clearly have a place, but the research I shall report here is of the Type II variety only. Specifically I was involved in bringing together people like myself who practised particular approaches to assisting others with their learning and development. It was not relevant to attempt Type I research in this case.

Dialogic research

This centres around the two-person interaction and uses the dialogue as a mode of 'finding out'. At one level it is a special case of collaborative research. However, there does seem to be something about the two-person mode which makes it distinctively different. At its simplest there is no group process to attend to, only the interpersonal relationship of two people.

Experiential research

By experiential research I mean research which uses as its focus the direct experience of the person/researcher. The researcher is thus the 'subject'. There can be two kinds of experiential research:

1   personal, where researcher and subject are one and the same;
2   dialogic, where experience and/or response to experience is shared
.   with others.

Heron (1981b) specifically uses the term 'experiential research' to refer to the latter mode, whereas I will use the term in a personal context (i.e. as for mode 1 above).

I want to argue that experiential research is an essential feature of human science activity, and *we as persons should learn to be effective researchers of our own experience.* As Torbert (1981a) comments:

> Under the new model of scientific research, valid social knowledge depends first and foremost on the development among persons of a new politics based on a shared wish to research their everyday lives together. Valid social knowledge depends secondarily on the development among persons of a new ethics based on the commitment to confront apparent incongruities in their common life. Valid social knowledge depends only tertiarily (but, of course, by no means unimportantly) on the development among persons of technical skills in discriminating the degree of trustworthiness of experiential-empirical data. (p. 151)

In my field of inquiry much of the published material is based *solely* on personal experience. The journals are full of articles and papers which relate to an individual's response to a particular programme he/she has organized and run. If the practitioner has not engaged in the other dimensions of interactive holistic research, or has not demonstrated a personal skill in experiential research, then I feel justified in treating such material with a low level of confidence. This stance does not, though, mean one should elevate traditional detached research. The outsider to a situation, for example in much classic evaluation research, is, by virtue of not experiencing the event as a participant, limited in his/her contribution to the research process.

One rationale for me studying me is the need I see to develop and promote self-awareness: the idea that we can study others and neglect ourselves seems to be genuinely in-human. As Schumacher (1977) has argued, self-awareness is what characterises human-ness: to deny it is to classify us as things not as humans.

My view of personal experiential research is that it is not old-fashioned introspectionism, as it is based on experience and not on armchair theorizing or limited projections. It is part of a wider scheme whereby such experiential research is linked to other methodologies. Specifically, as well as talking with others (dialogic or collaborative research) one needs to test one's personal research in action.

Action research

'Action research' is a well-known term and by and large I accept a great deal of the 'standard' ideas about action research (see Lewin, 1948; Freire, 1970; Revans, 1980; Torbert, 1981a). However, I am concerned that some action researchers still operate in a detached, disconnected mode in relation to others in 'the action'. This is not in keeping with principles expressed by myself and others in this volume. I am also wary of the dangers that the researcher becomes obsessed with action and ceases to do research. One may end up with an interesting impressionistic case study, but not a contribution to wisdom (Maxwell, 1984).

In my own research reported here I was specifically interested in using the action arenas of practitioners as the source of research material (the other three modes do not necessarily assume active 'doing' as *central* to the process, though the *evidence* of action will form the basis of other modes).

Contextual locating
This is not necessarily 'research' as typically conceived. I mean by this term that one feeds into and off the context within which one operates. So in this research there are people working in the field, writing about it, discussing it at conferences, etc. The theory developed in and through the other four modes will in part come out of this wider context and also feed into it. Hence there is an iterative, to-and-fro process which provides the basis for testing and evolving theory. I can map this situation as shown in Figure 8.1. The double-headed arrows show a mutual interaction, that is the ideal process is one in which the different research modes cross-link, weaving together wisdom developed in different ways. Thus in my research I have, for instance, thought of ideas from my experience (experiential research), talked with others about them (dialogic research) and tested and developed them in action (action research). I have also simultaneously drawn upon written material, and published papers myself (contextual locating).

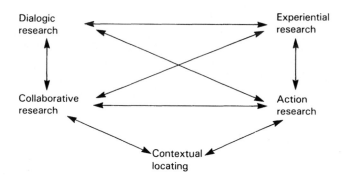

Figure 8.1   *Testing and evolving theory*

This could be plotted linearly, but it has *not* worked that way. I find linear, digital language a difficult communication mode for my purposes. What has actually happened in my research is that I have been working with numerous strands and I have been inter-twining research modes. Language implies a 'one-after-the-other' situation, which isn't how it happened.

I see interactive holistic research as an omni-focused activity. By this I mean that one keeps a focus on the person (as researcher); the problems to be addressed; other persons; and the context of the research (social, cultural, etc.). I want to avoid simplistic notions of 'person-centred' or 'problem-centred' – as they are *all* at the centre. In taking this stance I relate my research principles to the connectedness and ecology of Taoist philosophy. I believe we need to avoid either/or debates and instead concentrate on integrating aspects of our work. This doesn't imply a slavish working through of different methods. The five I have quoted here are identified by somewhat arbitrary distinctions, and I certainly wouldn't always follow the maps I've drawn here. The more important point is avoiding the trap of searching for 'the one right way' to do research.

Method in practice

In this section I will now get into the practical details of what I did for my research. When I started my research I was urged to have a research design, and to have a clear plan. I have written elsewhere (Cunningham, 1984b) of my views on planning, and have indicated my doubts about much traditional planning activity. I have counterposed the notion of planning as usually conceived with the concept of 'preparing'. What I attempted to do was to prepare myself well so that I had the necessary abilities and personal qualities to undertake the research. I attached little value to the idea of having a relatively fixed written plan/design. I spent a great deal of time on paper exercises exploring what I might do, and also checking my ideas with others (I produced, for instance, 61 pages of notes of ideas for research projects, and what I might do). In the end I rejected almost all of what came out of my 'paper-and-pencil' exercises, but they were nonetheless valuable as *preparation* (as they forced me to think through ideas and test them out).

What I produced eventually has perhaps a superficial neatness that was not evident during the research. In practice what I did felt very messy while I was in it, but I nonetheless always believed that something would come out of it.

What in the end became the pattern for the research was the integration of a series of projects each with their strengths and weaknesses which I could bring to bear on the research problems I was tackling. It is also inherent in my formulation of interactive holistic research, which I have argued requires the interplay of various methodologies.

In subsequent parts of this section I shall categorize projects and activity according to the five headings I used previously.

Contextual locating
This activity comes first as it provides the backcloth of patterns and ideas within which more specific projects are carried out. In my research I had already spent many years doing, thinking, reading, writing and talking about issues of learning.

As I have already emphasized, I wrote up the work linearly, but that is not how it happened. The above factors, and others, intertwined in providing a contextual basis for my work. Let me quote an example which linked

> me as a practitioner;
> my use of conferences;
> my use of a professional association (Association of Teachers of Management, ATM);
> my reading.

I presented a session at an ATM Conference. A practitioner with whom I had previously spoken, and whose work I had read, came to my session. Afterwards we chatted in the bar about linkages between his work and mine and he referred to some writers who had influenced him. As a result of this conversation I went away and read some of the books and papers to which he had referred. I talked over some of the ideas from these with colleagues and tested some interpretations of mine on course members with whom I was working. And so it goes on. One way to map this is shown in Figure 8.2. I hope it will be apparent that this essential contextual

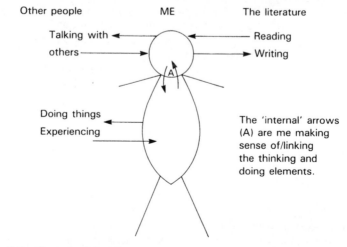

Figure 8.2   *Contextual locating*

locating is not possible without immersion in the field of activity. I do not believe that it is possible for, say, the one-shot researcher coming in to do a quick study to carry out this kind of research. That is not to say that the 'outsider' is valueless, but rather to suggest limits on it. For instance, it takes time to do things, write about them, get feedback, apply new learning back in the field, etc. Just the time scale of publications means that one has to be in the field for some years before a genuinely interactive process can emerge.

Action research

In the following boxed aside are extracts from my notes of a group as I wrote them up during and at the end of the day with only slight tidying up. This style of note-taking was typical of what I used in my action research work. (Taping would, in most cases, have been unacceptable, though I did use it in some groups.) The reason for putting this in here is to give the flavour of how I used such situations. I put in parentheses my asides to myself where I was making cross linkages.

27/7/83 (10 am–5 pm)
Notes from Principal Officers Workshop (set)
(Four people present)

1. Coffee at the start. I let people talk a bit to each other to unwind. I'm conscious that M has come from another meeting, so he needs to adjust to being in a new place. (So the process of 'entry to temporary system' is important. I've sometimes used exercises, e.g. relate a 'good thing' from the last 24 hours, but increasingly I just let an informal process happen. So there is a choice here – structure it or let it go informally.)
2. We talk a bit formally – well I open it by reminding people of why we're here – not exactly that – more business like. I ask people if I should stick up flip charts from last time. They say yes. I then suggest that they read them. (On them are the issues they raised last time for discussion. Some we discussed – much we left.) I suggest that they spend a minute or two (with a piece of paper) noting down new items or modified versions of items already down. They agree and start to do it. (So here I'm structuring it a bit more.) J and M don't have paper, so I give them some. (Important for trainer to have materials like paper to give people if needed – many people forget this.)
3. We go round the room. Some people modify/add/or delete items from the flip charts.
4. J looks to S who had raised a hairy problem last time. My assumption is that J wants S to go first, in order to get an update on what's happened since. I say that I think J would like S to go first – J's response indicates this (nodding, eyes brighten, etc.). S is OK to go first, so she does. (Here I'm *not* being intuitive, though an outsider might think I was. I saw J look at S, and from the way she looked, I read it as a desire for S to go first. I *interpret* J's response – or at least check an interpretation. But what triggers me is J's *behaviour*.)

5. S talks about her problem. I come in with a challenge re. her pessimism. I raise the concept of 'reframing' – can S look at her situation in a more positive way? General discussion around this. We get on to how to work the politics of the organization. We map her existing contacts – and I suggest she needs to improve her network of informal contacts. I also introduce Revans' 'Who knows/Who can/Who cares' model. She seems to find this useful as a mapping process.

(There were three more sections here – left out to save the reader.)

9. I'm sure other things happened today (I know they did). But this stuff is what I remember (No: In addition they agreed to continue to meet as a support group – that was a very positive outcome – I feel good about that.)

I used notes like the above (from a whole range of projects) as a basis for analysis. They make more sense to me than, I would guess, to the reader coming 'cold' to them. One reason for this is that such a session as this one-day meeting fits into a stream of events. This group had met before and also met afterwards. In discussion with colleagues, whose work I also used, they agreed that one could not make sense of, say, a set meeting in isolation from the set of activities as a totality, the context of the programme, etc.

This point was particularly relevant to situations where I did use taped material. Mostly I taped myself in various set meetings and then analysed the tapes (over 50 hours of them). However, I also taped two other events:

1 A set meeting in which I was a member of the set but not set adviser (this then could still meet the condition of understanding context).
2 A set meeting in which a colleague was set adviser. In this case a student who I was supervising went to the other set and did the taping. Then he transcribed the tape, and we produced three copies, one for him, one for the other tutor (set adviser) and one for myself. We had a three-way meeting to talk through the transcript. This then moved into an experiential/dialogic mode. We taped the discussion the three of us had about the transcript and then those (second) tapes were transcribed in order to give us further insight into the process. Also in the meeting of the three of us we replayed the (first) tapes at certain points in order to re-create the actual events (when the transcript seemed too 'cold').

Dialogic research

This research mode is based around one-to-one interaction; in this case between myself and others. My aim here was to engage in dialogue with other practitioners to explore issues of doing the work of a developer. I shall first comment on my choice of people to talk with, before discussing the nature of 'dialogue' and the content of dialogues.

Choosing people. I was not interested in talking to a 'sample' of the population of people doing this work. On the contrary, I was deliberately highly selective about the people I chose as a 'core' group for the research. I also talked with people who I identified as 'fringe' people: these were people who did not meet the central criteria of being highly competent *and* highly experienced in 'learner-centred management development'.

For the 'core' group I talked *only* with people who met *all* the following criteria:

1 At least ten years' experience in management development or related work.
2 Major involvement in 'learner-centred' approaches like self-development or action learning in at least two settings/contexts.
3 Acknowledged by others in the field to be competent.
4 Active involvement in the 'outside world' (e.g. outside their own organization/institution).
5 Involvement in publications (preferably a significant record of published work, but not necessarily).
6 Involvement in research. I treated such a term in a broad sense, i.e. I did not imply only 'academic research' as often normally defined but included, for example, in-company evaluation studies.

N.B. 'Fringe' people did not meet all the above criteria though most met *some*. In total I talked with 21 'core' people and 12 'fringe' people: typically each discussion lasted about 2 hours. Each meeting where possible was taped, though this did not always prove feasible. Also in one case the tape recorder didn't work.

The criteria I indicated above are, as with any criteria chosen, a subjective choice. Some were evolved prior to this work, some afterwards (that is it only occurred to me after talking to people that there were further criteria). The categorization 'core' and 'fringe' only came to me *after* I had conducted a number of dialogues and though, of course, arbitrary, it seemed useful as it allowed me to make comparisons.

Dialogues in action. I want to emphasize that these dialogues took place within a broader context, and I am only artificially isolating them here. Specifically I fed into the experience of the dialogues my own experiences from action/collaborative/experiential research and from the contextual locating process. Thus the dialogues provided, as with all the rest of my research, a place *both* to test and develop concepts/models/propositions produced from other contexts *and* to provide concepts/models/propositions to feed into other research contexts.

By virtue of picking, as a 'core' group, the people I did I could gain access to their action/collaborative/experiential research and contextual locating. Obviously the extent to which each person had engaged in such activities varied, though everyone did have rich experience *and* theory upon which they drew.

The centrality of this group in management development also allowed me to overcome what McLean *et al.* (1982) identified in their research on organization development consultants as 'The possible tendency of persons to describe their actions in a way which fits in with the literature' (p. 15). This was not a problem as this group has *created* much of the core literature in this field.

Questioning. I did not treat these meetings as 'interviews' in the sense that many researchers use the term. I did have some questions I wanted to explore, though, and in most cases I introduced nearly all of these into the conversation at some point. Thus I rejected the notion that the interviewer giving up the traditional controlling stance meant we should swing to an opposite pole of interviewer passivity. A dialogue means a two-way inter-action and, as well as commenting on issues myself, I also put in questions and initiated areas of exploration. However, if a person did not want to explore something (because it didn't interest them) I accepted that and backed off. In the feedback I received on the meetings, one person felt I had been somewhat pushy with my own views at one point. I don't know if this hindered the process or not, and I don't know if the person's comments were influenced by a view that the 'interviewer' should be more passive.

Collaborative research
I undertook a number of collaborative projects. Some of these involved groups of us as working colleagues stepping aside from our activity to explore and examine together the nature of our work (and how to do it better). I will elaborate below on another project which linked dialogic and collaborative activity, in a temporary 'stranger' group.

This project went in three phases. The first phase was to use material gathered in the dialogic research mentioned above. I made a loose analysis of this from the tapes of all the one-to-one meetings. I then fed this back to the people involved. In the second phase I invited a group to come to a two-day residential meeting, which I will discuss shortly. The third phase was a write-up of this meeting circulated to all participants for their comments.

Of the people from dialogic research in the 'core' group, eight came to the two-day meeting. As people were from all over the country, and very busy in their own worlds, this seemed the only mode open, that is to get the group together on a one-off basis, but to make it relatively intensive.

The meeting itself did produce a great deal of material, though analysis was tricky (over 12 hours of tape produced 91 pages of raw material – even after leaving out much redundant 'talk'). Immediately afterwards I didn't feel too happy with how it went (and I will indicate shortly some of the problems with the event). However, in retrospect it doesn't seem so bad. The plus points were that:

1 people came and gave up 2 days;
2 after a wobbly start we did work together on issues;
3 there was a fairly high level of trust, as evidenced by some quite sensitive and personal issues being discussed;
4 we lived with the uncertainty and messiness of absence of controls, of no fixed agenda, etc.;
5 it was a good-humoured event;
6 I did not notice any 'point scoring' competitiveness;
7 people did confront each other openly about issues and seemed to give honest responses to questions;
8 near the end someone asked, 'Could you work with people here?' The responses to this were positive, with some comments of the nature of: 'Yes, depends on the particular work'. This seemed to me to indicate a level of respect for each other.

The negatives were:

1 Sometimes the pace was too rapid to allow for full exploration of issues. I found that, on listening to the tapes, I could identify points where I certainly did not get a chance to explain clearly enough my point of view. I suspect this occurred for others too.
2 At one point early on in the meeting I did not push what might have been a serious disagreement as I felt that cohesion of the group was more important than the content point. However, someone listening to the tape might assume a consensus that wasn't really there.
3 The notes I circulated had only a small impact on the group. I received little feedback on them either before or after the event (despite a number of requests for comments). This seems to undermine a genuinely collaborative basis for the analysis of ideas (at least in terms of this sort of situation, though not for others).

The negative aspects mentioned above seemed to stem largely from this being a temporary grouping of people, most of whom are used to working a great deal on their own. In collaborative projects with work colleagues we did not experience any of these problems, though perhaps we were in danger of a cosiness and insularity. For me the value of doing projects of the two kinds (with temporary grouping and with colleagues) was of tapping into two different kinds of context, each with its strengths and weaknesses.

Certainly in retrospect I felt much more relaxed about the difficulties of making a temporary group work. I also had to accept that neither I nor the others in the group could think of a better way of doing things.

So if I wanted to get the benefit of the experience and ideas of these people I believe I had to go down this route. It was impossible, for instance, to get more commitment out of people who are busy; located all over the UK; in many cases self-employed (and hence losing income by taking time out).

I shall not comment further here on the more detailed aspects of this research mode as they are covered elsewhere in this collection (for example, Chapters 1 and 2). I can say that we adhered to the basic requirements of this mode that Heron and Reason spell out, for example collective decision-making; sharing facilitation; joint development of conceptual frameworks and models; etc.

Experiential research

The basic requirement, in my view, of experiential research is for one to experience one's own experiencing; to be aware of one's awareness and conscious of one's consciousness (see Ferguson, 1980). It is, then, a second-order process, out of which one needs to link to one's map of the field. It is not totally self-absorbed introspection since it requires linkages between one's self and the world around.

Thus in my research one of the techniques that I used was to audio tape set meetings in which I was set adviser. By going through the transcripts of the tapes I could then re-create the experience and create meaning from it. The *awareness* has to be translated into analysis: I had then to categorize and to use concepts to describe the experience. The 'experience' was not just in overt behaviour. Sometimes I would not speak for a long time, but inside me I was thinking about what to do, observing the action, feeling emotions, etc. Most of this would not be apparent to an observer. This is readily demonstrated on a video tape I made of myself working with a set.

I had used video recording as a training/development method for many years, and it occurred to me that this technique had value for my research. The specific situation I used was a set meeting (for which I acted as set adviser) of which I taped one hour. I then reviewed the tape with the set, and we processed what had gone on. I noted the issues raised, and then went away and viewed the tape on my own. I stopped the tape at short intervals (every few minutes) and noted down what I was doing on the tape and why I was doing it. I wrote this up and re-presented it to the set to check it out. I then used the video tape and my commentary with groups of experienced and novice set advisers in order to engage with them on the issues raised. It was clear that without my commentary the tape would, on its own, be quite misleading. There were long periods when it would appear from an analysis of my behaviour that I was doing nothing. In fact I would be observing, listening, processing internally what was going on, deciding if I should intervene or not, checking my feelings, and so on.

A number of points need to be borne in mind considering the technique of taping (audio or video):

1 Sometimes it was of value to me to replay the tape itself rather than just read a transcript as then I could get a better feel for the event. However, this was not usually necessary.
2 Set meetings that were audio taped needed to be located in context within a sequence of set meetings, and understood in that context.
3 Tapes only tape what went on. They do not show the range of human capacities available to persons present. In this context I could be aware that I was *capable* of behaving in a particular way but didn't behave in that way. This is an especially important point if a set adviser is operating in what I term an 'infill' mode, that is he/she 'fills in' aspects only if no-one else does. Thus if everything that occurs to the set adviser is done by other people in the set he/she may not need to say anything. One can only tap this through the person in the action, analysing and making explicit their internal processes.

A further problem is that a set may not create situations to which the set adviser could contribute. An example of this would be extreme conflicts. Set advisers may have different ways of dealing with heavy conflict, but if a particular set is always harmonious the ability to deal with conflict will not be tested (and hence one will not know what the person is capable of). Tapping into wider capacities may need other experiential modes or the use of dialogic/collaborative methods.

Research outcomes

What I have presented so far provides a few examples of the interactive holistic approach as a method. In this section I will indicate some outcomes of the research on set advising. Because of the constraints of space I will provide relatively disconnected micro-level examples. These in a way are distorting, as they may imply a reductionism that I would reject. But as I don't believe theoretical statements are about truth, I console myself that the examples I shall mention may suffice at least to show how the research method *works*.

A simple example

The reason I label this 'a simple example' is that the results obtained were triggered by one event, though as with everything there was a contextual basis for my analysis. The precise aspect of contextual locating was my interest in the use of questioning techniques from neuro linguistic programming (Bandler and Grinder, 1975). The specific objective of the techniques is to get to a level of unambiguous clarity, normally associated with locating sensory-specific data. The particular technique I used in the following example is called the precision method (McMaster and Grinder, 1980). The aspects of precision questioning I used were specifically to ask 'what?' or 'which?' of ambiguous, unspecified nouns or 'how?' of ambiguous, unspecified verbs. I also challenged a statement of universal validity to gain clarity on this.

The key occasion on which precision-type questioning came into its own in my collaborative research was in the two-day residential group meeting. Indeed the following incident was a major one for me in the two days. What it convinced me of was the centrality of language: that we had been tossing words around a lot of the time and that our language was imprecise, ambiguous and woolly, and that I could see little progress in this field unless we developed more rigorous and sophisticated ways of dealing with language patterns.

The actual incident seems almost trite, but I think it is indicative of a *major* fundamental problem. What happened was that the verb 'help' came up. One person said they were puzzled by the notion, but others said it was a 'yukky idea' to help others (in relation to management development work). I asked if someone in the group did agree with the idea of helping others in this context, and one person volunteered. I then used a modified precision questioning to try to elicit the meaning of 'help' to him. I asked for a sentence from him, and he said:

'I help colleagues'

This sentence is, like much of our language, unspecific, imprecise and ambiguous. It doesn't say which colleagues nor how he helps. My first question was to ask 'which?' of the noun 'colleagues' in order to get more data on this. His reply was:

'Those I get on with'.

This implies a universal (in 'precision' terms); that is that *everyone* he gets on with he would help. This may or may not be a valid assumption, so I checked on this to remove ambiguity. I asked:

'All?'.

He said:

'Yes'.

So now I had a more specific, less ambiguous statement: all the people that he gets on with are people he would help. I could explore what the process of 'helping' was that he would apply to these. The following was the sequence (my questions are the ones in between his statements).

Statement: 'I help colleagues'
Question: 'How?'
Answer: Helping out in the sense that there are some colleagues who would say 'Oh heavens I'm caught short tomorrow: we need someone to help in an interview.'

And I would say 'yes' even to other people I'd said 'no' for other things. Or it could be A's just had a meeting with B and he needs to kick a wall or two and he comes into my office looking distraught and he wants to talk.
Question: 'When he wants to talk, *what* do you do?'
Answer: Well, a lot of it is being prepared to stop whatever you're doing and just be there – as a friend, as a mate. It could also be something which wasn't just a sounding-off job. It could be helping him to take a different look at (things).
Question: *How* do you help him to take a different look?
Answer: Sometimes people want you to take their side. But sometimes it's not just that they want to kick the wall but it is actually about trying to work out in their minds why it is they get so angry with that person, or whatever.
Question: *What* would you do to help? How do you help?
Answer: Try the old sort of 'Is this happening?' 'Is this happening?' Try out ideas. . .I think it would be more, 'here is one way you could think about as to why this is occurring and why you get annoyed'. It's not impotent Rogerianism: I don't see myself as a Rogerian.

(This could have gone further, because we did not get a completely unambiguous, agreed, clear statement about 'helping' in its totality.) Following the above interchange people in the group who had said they disagreed with 'helping', all said they agreed with the process described. One person (who'd said helping was a yukky idea) said:

'I'd call that supporting' (which was an acceptable, indeed positive term to him).

So here we have a word commonly used in management development which people disagreed about, but in the group people could agree with a particular process of interacting with other human beings (as the person described above). The situation, as I see it, is that we have a *mass* of unclear terms used in 'management development' (including 'management development' itself) but which are allowed to masquerade as precise and with agreed meaning.

Following the two-day residential group I was able to go back to literature on language to develop further my ideas. I also tried, in writing about the research problem, to develop a language which was clearly clear or clearly unclear. That is, if I could write in concrete, specific, precise terms I did. Otherwise I emphasized, as clearly as I could, the open, ambiguous nature of my terms. An example of clearly unclear terms has been my use of Taoist and other Eastern ways of thinking. The idea of the 'Tao' is about as unclear as one can get since if, according to Lao Tsu, you can define the Tao then it isn't it. ('The Tao that can be named isn't the real Tao', is one typical translation.)

These two kinds of clarity (clearly clear and clearly unclear) avoid the trap of the unclearly unclear, such as the verb 'to help'. It's a trap because it isn't clear it isn't clear, and so we were in danger in our research group of debating rather than researching.

A more complex example

This example is 'more complex' as it involves a layering and interweaving of research modes. As always, contextual locating provides a backcloth to the exploration of an apparent dilemma. The insight came from collaborative research, and action, experiential and dialogic research provided confirmatory 'evidence'.

Supportive confronting.   In sets, the idea that the set adviser should be supportive to the group and/or individuals in it is a commonplace assumption (Kolb and Boyatzis, 1984). Also there is a well-understood and accepted idea that the set adviser may need to confront people about issues (Corfield and Renney, 1983; Heron, 1977a). Lessem (1983) expresses a commonly held view that supporting and challenging (confronting) people are both desirable activities in sets (and other learning groups).

What I have found confuses novices is the notion of supporting *and* confronting going on in a set, and how a 'set adviser' could actually do both, since to the novice they seem mutually exclusive.

I analysed much of the research literature (Rosenshine and Furst, 1973; Berenson, Mitchell and Laney, 1968; Kurtz and Jones, 1973). What I felt was lacking in the authors I have quoted is a recognition of the support–confront dilemma.

One way out of this problem seemed to be to use a model developed by Peter Smith from his research on T-groups (Smith, 1979, 1980). My modified version of his model is shown in Figure 8.3. The evidence of Smith's research was that, for example, a cosy highly supportive but non-confronting group would learn most if the trainer was relatively highly confronting. Or conversely a highly confronting group that wasn't very supportive would learn best if the trainer was highly supportive. The implied 'ideal' group is one which is high on both (then life is easy for the trainer). In a group that is low on both the trainer has to work on both dimensions.

TYPES OF GROUP

Supportive ↑	Hi support	Hi support
	Lo confront	Hi confront
	Lo support	Hi confront
	Lo confront	Lo support

Confronting →

Figure 8.3   *Modified version of T-group model developed by Smith (1979, 1980)*

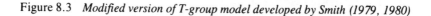

This seemed to hold out the possibility that people could analyse their sets in terms of this model and then adopt behaviours appropriately. It appeared to help up to a point, but there were still issues around how to do it. Then in a collaborative research group with colleagues the solution came to me in very simple terms:

One *supports being*
One *confronts doing*

By this I mean supportiveness is related to a whole range of factors concerning persons as persons: caring about each other, trusting one another, etc. 'Support' is then at a different level from 'confronting' which is best done in relation to what a person *does* When I checked both tape transcripts of sets and my notes from set working I found that the evidence was already there, and I hadn't put it together. For example, in one set I had (I believe) shown my concern for the person as a person. I had expressed my desire to support her in what she did. On one occasion she was upset about a presentation she had to do. I asked her whether she had to do it or not, and she wandered around the subject without really answering.

I said to her, quite sharply, 'You're not answering the question'. I felt I needed to confront what she was *doing* at that juncture. (The tape shows that my confrontation worked in getting her to focus.)

Similarly in another set, we had all been very supportive of someone who had to make a difficult decision. The conversation seemed to be going round in circles, and the set was playing a 'Why don't you, yes but' Game (Berne, 1964). In the end I came in with:

'OK, you are saying you are still wanting to think but you are not giving answers at the moment, are you?'
The person said 'No'.
I continued:
'Ideas have been put to you and you are fending them off. So I'm hearing you say you want to think about it, but haven't got long . . .'
Again I was confronting what she was *doing*, not who she was.

I can exemplify the issue by quoting two different, hypothetical, support/confront statements:

A. 'That was a brilliant piece of work you did. I don't know how such an unpleasant person can produce such work.'
B. 'I care about you and what you're doing, but this piece of work is unreadable.'

A is support doing, confront being.
B is support being, confront doing.

In practice I believe that I show support more in non-verbal ways – by paying attention to people, treating them seriously, using my voice and body posture, etc. So tape transcriptions don't show too well how I've worked in sets. My notes of set meetings, however, did pick up these issues. I reproduce in the boxes below two bits from such notes.

> 'I will confront people quite strongly on their work, but I will always try to do so from a basis of caring and support. I tell people I believe they will get their diplomas or degrees – I'm not conning them; I do believe it.'

> 'I am quite clear about confronting people about their failures. The crucial issue, though, is that the learner sees that it is a particular project that has failed, not that he/she is personally a 'failure', i.e. the person identifies why they failed to achieve what they set out to do, rather than take on the label of 'failure'. Failure must be associated with a task, an enterprise, a project *not* a person (though the person needs to recognize why they failed to do something).
>
> Typically what happens in the set is that someone will, say, fail to produce a piece of work by the date they voluntarily agreed (N.B. deadlines must be voluntarily agreed – the person must themselves pick a deadline so that any failure to meet the deadline must be down to the person concerned). When a deadline is not met, I will tend to ask the person for their views as to how it happened. There are, of course, genuinely external events, such as illness, which can prevent a deadline being met. However, allowing for those (minority) cases the person then has to account *to themselves* for their failure. It may be the person used their time badly, failed to get organized, failed to get necessary background data. Whatever the reason it is for each individual to face their own failure, analyse it, and see what they can learn from it.
>
> It is important that people are not personally criticized for failure. I tend to confront people about failure to achieve particular goals, but avoid personal attack. This is an important distinction. Indeed sometimes I will praise people for their failure; for example when a student sets goals which are quite challenging and fails to meet them. Such a situation can occur when a student takes on a difficult project which they then write up, but fail to meet their goals in full. I will tend to be concerned to acknowledge the achievement of completing such a project, even if the final piece of work is not good enough. As Harrison and Hopkins (1967) suggest, 'to "goof" is all right: to "goof off" is not'; that is, to have a go at something and fail is great; not to try in the first place is a much worse failure.

When I checked the tapes of my dialogic research I found comments from others such as:

> 'I'm learner-centred and business-like: being supportive doesn't mean pandering to the set.'

'I'm increasingly comfortable with the two bits (hard and soft).'

'I use a counselling mode, plus I tell people (things).'

So by a bringing together of different research strands I could illuminate the problem more adequately, and feel more sure about my stance. This one issue also added to a wider consideration of the separation of 'being' and 'doing' factors in studying human beings and their actions (doings).

Conclusion

I have tried to show something of the interactive holistic approach in use. I have wanted to emphasize the value of a method of researching which uses:

1 existing theories and ideas (contextual locating);
2 the situations and contexts of human action (action research);
3 the interaction with others (dialogic research and collaborative research);
4 and acknowledges and utilizes one's self (experiential research).

The ideal is to run these modes almost concurrently. As I am talking with others I am aware of myself as well as the other(s); I am aware of existing theoretical and conceptual schema and I am aware of the context of the action. However, the ideal can only be 'almost concurrently'. Hence the need for the interactive interplay of modes of research.

9

Impressions of the Other Reality: a Co-operative Inquiry into Altered States of Consciousness

John Heron

There is a strong case for the use of co-operative inquiry in altered states of consciousness (ASC) research. The basic argument of using a research paradigm that honours the self-determination of persons applies as much here as it does in any other field of human inquiry. And it is strengthened by some considerations peculiar to the ASC field.

First, you cannot properly research altered states of consciousness exclusively in terms of constructs derived from ordinary states of consciousness, since by definition the former go beyond the conceptual parameters that delimit the latter. Thus, second, it makes sense for ASC researchers to be involved in the altered states they are studying, if they want to generate appropriate categories of understanding and methods of inquiry. It is unsound to map an unknown country by never visiting it yourself, and by trying to make sense of the reports of others who have visited it.

Third, there is the all-important issue of intentional entry into (and exit from) altered states. Gaining knowledge about *how* to enter an ASC, and know that you are doing so, is surely best done by full participation of the researcher in the entry process. Thus the traditional, externally managed research into extrasensory perception (ESP) by card-guessing experiments threw no light on how successful subjects could use their ESP ability intentionally and awarely. Nor did it help subjects to differentiate – at the time of making them – right guesses from wrong guesses.

So fourth, we need a research method that will generate criteria for distinguishing between the real and the imaginary, the sound and the unsound, in the domain of altered states. Since many of these criteria may well be subtle and peculiar to the field, participatory research again seems to be the answer. The researchers need to get into the appropriate states of consciousness in order to learn how to winnow out the chaff from the dross. So the research becomes at the same time a training in entry into and use of altered states.

All this being said, co-operative inquiry in this field is a baffling and challenging enterprise. Once a group has launched itself beyond the familiar parameters of everyday states of mind, it seems to get caught up in processes and energies that scatter and diffuse ordinary thought. So the inquirers have a double challenge. In the reflection phases of the inquiry, which are in an ordinary state, they need to find subtle forms of thought that do justice to an altered state. But the legacy of the altered state is to scatter the thought processes of the ordinary state. The inquiry which I now report was very much beset by this effect.

Membership, time structure and location
There were 20 people in the inquiry group, four men and 16 women, with ages ranging from the 20s to the 60s, with a mean in the late 30s. The majority had considerable interest in and diverse experience of altered states. Over half those attending lived locally, and were part of a local community of persons who knew each other, were involved as practitioners and/or clients in various forms of radical psychotherapy, and were open to occult belief systems in general and about Cornwall and its ancient stone circles in particular. The participants were recruited by a programme brochure advertising a workshop, facilitated by myself, as a co-operative inquiry into altered states of consciousness. The blurb gave a brief account of what this would involve.

The group ran as a five-day residential workshop in October 1981, at the Centre for Alternative Education and Research in Cornwall. This Centre is in a country house on the site of an iron age settlement, including a *fogou* – a stone passageway running under the ground and out, with a chamber (the creep) to one side, the whole structure being thought to have had some important if obscure ceremonial function in Iron Age culture. Ancient stone circle sites were nearby.

The initial idea, and the overall design
The inquiry opened with a series of introductory rounds, in which members in turn shared with each other various aspects of themselves and their experiences, including altered states of consciousness. I then introduced the theory and practice of co-operative inquiry as a research method. This was discussed and debated until it seemed there was sufficient grasp of it, and assent to it, for the inquiry to be viable.

Our first reflection phase considered different possible areas of inquiry within the total field of altered states. I presented the following list: psi fields of physical entities; subjective ASCs such as dreams; ESP in its various forms; out-of-the-body experiences; mediumship; the other reality; the domain of archetypes; the divine as such.

After much discussion, we decided to inquire into that altered state in which we have impressions of the other reality while still functioning awarely in this reality. So our starting idea was that it is possible to function awarely in two worlds at once: this physical world and a non-physical, subtle energy world of presences and powers that is somehow within and around the physical world.

We then embarked on a series of six cycles of experience and reflection. The plan for each experience phase was devised co-operatively within the whole group. All the experience phases were done collectively by the group in the same large room. Some of these phases involved group interaction; in others group members did solitary things side by side. The reflection phases, too, were all done collectively: individuals shared their findings and impressions verbally in the presence of everyone else. These findings were recorded.

We completed four cycles by the end of the third day. The fourth day was devoted to a very long extension of the reflection phase of the fourth cycle. We applied a rigorous devil's advocate procedure (see Chapter 2) to impressions gathered in the previous cycles – mainly but not exclusively the fourth cycle in the fogou.

The fifth day included a very important and powerful fifth cycle, and the concluding sixth cycle. Reflection on the sixth experience phase led over into a final and closing reflection, but this was a shared celebration of the workshop experience as a whole rather than a formal deliberation about the findings of our inquiry.

Validity procedures were included during and after the second cycle, during and after the fourth cycle, with an unexpected validity event occurring in the middle of the fifth cycle. In what follows I shall report firstly on the cycles, secondly on the validity procedures, and finally on the findings.

The findings given at the end of this chapter have been distilled by me out of all the recorded data, especially the data on the devil's advocate procedure. The chapter has been written exclusively by myself, and has not been circulated to group members for their comments.

N.B. Including myself there were 20 people in the inquiry group. But some of the local participants had commitments that made their attendance variable. So in some of the cycle reports below, less than 20 people are referred to.

The inquiry cycles

Cycle 1 (Day 1): A ritual for receiving impressions of the other reality
In planning this cycle it was proposed by one group member, and readily agreed by all, that ritual activity is a way of acting awarely in this world while at the same time eliciting impressions of the other world. A number of different people in the group spontaneously improvised a ritual, and one person took us through it.

Experience. We stood in a circle with hands on each other's shoulders. We then moved in a counterclockwise circle step by step saying together 'East to West it behoves the rest', moving faster and faster. Next we sat in a circle, relaxing for ten minutes; then held hands and visualized energy moving from left to right. Finally, we centred ourselves and became open to impressions. After some time we shared these impressions.

Reflection. Seven people received no impressions, ten members received some impressions. Of these ten, four got mental pictures – of eyes, birds, pyramids – and three received 'instructions' from 'unseen presences'. One of these three received several 'instructions' very strongly. They were for the group: to use catharsis and shamanistic ecstasies; to spend two days indoors; to polish the floor; to inquire where the birds flock in the garden; to use chants and music.

Discussion then focused on whether this set of instructions was from a person or persons in the other reality; or whether it was bizarre phantasy material of a purely subjective kind. No conclusions, or tentative criteria for distinguising genuine from spurious instructions, emerged. The issue was left open, with several members willing to give the 'instructions' the benefit of the doubt. Others felt that whatever their status, they were interesting, if odd, guides to future action.

Cycle 2 (Day 2): A ritual for receiving impressions of the other reality
In planning this cycle it was agreed to use again ritual activity as a way of becoming aware of the two worlds at the same time. This led rapidly to several people – not all the same as those who designed the first ritual – devising a ritual sequence that included activities derived from the 'instructions' strongly received by one member in the first experience phase.

Experience. Each person in the group divined for water sources or streams (which were known to be plentiful) in the ground under the wooden floor of the large room in which we were meeting. Every member, having thus chosen a spot on the floor, polished it with a cloth for 20 minutes, then danced on the same spot to music for another 40 minutes. We sat in a circle and practised glossolalia (speaking in tongues); and then used ordinary language for impromptu prophetic utterance. We shared impressions and reflections.

Reflection. We agreed that the first two experience phases had been concerned with preparation and sensitization: the bizarre activities were for loosening us up, disarming us and getting us ready. Impressions that occurred in the second ritual were then shared: they were mainly received during the polishing of the floor and the dancing on the same spot. Nine people had various experiences to do with 'energy', ranging from trance-like altered states to erotic ordinary states. Two members were preoccupied with feelings of distress from past experiences; one other reported simple enjoyment.

Most of the ostensible altered states reported were ambiguous. Did they portend another reality, or were they simply subjective sensation and imagination stirred up and heightened in their impact by rather unusual activity? We were aware of this issue, but did not address it with any rigour. There was a general tendency to give the ambiguity the benefit of the doubt. We assumed or hoped that maybe some impact of the other reality was evident in some of our experiences.

During this cycle considerable agitation and distress of the ordinary sort – both interpersonal and intrapsychic – started to surface. We took time out to deal with it, both during and after the cycle, as reported in the section below on validity issues. It was important to attend to this, but it did rather distract us from rigorous reflection.

Cycle 3 (Day 3): Noticing the other reality at
the edge of the visual field
During the first two cycles we had all been very divergent and idiosyncratic in how we gathered in impressions of the other reality. Because of this, I proposed a convergence: that each person would gather impressions in the same sort of way. I suggested we try out the following procedure and this was agreed.

Experience.   For some 30 minutes we each practised noticing extrasensory impressions at the very edge of the ordinary physical visual field. We did this first standing, sitting or walking, in silence and without social interaction, while being altogether in the same room. Then we tried it while chatting to each other about mundane things. In these two parts we were trying to combine ordinary sensory perception of this world with extrasensory perception of the other. We shared our impressions and reflected on them.

Reflection.   Four members reported that they entered a daydream state while silently wandering about the room; and that this state was pregnant with potential extrasensory perception. They said they had experienced this state earlier in their lives, and had felt guilty about it – as if there was strong social disapproval of it. They felt that the extrasensory potential was about states of affairs in the other reality that precipitate events in this world.

Another person said he found a chink between the daydream and sense perception of the room – 'where they transform each other' – and 'saw' a cherub there. Someone else said she 'saw' 'entities and women in white' at the edge of her visual field. Most found that talking to each other about everyday matters constricted their ability to attend to the edge of their visual fields.

There was a marked reduction in the sense of ambiguity attaching to the impressions reported in this cycle: those who reported some unusual experience did so with more conviction. But this conviction was still not defined in terms of criteria for picking out genuine from spurious ESP.

Cycle 4 (Day 3): Procession and entry to the other reality in the fogou

In planning the next cycle the group was again taken up with the 'instructions' received in the first cycle. We had followed several of these: we had used catharsis, tried shamanistic-type utterance, polished the floor, used music, and spent two days indoors. It was agreed that we would now chant, and 'inquire where the birds flock in the garden'; and that this would lead on to the main event in the fogou, also in the garden. The following sequence was put together by several group members, each of whom conducted a part of it.

Experience. We gathered round a large tree in the wooded area of the grounds. This was a tree where the birds flock. One member introduced us to a chant. We stood round the tree chanting, then proceeded in single file along a sinuous path through the wood, still chanting. This path took us to the fogou, which we entered.

We lined up on each side of the underground stone passageway, holding hands in silence, opening ourselves to impressions of the other reality. Subdued daylight filtered down from the openings at either end of the passageway. After some time we filed out of the fogou and stood in a circle in the garden over the top of the underground chamber that runs off the side of the fogou passage. One member was inside the chamber, reciting prayers aloud. We were all silent for some time, receiving impressions. We then went back into the house and had a long session sharing our impressions and reflecting on them.

Reflection. There was a dramatic increase in the number, range and intensity of the impressions received by group members in this cycle. There was a very strong sense of the impressions being *impacts* – coming *into* ordinary consciousness. They were all received when the group was inside or just above the fogou.

Inside the fogou six members reported powerful trembling and shaking, with energy coursing through the physical body, both up and down; three people experienced a mental and physical cleansing; eight members had impulses to act in various ways, and six of these acted on their impulses, moving and gesturing in various ways; two people had a sense of two presences in the other reality within the fogou; and two others had a sense of a lot going on in the other reality within the fogou; five members had strong images of various kinds, especially faces emerging out of the stone walls of the passageway; one person heard 'sounds'. Many people experienced very considerable power, leaving them somewhat in awe and positively shaken: 'overwhelmed' as one person said. Other used phrases like 'wonderful', 'very good feeling', 'like a cool dip'. There was considerable overlap among these different sub-groups.

Above ground, standing over the underground chamber, four people 'saw' and/or sensed subtle energy like flames or swirls coming up through the ground out of the chamber and rising up into the sky, yet in the other reality.

There were thus basically five different kinds of experience reported: (1) streaming of energy in and out of the energy field of the physical body; (2) visions: pictures or images of faces and symbolic objects; (3) a felt sense of presences, and of their energies and activities, in the other reality *within* certain areas of physical space; (4) a sense of the numinous, of pervasive spiritual power; (5) emotional uplift.

As the group members shared all these sorts of experiences, we realized in our further discussion that our sharing was based on the very strong implicit assumptions (1) that our procession into the fogou had activated events in the other reality in a way that interacted with us and our location in this world and (2) that we were genuinely noticing these occult events in a variety of different ways.

This reflection then moved into a deep concern, widely shared within the group, that we had all fallen victims to a massive consensus collusion. We feared that we were confusing our own hysterically activated subjective phantasies with real impressions of another reality. Had we become unhinged by three days of bizarre activities, lost in a collective delusion that gave vent to all kinds of unnoticed but quite ordinary pathologies?

So we devoted almost the whole of the next day, the fourth, to an elaborate devil's advocate procedure, in which we tried to find ordinary explanations for our claims to extrasensory perception. This often meant seeking to reduce assumed altered states of consciousness to somewhat pathological ordinary states. Details of this procedure are given below in the section on validity.

This procedure, once completed, led over into a central discussion on criteria for distinguishing between authentic impressions of the other reality, and subjective illusions. This was an important time of conceptual convergence in our inquiry, and a main source from which I have distilled some of our findings. But the discussion also pulled up a lot of emotional agitation to do with the conflicting claims of analytic inquiry and human sensibility. So we chose to follow it with a long session in which these feelings of distress were identified, released in catharsis, and followed by a measure of insight.

Cycle 5 (Day 5): A sword in the other reality

This cycle was not at all planned. It arose spontaneously out of some individual psychological work done by one member in a group session to explore feelings, at the start of the fifth day. This woman was in the midst of considerable personal crisis, which interacted with the dynamic of the group.

Experience. With myself facilitating, and the rest of the group gathered round to give supportive attention, she began dealing with her present crisis, then regressed to early childhood experiences, and worked on these for quite a while. Then she suddenly embarked on a spatio-temporal extension of consciousness beyond her own personal history. She began to resonate with the experiences of a 14-year-old girl undergoing some kind of psychic training in an Eastern country in an earlier historical epoch. After recounting details of this training she came back into the present, bringing with her a sword – that is, a sword in the other reality, yet strongly focused *within* this physical reality, interpenetrating it yet invisible to ordinary physical perception. This sword was ceremonially passed round the group from person to person until it was held again by the one who had brought it from the past into the present. She held it out straight in front of her for a while.

The owner of the house and Director of the Centre sponsoring our workshop had a large and friendly dog, which had spent a good deal of time with us in our indoor meetings. It now got up, advanced towards the sword, sniffed at a point in space roughly where the sharp end of the blade would be, then backed off very quickly with a jump and start – and a yelp *as if* pricked on the nose. It then prowled warily at distance from the sword, keeping an eye on it. The sword was finally placed in a mirror on the wall. We opened a phase of reflection.

Reflection. Discussion centred entirely on the sword incident. Almost everyone had experienced the dog's behaviour – in advancing curiously, sniffing, jumping back with a start and a sound, then prowling warily at a distance – as a striking confirmation of the presence of the sword. This event had had a powerful and immediate evidential impact. Several people reported that the dog's reaction jolted them out of their scepticism about the invisible sword. No-one came up with any ordinary explanation that seemed more plausible than the sword explanation.

Perhaps the group was colluding in a collective hallucination, and this hypnotically induced in the dog behaviour consonant with it. But no view like this was advanced at the time. For rather than the group's strong belief inducing the dog's response, it seemed to be the other way round: the dog's strong reaction changed the group's half-hearted belief into something much firmer.

There is, of course, an anomaly here, to say the least. For a dog's experience suddenly becomes central to the inquiry process. Yet the dog was not a member of the group. It came into and went from the group. It came into and went from the group room when it felt inclined, and no record of these movements was kept; nor did anyone notice its responses to previous group activities. Then suddenly its supposed reaction to the unseen sword counts for more than group members' reactions to it. This is experiential validation of a very curious second-hand nature: as if responsiblity for authentic ESP has to be delegated by humans to a dumb beast. Nevertheless – and for what it is worth – the humans' experience of the animal's reaction was collective, convergent, and virtually unanimous in its mixture of conviction and shocking surprise.

Cycle 6 (Day 5): Closing ritual at a stone circle
This cycle was co-operatively planned by several group members. It was much more like a concluding ceremony – a celebration and an affirmation – than a formal part of our inquiry.

Experience.   We walked from the house half a mile or so to a large, ancient stone circle standing in a field. Each person stood beside a stone. We held hands and weaved in and out of the stones, moving around the circle three times. A physical sword had been stuck in the ground in the centre of the circle. We spiralled in and out three times from the stone circle to its centre where the sword was. We then stood in a wider circle, and each person, outside a stone, assumed a symbolic posture and said aloud one word. After a period of silence we returned to the house for discussion and reflection.

Reflection.   For many, the stone circle experience was mystical, religious: feelings of peace, stillness, of opening up to love, of the interconnection of all things, of stepping out of ordinary time, of the unity of Atman and Brahma, of being powerfully energized, of the source of things. Sharing these accounts led over into spontaneous reports of what the whole workshop experience had meant to people. We had a closing circle of meditation, followed by appreciations.

The validity of the inquiry

The inquiry ran into some classic problems. In the last cycle the experience phase transcended the claims of the inquiry: it was devised and pursued more for its own sake, almost as a form of worship, than it was as a way of concluding a process of research. It led into celebration and bearing witness, rather than winnowing out conclusions. Unless, of course, you choose to see the celebration itself as a special kind of conclusion drawn from the inquiry.

In the early reflection phases it was difficult to move beyond *describing* impressions, ostensibly of the other reality, to *evaluating* them. It was as if people had to go with these occult impressions, nurture and encourage them, without prematurely challenging their ambiguity. To believe anything at all in this field you sometimes have to believe a bit too much. This means you often have to assume much more is going on than you are entitled to assume on the basis of available evidence, in order to get the kind of experiential evidence you need. To have any experiences at all of the other reality, you have to entertain them in an open, receptive and uncritical spirit – for a period at least. Extrasensory perception at the outset may be confused, obscure and messy. And it is no good pressing too soon to find out what precisely is wrong with what, at best, may only vaguely be right.

I will now review the inquiry in terms of the different validity procedures proposed in Chapter 2. I refer the reader to that chapter for detailed accounts of these procedures.

Research cycling. We covered six cycles in five days. The first four were planned, the fifth was impromptu and important, the sixth was a closing which transcended the claims of the inquiry. The number of cycles seems adequate and reasonable, considering the other activities to do with validity issues also covered that are discussed below.

The research cycling was all collective, that is, both experience and reflection phases were done by everyone together. It was very much a group inquiry. This may not always have been in the best interests of fully individual work during the reflection phases, a point I take up again in the discussion of authentic collaboration below.

Divergence and convergence. The inquiry was highly divergent. Each of the group rituals was very different; and two of them were more determined by 'instructions' received by one member, than by principles of research method. Every cycle adopted different methods; and in every cycle except the third each person gathered impressions in their own idiosyncratic way.

No one way of generating impressions by one particular ritual activity was pursued rigorously over several cycles. And no one way of receiving impressions was pursued rigorously over several cycles. This extreme divergence did indeed give us a multi-faceted view of how humans may pick up intimations of the other reality while engaged in a variety of different activities in this reality. But the results were highly impressionistic: the overlapping of diverse blurred parts made for a certain vaguely systematic comprehensiveness – but at the expense of a substantial experiential warrant for any one part.

This excess of divergence in the experience phases was offset and counterbalanced by an important conceptual convergence in an extended reflection phase in cycle four – when we devoted nearly a whole day to the use of the devil's advocate procedure. What we were systematically converging on here were criteria for picking out genuine from spurious impressions of the other reality.

There was one important occasion of complete experiential convergence – when we all witnessed the apparent psychic reaction of the dog to the invisible sword in the fifth cycle. This did curiously bring the inquiry to a sharp moment of close accord. But as I have already pointed out in the report on that cycle, the convergence had a highly anomalous second-hand quality.

Experience and reflection   The time spent on experience phases and reflection phases was about equal, with the exception of cycle four, where the reflection phase was extended to a whole day with the devil's advocate procedure. This extension made up for the fact that in earlier cycles not enough time was spent on reflection in order to move beyond description of impressions to evaluation of them. One of the major difficulties with ASC participative research is that there is a tendency to come not quite fully back from an altered state, and so to fall short of sufficient critical discrimination, in an ordinary state, about what was really going on. Reflection phases may need to be rather longer than the experience phases, to allow for a full return, and for the shift from description to evaluation. But at the same time it is also important, when returning, to remain sensitive to the sort of criteria it is appropriate to use for evaluating altered states. It is a delicate balance.

Aspects of reflection.   As mentioned above, the inquiry, in the first three reflection phases, had difficulty in moving beyond the description of impressions of the other reality to evaluation of them. This failure to evaluate meant that it was only after cycle four that we really got down to the business of identifying criteria for picking out genuine from spurious altered states. It seemed to me there was not a lot of conscious transfer from the reflection phase of one cycle to planning the experience phase of the next cycle. In a way the inquiry rather bypassed such transfer, certainly in planning the second and fourth experience phases, which simply took account of 'instructions' received by one member in the first experience phase. The momentum of the early cycles was too experiential, with action generating more action: later action was not sufficiently influenced by learning distilled by thorough reflection on prior action.

Falsification. As mentioned above, at the end of the reflection phase of cycle four we realized we had been carried away by the other world assumptions of our impressions in the fogou. We feared we were all colluding in passing off our pathological material as genuine impressions of the other reality. So we spent the better part of a whole day on the systematic use of a devil's advocate procedure, in order to subject our claims to extrasensory experience to a reductionist critique.

The procedure was as follows. Each group member in turn sat in a chair in front of the group and had read back to them what they had reported as impressions of the other reality during cycle four in the fogou (sometimes their reports from earlier cycles were used as well). These reports had been recorded in writing at the time they were made.

Then anyone else in the group could come forward, stand before the chair as devil's advocate, and give a reductionist interpretation of what had been read out, invoking an explanation in terms of ordinary phenomena and ordinary states of consciousness – usually more or less pathological states. The person in the chair was then asked to reply to the devil's advocate in one of three forms: (a) to assent to the force and plausibility of the devil's advocacy where it seemed honest and rational to do so; (b) to present a well-argued rebuttal of the advocate's case, and to uphold the ASC view with good reason; (c) to insist on the intuitive claims of the ASC view, while admitting that they could find no supporting argument to rebut the devil's advocacy.

This whole procedure was applied with great thoroughness for each person in the group, and so took up a considerable time. I found it one of the most interesting parts of the inquiry, in which discrimination between the worlds was brought to a finely honed point. I give here only a small sample of the sort of devil's advocate points made, with abbreviated versions of the sorts of replies made.

Devil's advocate: Your so-called ASC impressions are nothing but a form of attention-getting through promulgation of the bizarre.
Reply: This is possible; but other attention-getting activities are less strenuous and less likely to be rejected.
Devil's advocate: Your so-called ASC impressions are a phantasy projection of your longing for the non-existent mystical.
Reply: I accept that some part of my experience may be just a projection of my longing; but equally such longing may exist precisely because of the reality of what is longed for.
Devil's advocate: Your so-called ASC impressions are nothing but a phantasy projection of your own unexplored libido, sexual energy. The felt sense of a 'presence' in the other reality may be just a displaced longing for a yet-to-be-experienced, liberating lover.
Reply: I accept this as a possibility; I don't believe it applies.
Devil's advocate: Your so-called ASC impressions are nothing but unexplored aspects of your own psyche projected out, and sucked into the mass delusion about another world which afflicts some of you people in Cornwall.

Reply: I accept this as a possibility.

Devil's advocate: Your images of a warrior and a guardian are a displacement of your denied rage.

Reply: I am in touch with my rage; I have had no such images prior to the procession; I did not and do not identify with the warrior trip.

Devil's advocate: Your images of swords are but a projection of your psychological armouring and rigidity together with blocked sexual energy.

Reply: I am not heavily armoured, having worked on it a lot; and I am in touch with my sexual energy.

Devil's advocate: Your ASC mythology about the fogou is a defence against all the insecurity and anxiety you have about being here.

Reply: I am not clinging to being here. I have a loose and open attitude about going or staying.

Devil's advocate: You are not in touch with another reality, you are just unable to cope with this reality.

Reply: I do not accept your dichotomy. There is just one comprehensive reality.

Devil's advocate: Your feeling of cleansing in the fogou is nothing to do with being psychic or having an ASC. It is entirely a physiological response to the physical conditions in a damp cave.

Reply: But I have been in other damp caves in which I have not experienced any kind of cleansing of this sort.

Devil's advocate: Your experience of spiralling energies through your body was but a physiological response to fatigue.

Reply: But I am in good physical condition.

After everyone had taken a turn, and from all the perspectives which the procedure generated, we winnowed out a set of possible criteria for distinguishing between a genuine impression of the other reality, and subjective illusion. They are given in the section below on our findings.

Chaos and order.   There was considerable emotional upheaval of various kinds during the course of the inquiry and this is referred to below. One person had a brief semi-psychotic episode one evening half-way through the workshop, and this required a lot of attention. It also brought out the de-stabilizing, de-egoizing, disorienting impact of this kind of inquiry.

There was much conceptual chaos and ambiguity in the early cycles. We generated a mass of divergent impressions whose ambiguous status remained totally unresolved for three days. We had the devil's advocate procedure on the fourth day because we could no longer tolerate the ambiguity. This intellectual closure was not premature, rather it was overdue.

Indeed, it is a moot and interesting point whether we *would* have had a better overall intellectual closure if we *had* been more rigorous about evaluation rather than mere description in the early reflection phases. Perhaps the conceptual chaos of the early cycles led to a more fruitful kind of order in the end.

The management of research countertransference. We assumed that individual emotional distress, entwined with interpersonal tension, would be called up during the inquiry. And that this might both interfere with our planning and reflection phases, and fog our capacity to receive impressions of the other reality. So at the end of the experience phase of cycle two, and before the reflection phase, we had a round of disclosures about the emotional state of each person. This led immediately into a one-hour session of exploring feelings being evoked by the inquiry, using bodywork exercises, with some members having a cathartic release of distress. Then after the reflection phase of cycle two, we had a long session on interpersonal work in the group, dealing with issues of attraction and antipathy.

This was all on the second day, and it sustained us through cycle three and the central and all-important cycle four, both on the third day. But after the very long devil's advocate procedure on the fourth day, the critical discussion on criteria for distinguishing between authentic and illusory impressions of the other reality, stirred up a good deal of emotional agitation. This was to do with the conflicting claims of inquiry and analysis on the one hand, and human feeling and process on the other. We released some of this tension through vigorous physical activity and some dancing, for a short period. Then we had a much longer session in which several members took a turn one after the other, facilitated by me in the middle of the group. They were tracing back their current upset to past distressful experience, with resultant catharsis and insight

On the fifth day, in the morning, a life-crisis involving one member criss-crossed with the dynamic of the group. The fifth cycle arose spontaneously out of deep personal work done by this person in the middle of the attentive group, as I have already described. What is really important here is how what was for many people one of the most evidential parts of the inquiry emerged from what started out as a piece of individual regression.

Given the brevity of a five-day inquiry, and the demand of the research cycles themselves, our management of research countertransference was thorough. That is, we did take enough time to identify work on obvious distress called up by the inquiry. This thoroughness, in my view, enabled us both to sustain the inquiry, and to give it more depth and validity than would have been the case without it.

Authentic collaboration. The group took to the inquiry method speedily and eagerly. I did not run, manage or design the various phases of the research. The third cycle only was based on my proposals. For the rest a remarkable degree of co-operative creativity in the group took over.

The one time I did try to push hard on what I considered to be an important methodological issue – to do with getting beyond mere description of altered states to evaluating them – the group resisted it as unwarrranted pressure. They came to deal with this issue in their own time, on the fourth day as I have already reported.

In some ways members took the method on board too eagerly, impatient about its finer points, so that, for example, some of the early reflection phases were in my opinion too impressionistic and superficial. Yet their commitment to some of the validity procedures – such as emotional housecleaning and devil's advocacy – was impressive.

The use of collective research cycling, especially in the reflection phases when members in an impromptu manner gave their verbal reports in the whole group, may not have been the best way of distilling individual learning. It was probably too loose and unfocused. And in the planning of the next cycle, my recollection is that most of the creative work was done by different people in that half of the group that was most experienced in the ASC field.

This report has not been written collaboratively with the group, but exclusively by myself. And this is a clearly a limitation on any claim that the findings of the inquiry are based on authentic collaboration.

While the group worked largely under its own steam, it is also noticeable that it did not take time out to ask just how adequate individual contributions were, and so to find out how widespread the collaboration was.

Findings of the inquiry

Our starting idea was that it is possible to function awarely in two worlds at once. Our conclusions or findings were a very tentative set of criteria for distinguishing between genuine and spurious impressions of the other reality. These criteria have been distilled by me from my notes on the devil's advocate procedure after cycle four, on the fourth day. They have a provisional, but not a substantial, claim to validity. And for the following reasons.

The inquiry was very short, only five days. Within it, only four of the six research cycles were intentionally planned for research purposes. The experiential phases of these four cycles were highly divergent, with no repeat cycling of particular ritual methods, or particular ways of receiving impressions. There was one important, but only one, convergent reflection phase that really addressed the issue of criteria. And there was only one fully convergent experience phase when everyone was presented with the same phenomenon (the supposedly psychic dog in cycle five); but this, as I have mentioned above, is in part vitiated by its anomalous and second-hand status. So the validity of our findings cannot be claimed to be substantial.

But it can be claimed to be provisional. There was a widely divergent spread of interlocking impressions yielding, when analysed, an interlocking, mutually supporting set of criteria. The devil's advocate procedure was thorough, attention to counter-transference material considerable, premature closure on ambiguity was avoided, and collaboration was reasonably authentic.

The criteria need to be seen as mutually supporting each other. They make their provisional claim *when taken all together*. They are as follows:

1 *Agreement*. Two or more persons have the same or similar impressions of the other reality.
2 *Heterogeneity*. Very different sorts of impressions of the other reality, which occur both simultaneously and serially, in the same person and in several persons, are compatible. The main sorts of impressions in our inquiry were: (a) feelings of subtle energy streaming up and down and around the physical body; (b) visions, pictures or images of something in a subtle domain; (c) a felt sense of presences, their activities and energies in the other world; (d) a felt sense of pervasive spiritual power; (e) emotional uplift felt to come from a liberating unseen ambience.
3 *Synchronicity*. Impressions of the other reality occur simultaneously to two or more persons, and are meaningful to them in the same or a similar way.
4 *Spontaneity*. Impressions of the other reality often come unexpected and unbidden; are often surprising in their content; and the recipient did not want or intend to produce them in the way in which they occurred.
5 *Independence*. Impressions of the other reality have a life of their own and are not amenable to manipulation and interference.
6 *Spatial reference*. Impressions of the other reality have reference to locations in a subtle and inwardly extensive space that is somehow *within* physical space.

The discussion after the devil's advocate procedure led to some views which we felt we would want to take into account in any future inquiry in this field.

Sometimes there is an obvious discrepancy between the content of an impression of the other reality and its supposed status as a purely psychological projection, which makes the latter account unsatisfactory. And in general, the sceptical, reductionist account that explains away extrasensory impressions in terms of ordinary states is often less plausible than the explanation of them in terms of the other reality.

Emotional projection and extrasensory perception of the other reality are not mutually exclusive: the former may get mixed up with and mix up the latter. Thus heightened self-insight and cleansed emotional states may help to clarify the process of extrasensory perception of the other world. But quite apart from all projected material, emotional longing for the other reality may be part of the evidence for it.

It seems that perception of the other reality is cast in more idiosyncratic subjective form than is the case with the perception of physical reality. The same person may have diverse impressions, in different modalities, of the same occult scene; and this diversity may be multiplied greatly when different persons are attending to the same occult scene. This may be in the nature of the case – in the sense that the other reality is much more obviously a subjective–objective creation, or it may be due to lack of practice and skill, or it may be the result of emotional interference. Or it may be due to a mixture of any two of these, or of all three.

10

Reflection in Action:
Exploring Organizational Culture

Judi Marshall and Adrian McLean

This chapter is an account of research conducted in a Local Authority in Shropshire, England, between February and December 1987. Our intention was that this should be a co-operative inquiry (Reason and Rowan, 1981a). Here we shall describe the unfolding process of this project, and highlight some of the issues and dilemmas that we encountered. The chapter is therefore written with two parallel threads: the one a descriptive narrative telling the story of the project, the other a reflection on the broader questions raised and the choices made concerning what in its loosest sense might be termed the 'management' of the research. We have chosen to report the research in some detail, in order to go into some of the practicalities of working with processes of co-operative inquiry, and thus complement the more inspirational literature in this area.

We are members of a staff–student Postgraduate Research Group at the University of Bath (with Peter Reason, our close friend and colleague). We had a number of discussions with this group during the course of the project. These were both challenging and supportive, helping us to reflect on our roles in the research and the nature of the collaborative relationships we were developing with our co-researchers. This proved very valuable.

We begin then with an account of our first visit to the organization, the Wrekin District Council.

First encounters

Early in February we drove up to Telford in Shropshire and had lunch with the Chief Executive and Personnel Manager (Roger Paine and Norman Rollo) of Wrekin District Council, an organization of 1200 people. We were there to negotiate permission to conduct a case study of the organization culture at 'the Wrekin', having been commissioned to do so by another agency, the Local Government Training Board. The Wrekin had been chosen for our case study as they have a reputation for innovation in local government circles.

We were warmly received and talked over an excellent lunch. Both parties knew of each other's work and this was an overdue opportunity to meet. They described the changes they had been trying to achieve in the organizational culture over a period of four years or so. A participative exercise had been undertaken to identify a set of 'core values' in the culture. The outcome of this process was three words – Quality, Caring and Fairness – which were now used as an essential element in internal and external council publicity. They saw themselves as working practically with a cultural approach rather than as experts in the theory of cultural change. We shared with them some of our experiences of working with cultures and the ideas these had generated. There was a ready rapport between us; we easily translated between each other's experiences and built on each other's ideas. This in itself was enjoyable, exciting.

When we came to talk about the possible study, both Roger and Norman gave their ready agreement. They wanted to be identified by name in any publications. We explained that we preferred doing research *with* people rather than *on* people, and outlined what this might mean. We wanted to set up a group inside the authority to do the project with us. This too was well received. They had hoped that we would not take a traditional, distanced approach as this would 'not fit with the culture' – a phrase we would come to know very well as the research continued.

We discussed the composition of the group that would work with us. We asked that it should include representatives of different organizational levels and departments, and be balanced in terms of gender and any other characteristics (such as length of service, locals vs incomers) of significance within the Council. We talked together about inviting people who would be able to work in a collaborative way. The phrase 'who would be positive' was used. It transpired that this meant different things to the two parties. To the researchers it meant people who would be willing to act as researchers, whereas to those inside the organization it had connotations of being committed to the Council. We were to discover this and explore its implications later.

Roger and Norman had clear purposes of their own for wanting the research to happen. They wanted to learn about the effects of their work over the past four years and to find out if the organization had 'really' changed much. We talked about the idea of there being a darker, 'shadow' side to any culture. They liked this notion and stressed their desire for the research to portray both facets in a balanced way.

A member of the Personnel Department – Danny Chesterman – was nominated as our regular contact and as internal co-ordinator. A full schedule of visits, including an early meeting with the Departmental Directors, was agreed on the spot. The research was moving ahead more quickly and in a much more straightforward way than we had envisaged; driving home we wondered if it was all 'too good to be true'.

One reservation about our proposals had been expressed by Roger which we had to think through. He felt that the word 'culture', which we were using as our core concept, had already been over-exposed in the Wrekin during the various change exercises. He strongly suggested that we find an alternative, such as 'style'. At the meeting we agreed reluctantly to this, but later realized that we would feel restricted in having to control our language in such a way. We saw dangers in having the notion of culture lurking in the background but un-named, and thought that this fundamental inauthenticity on our part could be confusing to other participants and could well be reflected in any data gathered. We wrote to Roger and Norman explaining our concerns, and they gave their agreement to us using our own language. We were already having to work at achieving a balance between our interests and those of others involved in the research.

Overview of the research process

The research we organized in Wrekin District Council had three major and intertwined strands for us: our work with the research group, interviews we conducted with other members of the organization and 'being around', collecting ethnographic data as we moved about the organization. This chapter concentrates on our work with the group, which represented the mainstream of our activity and sense-making. The other strands fed into our work with them.

Our meetings with the research group were each a day long, and were at roughly monthly intervals. There were four main meetings and a shorter meeting directly before the presentation of the research findings to the Management Team. As we write this chapter a further follow-up meeting is planned, we will talk about this below. Figure 10.1 shows the overall shape of the research schematically.

Planning the first meeting with
the co-operative inquiry group

Before our first meeting we talked through the issues we saw at this stage in the research, what our objectives and feelings were, and drew up a tentative programme for the day. We discussed our plans with the staff–student Postgraduate Research Group at Bath University.

The main dilemmas we saw at this stage were:

1 our academic language might get in the way;
2 the notion of 'research' might be alien to the group, too impractical, 'over their heads';
3 whether they would really want to take part and whether they had had any chance to say 'no';
4 how to honour our expertise in relation to culture and research and yet do the research collaboratively;

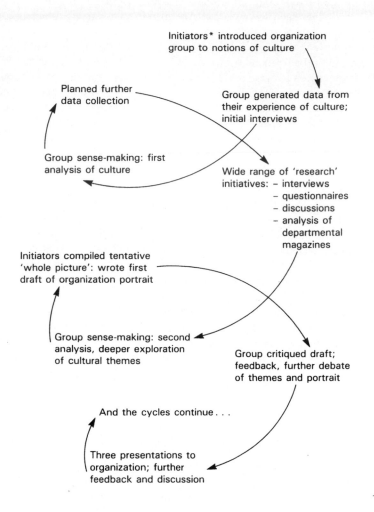

Figure 10.1 *Cycles of activity and reflection in collaborative
analysis of Wrekin District Council's organizational culture –
February–December 1987*
* Initiators were Adrian McLean and Judi Marshall

5 the pressures of allowing sufficient time and space for repeated cycles of data collection and analysis in a busy organization;

6 how much we should control what the group did, and how much we could let go and engage with the creative possibilities; how collaborative we could be;

7 we had already pre-empted the process by signing a contract to write this chapter, we felt embarrassed at this and realized that we had moved ahead unilaterally;

8 whether doing the research would meet their needs; it had clearly been initiated to meet ours;

9 would the interviews with other members of the organization we wanted to conduct diminish the importance or centrality of the group?

10 would the organizational hierarchy be reflected in the group, would some people dominate?

11 would they only be interested in implications for change whilst our main interest was in portraying the organization culture as it was?

With this intimidating list of concerns we planned the programme for the first meeting with the group, deliberately choosing to take clear charge of the process and to own our relative expertise as both researchers and students of organizational culture. We were aware that this gave us considerable power in the group, but we saw this as the reality and sought to acknowledge the power imbalance as inevitable. Our view was that it was necessary for us clearly to take power and initiative at the start; we hoped then, through a process of sharing our thinking and methods with them, gradually to empower them to take their own initiatives within our overall paradigm.

The first meeting with the research group: April

Prior to the first meeting, members of the group had been briefed by the Personnel Manager. He stressed the organization's commitment to the project, and that senior management wanted people to be 'blunt' in expressing their views. The members of the team were:

Joy Bailey – Play Leader
Terry Brookes – Principal Engineer
Danny Chesterman – Personnel Officer (and our internal link-person)
Pam Edwards – Housing Welfare Officer
Anne Hewitt – Employment Development Assistant
Annette Lewis – Print Room Supervisor
Gordon Little – Street Lighting Technician
Mick Paish – Bricklayer
Brian Piper – Senior Estimator/Surveyor
Derek Shaw – Housing Centre Manager

Tony Smith – Area Foreman
Brian Wright – Janitor

A few people knew each other in advance, but some knew no-one else in the group before we started.

We began the meeting by introducing ourselves and saying briefly what the day was about, describing ourselves as *issuing an invitation for people to join us*. Members of the group introduced themselves and said why they were there, how they felt about being there and what they anticipated. No-one expressed reservations about being in the group. Someone said that it was 'akin to an honour' to be included, and others seemed to agree with this. People were not at all clear what was about to happen, but were willing to 'wait and see' and to join in.

We then told our story of how our interest in the area of culture had developed, how we had come to believe in the importance of fully understanding an organization's culture in order to be more effective within it and to facilitate change. We outlined our proposal that the research be conducted collaboratively. People were attentive and interested, nodding agreement at the idea of a co-operative inquiry. We then introduced our plan for the day: we would present some ideas about culture and research and then the whole group would plan what to do next. We emphasized the importance, as we saw it, of them being able to decide what involvement they wanted – if any.

We had planned to use small, 'base' groups during the day for them to discuss with each other how they felt about what we were saying and to explore what they wanted from the project. It was also a less formal way for them to get to know each other. This device was also intended to reduce any possibility of them being steam-rollered by us, something that the Postgraduate Research Group had confirmed as a risk.

Having thus set the scene, we asked them to form the base groups. We took this opportunity to confer as facilitators, processing how things were going and our reactions. We suggested the following questions for the groups to cover:

Does it make sense so far?
How do you feel about it?
Do you have any questions?
Do you have any concerns?

What the groups did with this list varied; they joked that people in the Wrekin do not always follow instructions, they make up their own agendas if they choose. So some groups started talking about the organization culture, the strength of the values of Quality, Caring and Fairness, the changes that have happened in personnel and so on.

Several groups were concerned that during the initial round of introductions no-one had expressed reservations about taking part. They thought that the group had been specially chosen to 'be positive' and enthusiastic about the Wrekin, and were worried that the group could become too 'cosy' and complacent. They said that there were 'cynics' within the organization, people who do not approve of the way the council operates, and that they were not represented in the group. We debated whether it would be useful to invite a few such people to join us. We decided to note this concern, for the time being, and make a final decision at the end of the afternoon. By raising this issue, people had already begun to reflect on the validity of the research – could the group as constituted produce a full portrait of the organization?

Another concern expressed by one group was about confidentiality. They did not want to be quoted personally in any reports, especially if their views were 'negative' or if they were involved in identifying 'deadwood'.

The general feeling from this round of feedback was of people saying that our proposals made sense, and that they would be very happy to progress with the agenda rather than wondering whether it was all all right. What we were encountering, without realizing it at the time, was a cultural propensity towards action. An impatience to 'get on with it', and to 'make it happen'.

The rest of the morning was spent with us presenting our ideas about organization culture: what the concept means, how we can become more aware of it, some of the major influences on its shape. Throughout, the group were involved and participating fully, they offered examples to illustrate the frameworks we were presenting. They found the notions we were using easy to become involved with; this way of seeing the organizational world seemed to 'fit with the culture'. Their examples represented rich data about the culture in the Wrekin. In some ways they were acting as informants, offering us their understandings as members of the culture. This made us realize, however, that in thinking of them primarily as co-researchers, people who would go out and explore the culture, we had not anticipated their desire to surface their own understandings. At lunchtime we used this realization to modify our plans for the day.

Lunch was delivered to the room in which we were working. As part of the discussion of culture we had been discussing how the importance of an event is indicated by cultural symbols. Two of the indicators of importance in the Wrekin, they told us, were the quality of the catering and whether the Chief Executive takes an interest. The lunch trolley was therefore greeted with more than gastronomical interest; it showed us that the culture project was considered fairly important – we had the menu that included chicken legs! During lunch we were to have a further indication, the Chief Executive and one of the Directors called by for a few minutes to see how things were going. This was clearly a promising sign to all!

Group members paid attention to the project's organizational importance throughout the research. They looked first to senior management and then to other organization members for signs. Their awareness reminded us of the organizational, political context within which the research was being conducted.

Revising our plans

During lunch we (Judi and Adrian) discussed our proposed plan for the day, which was already looking too ambitious and inappropriate. Our original intention had been jointly to plan a phase of 'outward-looking' data collection. Our new thinking was that, before extending the inquiry beyond the boundaries of the group, members needed time to explore their own perspectives on the culture, in doing so deepening their familiarity with the concepts and possible research approaches.

Our presentation material was based on the draft of a 'Workbook' on organization culture which we were preparing for the Local Government Training Board (McLean and Marshall, 1988). This contained exercises to enable the readers to learn about their culture. We offered the group copies of the Workbook and invited them to do some of the exercises to produce material for our next meeting. This new plan proved acceptable, and greatly relieved the time pressure on the afternoon.

Introducing notions of research

At the beginning of the afternoon we talked through some key issues about doing research collaboratively. We particularly emphasized the notion of going round the research cycle several times, coming to tentative conclusions and re-cycling to test these out or refine them further (see Chapter 2). We also talked about the need to develop 'critical subjectivity' as a way of owning and making best use of one's own perspective, and recognizing that there are different perspectives. We then discussed the next steps in the research.

The issue of how to include the views of cynics was raised again. We decided against co-opting additional people into the group which was beginning to feel cohesive, particularly as any newcomers might become 'tokens' for alternative viewpoints and this would not be 'fair' (one of the three stated values). Instead, we resolved to ensure that 'cynical' viewpoints were incorporated in the project by other means.

The group also explained their understanding of the organization's sub-cultures, advising us on appropriate groups to visit. They were particularly keen that we should not exclude people such as manual workers who are based outside Head Office, as one person put it (referring back to our discussion of catering as culturally symbolic), 'the people who have their tea in tin huts'.

For the final stage of the day, people returned to their base groups and we asked them to review whether they wanted to be part of the project and what involvement they would like. They were not very interested in our repeated questions about whether they wanted to take part. Some said that if they were not interested they would not have come back after lunch.

They did, however, talk about the difficulties they envisaged in finding sufficient time to do any work on the project. It was all very well to be given their managers' approval, they said, but when it came to a choice they would not be able to set other work aside without being criticized. We discussed strategies for dealing with these issues, and agreed to circulate a letter to managers explaining the commitment required and requesting their support. They also thought that there might be growing resistance in the organization to the world 'culture'. Some people asked for clear guidelines about how to use the Workbook, seeming overly concerned with details compared to earlier discussions.

During our closing discussion one of the group asked us whether we had achieved what we wanted from the day.

Reflections on the first group meeting

At the end of the first day we tape-recorded our reflections.

We were generally very pleased with how the day had gone. It had surpassed our greatest hopes, particularly in terms of how involved people were, how able to use the notions we had introduced, and how members of the group were raising and working with issues of group and research process. We were not unilaterally 'in charge', there had been a two-way flow of energy. We felt we had all built a solid foundation for doing research together.

We both felt flat and disappointed at how the day had ended, however. The group had raised a lot of obstacles about doing the next phase of research and seemed relatively intimidated by them. Their questions about how to use the Workbook felt overly detailed and dependent. We wondered whether this was an expression of anxiety about their competence as researchers, or doubts about being part of the inquiry. Perhaps their comments reflected a need to digest after the first intensive day of input and discussion. Perhaps their dependence was a response to the largely expert stance we had taken for the day. Unable to resolve our speculations, we hoped that this pattern would shift as the other members felt more comfortable with the ideas and the approach. Valuable proposals had came out of the discussions; for example some subgroups decided to find a room away from their desks to meet and concentrate on the research without interruptions. We were reassured by various people's comments that they wanted to see the venture through, despite foreseeing difficulties and conflicts with workload.

We were impressed with how the group had worked and with their awareness of process. Everyone had contributed to the day, there had been little sense of hierarchy or pattern of deference within the group. They seemed neither intimidated by us nor deferential towards us. Our hopes were high that the process could be collaborative throughout. The late question regarding whether we were 'getting what we wanted' was pleasing, since we took it as a supportive attitude, and as reflecting their developed abilities to work with process issues and willingness to be responsible jointly with us. The whole group had discussed and evaluated the process for the day. (This ability seemed to link with high levels of awareness about the *style* with which things are done – as in 'the Wrekin way' – and with widespread training on service delivery and other topics.) It felt easy to raise our concerns, to talk openly to the group. They had been hard and clear about confidentiality – and had raised it themselves. This was encouraging to us as it indicated that they were prepared to be resolute parties to the process.

We were glad that we had not rushed through the day with our initial plan. We were pleased with how we had worked together, keeping in touch, discussing things openly. This felt healthy. While we had not set out to contrive this, we realized that we had been modelling choice and dialogue around the process.

We were very excited by the wealth of data and insights that they had already given us into characteristics of the culture. We talked through what had been said, making sense of our experiences so far, pondering some of the paradoxes.

Reviewing the day, we thought that the group, and therefore the research, had already established a life and momentum of its own.

During the next month

The group were doing what they thought fit with the worksheet exercises.

We, meantime, talked to the Postgraduate Research Group about the first meeting. They were suspicious about whose needs the Wrekin inquiry group was serving, whether it was really participative, and whether we had controlled and pushed through the agenda too much from our own research needs. We said it did not *feel* like that, but fed this possibility into our review of the project. They also challenged us about whether our change of plan for Cycle 1 of data collection meant that we had put members of the group into the roles of informants rather than of co-researchers, thus accepting the roles of trainers rather than affirming ourselves as researchers. We and the Postgraduate Research Group were very aware of how little time we had allocated to do the research and were concerned that this could prove difficult; we had already extended our schedules.

Second meeting – May

We had prepared a potential agenda in advance for our second meeting with the Wrekin inquiry group. Our hosts were a little less organized than for the first meeting; as we gathered we all speculated jokingly about whether the prestige of the project had dropped.

Re-establishing the group

We began with a round of 'hellos', inviting people to say something about what they had been doing since we last met. We encouraged them not to talk about work but to share aspects of their non-work selves. There was a positive, relaxed and friendly feeling in the group from the start.

We invited people to meet in base groups. The groupings from the first day were largely maintained throughout the project, including times when they undertook joint data collection in groups between the main meetings. Our questions for the base groups were:

How did you find the Workbook?
What have you been able to do?
Were there any problems with managers about time for the project?
Other thoughts about the project, your involvement, what you want out of it?

In the plenary discussion that followed they were very frank with us about their experiences of reading the Workbook. They had found it difficult in places, and some of the exercises were too abstract or intellectual. Some had adapted and changed the exercises to make them more appropriate. They offered us a great deal of helpful advice on how to arrange the Workbook differently, especially to use layout to make the key messages clearer. In spite of these detailed criticisms they found it a helpful reminder of what we had discussed at the first meeting.

We were impressed at their creative improvisations of the basic principles for accessing cultural understandings. Although we felt vulnerable during this discussion – and said so – it showed that they were not dependent on us or willing to defer to our supposed expertise. Their openness was much appreciated; this, and our preparedness to be vulnerable, added to the growing climate of trust in the group.

Reviewing the past month

People had initiated a wide range of activities during the month. At the same time there had been quite a lot of last-minute preparation for the meeting. Some had talked to other people, not just exploring the culture from their own perspective. Some of their superiors had proved difficult and unco-operative, piling on conflicting work. Members of the group were so involved at this stage that they were not very interested in the questions about what they wanted and what sort of commitment they wanted to pursue. This was reminiscent of the first meeting. They were clearly fascinated by the work and the 'results' of this first cycle of inquiry. The group was being called 'The Culture Club' within the Council. There was a discussion as to whether this project represented another 'seven-day wonder'.

Sharing findings
The base groups were reconvened with the task of sharing the material that had resulted from their various activities. The main observations and issues were listed on flip charts. Later, each group (including Adrian and Judi) presented their summaries to the rest of the group and these were discussed. We encouraged a climate of noting the information thus generated, its consistencies and contradictions, and adopting an open, questioning attitude as to the deeper significance and more general themes evident in each presentation. At this stage we wanted to discourage premature interpretations of underlying cultural patterns. Flip charts, including ours, did not become fixed interpretations of the organization culture, but served as prompts for debate.

Some of the key topics emerging at this stage were as follows.

Subcultures.   There was a lot of material about subcultures within the Authority. People described a number of cross-cutting groupings and allegiances in the organization which make for a complex tapestry of super-imposed subcultures. Whether there are significant differences between manual and staff employees was debated at some length, especially in the light of recent steps towards 'harmonization'. Another aspect of discussion was the threat that various subcultural differences might pose to the recent consolidation of a more corporate image and unified value system.

Open communications – interruptions.   Communications are predominantly conducted on a very informal basis. They both rely on and express a basic level of trust between people. This characteristic of the culture was graphically described by several groups. During one such presentation the Print Room Manager was called away because a machine had broken down – illustrating the point well, and the interruption-based style of working it fosters.

Quality, Caring and Fairness.   QCF – the Council's value statement of quality, caring and fairness derived from a participative process a few years previously – seems to be embraced in the organization's practice, as well as being part of its espoused philosophy. Values are enforced by colleagues and subordinates rather than imposed on the organization from the top – this was most apparent at manual and director levels.

Vulnerability. One of our themes was the culture's apparent fragility or vulnerability. Major changes had been made during the past four years, and were still in progress. These had largely been carried by a few key people. Other members of the organization hoped that they would succeed, but were concerned that the changes were still very reliant on a few people's energy. Given this situation, we saw ourselves (through the research) as having the potential to damage the culture, to burst the bubble of what it told itself and others it was achieving. It felt easy to say that, and it linked for us with feeling that we were being given people's trust; we were also saying that we would do our best to treat it responsibly.

The open explorations of the above and other material created an engaging discussion which we saw as an encouraging indication of the emergence of a co-operative community of inquiry.

People were highly involved throughout the day. Our discussions were rich and exciting; we hardly stopped for lunch (a more modest affair which we interpreted as a sign that we were being left to get on with the job). Part way through the afternoon we paused to reflect on what we had done and plan the next steps.

Someone made the comment that the view that was emerging was from 'inside' the Council itself, and that the elected Council members would not necessarily share this view. How much of the organization we could speak for was a continuing issue.

Planning further data collection

To take our explorations further, people identified various other groups or individuals in the organization who should be included: cleaning staff, possible 'cynics', people at outposts such as sports centres, manual workers, elected members and so on. We were particularly being reminded to include and explore the viewpoints of those at the bottom and on the periphery of the organization, people in close contact with the public, to balance the views of senior people at the organization's centre. Members of the group volunteered to cover the various target groups, some deciding to design or amend a questionnaire as a basis for discussion.

Other sources of potential data were identified. For example someone decided to look through some unofficial departmental magazines which had expressed satirical views, to glean indications of changes in the culture. One person had a lot of contacts with suppliers to the organization and agreed to ask them for impressions of the Council.

It was also decided to write something in the weekly organization newspaper, the *Wrekin News*, telling people about the 'Culture Club' and inviting people to express their views to members of the team. This would open the research to still more people's influence; the group also hoped that it might pave the way for discussions with target contacts and reduce the chance of them dismissing the project as the latest fad.

We (Judi and Adrian) suggested that the group might like to have a drink together in the evening after the next meeting. This sort of 'thank you' for your contribution is a characteristically Wrekin way of doing things, and we noted with amusement how we were acting out this feature of the culture. It also fitted with our views that it is valuable to relax together after hard work. We debated when and where this should happen in order to achieve the qualities we wanted – another discussion of process.

Reflections on the second group day

Once more, when we returned to our hotel, we tape-recorded our thoughts on how the day had gone.

Group process
We were very pleased with how the group had started in the morning; it felt relaxed and friendly. We noticed how much more casual and informal we had all become with each other. Other members of the group, not just us two, were increasingly sharing responsibility for the process, saying when it was time to move on, or indicating that someone had spoken for long enough. They were certainly not leaving us to do everything. We felt that in part the culture had made it easy for us, that the project would take a very different form in another organization.

The nature of collaboration
Most pleasing was the realization that the group had not been 'merely' a collection of informants. They had been fully involved in joint sense-making with plenty of debate about the data collected and its meanings. There had been numerous times when the discussion did not centre around either of us, as it had mainly done at the first meeting.

This second meeting had been like a transition; there was a shift of power towards the group. We had been much less directive and central in managing the process; the group seemed to be much more independent of us. This was apparent from the different ways in which they had used the Workbook, and from their more grounded awareness of cultural phenomena. The pattern of discussion was a further indication. In this meeting it felt more as though we were working alongside each other, sharing, exploring and jointly puzzling the fascinating material that had been gathered. This was encouraging, and it raised other issues for us.

We debated whether they were doing too much and whether we should be taking a more directive leadership role. We no longer felt completely in control of the project. It was both a thrilling and disturbing feeling. People were now setting off on their own initiatives in many different settings, and examining a wide and diverse range of data sources. While the prospect of so many simultaneous inquiries was exciting, we also felt a little concerned and bemused that we would probably not see all of the data thus generated, or know exactly the questions asked and the methods used. Had we become the Sorcerer's Apprentice, invoking some magic that we could not control?

We were aware that the need to exercise control could be interpreted as a defence against anxiety. This awareness did not prevent us from still feeling some concern, however. Here was a confirmation of how doing collaborative research can challenge our identities as researchers.

Integrating reflection and action in the research process
It was interesting that, as a group, we had spent little time reflecting on the research method. There had been scant interest in this form of discussion, particularly compared to the fascination shown in the lengthy explorations of the research material itself. We noticed – we would have had to have been dim not to – that they did not want us to keep on asking whether it was a good idea to do such and such – they wanted to get on.

The group seemed to be taking its own line, doing what was intuitively right rather than carefully discussing and planning the research process. The emphasis was more on *reflection in action* than on addressing each as distinct and separate. Once more we realized that here was an expression of a cultural quality; in this case, what came to be called the 'right brain' property of the culture. Things tend to happen as a result of intense and at times chaotic activity and less as a tidy culmination of systematic planning. One of the ironic catch phrases in the Wrekin is 'Ready? Fire! Aim' alluding to this action emphasis. The impressive creativity of people within the authority, and the importance placed on the need for things to 'feel' right, is a further indication of the dominance of more right brain thinking.

The dilemma that this posed for us was whether we should be pushing the group for more discussion of research methods or moving forward with what 'felt right', allowing process issues to emerge *as they become relevant to the group*. We had some confidence in taking the latter approach as this seemed to be how the group was already working *and* had resulted in discussions of possible collusion, confidentiality and so on. We felt that they had 'a fund of knowledge' about how to do research which our presence was helping them to tap. For example someone had summarized the Workbook in two pages, to make the material more easily shared with people they talked to. Another person had used the material to prompt a discussion about possible changes in her work team. There had been issues she wanted to address; in notions of culture she found something she could use and without hesitation had started to work with it for herself. Individuals were doing what seemed practical to them with the material, not taking a detached intellectual approach, but not excluding the intellect either.

Were we being co-opted by the culture?
We admitted to each other being impressed by the culture, despite ourselves and despite an initial scepticism. This was a particularly interesting struggle between feeling that we were becoming acculturated – that we increasingly knew how to do things 'in the Wrekin way' – and simultaneously seeking to retain a detached and more discriminating view. What mattered to us was our ability to be critically subjective in the midst of the inquiry process. In this case it did not mean maintaining our independence of the Wrekin culture but being able to notice when we were behaving in ways that were consistent with its characteristics. In fact, only by becoming in some ways party to it could we understand its full nature. Thus, we saw the realization that our proposal for a drinks evening was uncannily typical of common Wrekin practice as an encouraging sign of our critical subjectivity, and not as an indication that our 'objectivity' had been compromised. At the same time our fears about being 'co-opted' might be seen as the shadow of our positivist selves, since they imply a loss of objectivity.

Third meeting: June

We made very few plans for the June meeting. By now it felt inappropriate and unnecessary for us separately to devise a structure for the day. We felt confident that this would be agreed collectively. Our main aim was to review the work we had all done during the second cycle of data collection, and jointly to explore what our information was revealing about the culture. We wondered, but did now know, whether these could be drawn together to give a total picture during the course of the meeting.

The day was more fragmented to begin with than previous meetings. Our round of 'hellos' was in terms of what people had been doing towards the research; this revealed a wide variety of activities, expressing people's individuality and different interests. It transpired that during the day we reached into more diverse views of the organization, and into what we would call its 'shadow' side.

Building an agenda together we again moved into people's diverse concerns. One of the first items posed was who in the Wrekin to present the final organizational portrait to, and how this should be done. We (Judi and Adrian) wanted to discuss how the case should be written. We asked what work others had done. The group wanted to know where *we* were, to see and to debate the material and sense we had been making of our visits to the Council. At previous meetings we had played down the importance of our interpretations of the culture and had not wanted to overpower the group. Now they wanted us to be more open with them by putting our current picture together, and we agreed – although we had not come prepared. We welcomed the opportunity for feedback and debate on our emerging ideas.

The bulk of this meeting was spent in another cycle of sense-making through small group work, presentations and discussions. We shall briefly describe some of the highlights of the day.

Reports on research initiatives

The cynic phenomenon. Several of the group had approached supposed cynics only to find that 'underneath' they were not at all cynical. While their way of presenting themselves suggested a lack of commitment to the Council and its values, further discussion revealed that they expressed a similar commitment to the Wrekin as other apparently more positive souls. As one person put it, they were 'passively pro-Wrekin'.

Assorted difficulties. Some people had found that work colleagues they approached were not very willing to give up time for the project; there had also been very little volunteered response to the item in the *Wrekin News*. Some members of the team were being criticized for being away working on the research and had to explain and justify their behaviour. This was interpreted as some people having a more instrumental attitude to the authority, not being willing to give up their time, or being more involved in their personal agendas such as looking for a new job.

Encouraging developments. But generally the response to the research team had been positive. They had tailored their ways of asking for material to their various audiences, someone had even given a contact the whole Workbook to look at, another group member had devised short question-naires, while others had held informal discussions. The range of people in the authority who had now been covered was extensive and impressive. We also heard how people were beginning to use the notions of culture in doing their jobs and finding them illuminating. Some said that they could not help looking at all they are doing in terms of culture.

Resisting a second cycle of interpretation. The next stage of the day was to work in base groups on the new data collected and to organize it for presentation to the whole group. This was the main purpose we saw in the meeting, but the other members of the group were resistant. They saw this as unnecessarily repeating the exercise they had gone through last time, they felt that nothing new would come out, they already had an idea of themes in the culture. We persisted in our suggestion that the new data had to be engaged with in its own right, setting the previous interpretations on one side for the time being. We added the justification that *we* needed the time to organize our thoughts if we were to 'reveal' to them, as promised, what emerging notions of the culture we were working with.

Sensitivities.   As an aside we asked them to put their names on the flip charts they then produced so that we could easily identify them. To our surprise there was much joking about this, and mentions of 'confidentiality' and whether people were 'expendable' – not issues which had been of that much concern earlier. We were now entering a new phase, when the data went more clearly into controversial issues.

Sense-making: second analysis
We presented our material first. There was much debate about the issues we raised. New material and interpretations and linkings emerged in ways that both confirmed and expanded on the first analysis. As one element we reflected back that we were getting a strong sense that we had been 'around too long' for them. This was by no means a defensive or distressed observation, but one offered as another indication of how things are done in the Wrekin. In the immediate-action culture, ours looked like a long-drawn-out project, and there seemed to be impatience to finish it. The group confirmed this to some extent, agreeing that they were now impatient to look at implications, and that other people were quizzing them about 'how much longer' the project would take. We then went through similar processes of debate, confirmation and elaboration based on the other sub-groups' data.

The general flavour of the day's work was of getting to grips with some of the conflicts and paradoxes of the organization's culture. Some of its impressive attributes have darker, shadow sides, and we considered these at some length, uncharacteristically for the culture, dwelling on some of the more negative repercussions for a while. For example, there was strong consensus across the organization that 'caring' was the most significant of the three stated values. At this meeting it became apparent how difficult it is to create or sustain any more formal organizational systems in the face of this priority. Caring can be the ultimate organizational excuse for not doing other things. Similarly the very open style of management, and having freedom within one's own patch, can also sometimes have a darker side, with some people 'getting away with murder' because they are not more tightly controlled. Later, someone would explicitly question the 'balance' we had achieved, and prompt us to reintegrate the total picture by seeing the culture's limitations in the context of its achievements and distinctive styles of working.

A lot of the discussion reflected tensions and conflicts that are lived with rather than being resolved, and a recognition that these are essential aspects of the authority's nature and that not resolving them contributes greatly to its abilities to be innovative and to gain people's loyalty and commitment.

Validity and next steps
Towards the end of the day we had a discussion about validity – initiated by members of the group. They were concerned about what they could

claim for the portrait we were arriving at, anticipating that we would meet criticism and cynicism from others. They thought we might all be accused of 'locking ourselves away' (not approved in the open-access Wrekin culture) and being too academic or cosy. It helped that, with the exception of the representative from Personnel, the group were not normally seen as being in the confidence of management or likely to collude with them.

There was a sense that we could not 'convince' everyone, but that we had all worked hard, had involved a lot of other people and were satisfied that we had achieved a full picture of those parts of the organization we had collectively studied. We had relatively little information on the councillors and the public, and would have to state these boundaries when we presented the material.

At this stage, a member of the group summarized, we could judge the validity of the process and were very satisfied with this. They felt that they had been able fully to influence the course and outcomes of the work. Several people said that it was also important to judge the validity of the product, that is, when we had one we could review as a whole.

The group discussed how involved they should be in feeding back our understandings to the organization. They decided that they wanted to be involved in this aspect of the project, and that a format of presentation and discussion to a range of interested groups would be the most appropriate for the Wrekin.

What we had not done during the day was put the wealth of material together to produce a complete portrait of the culture. This seemed far too difficult to do in the whole group at that stage. We jointly agreed that Judi and Adrian, the two academics, would produce a first draft of the case study for discussion, based on all of the material that had been shared and discussed during the two data analysis meetings. We were happy, indeed keen, to agree to this. There was a tacit collusion apparent here that we did not fully challenge. The rest of the group argued that it was only right, as we were the 'experts' in such matters. We agreed, however, on the condition that we would discuss the draft fully with them and that they could add further sections if they wanted to. They said that they might write some other documents or digests for internal consumption.

We then reviewed the group process for the project as a whole. People said: that it had been fun, that they had learnt a lot about other departments, that they had felt very much part of the group, that they liked the informality, that we had joined with them but retained some role in shaping what happened.

By then we were relatively pleased with the day and with our work on the project as a whole, although some people were a little concerned that our discussions about the organization's shadow side might lead to a more negative portrait, and would so be 'unbalanced'. In the Wrekin, committed people should 'be positive'.

It is fascinating how such reflections of the culture appeared throughout our work. As long as we worked with process and were sensitive to it and ready to question or at least reflect on it we could learn more about the organization and about our research 'topic'. If we began to see them as 'facts' we lost our ability to tap this dimension of data. This link is especially apparent in a project on culture, because it seems relatively obvious that the nature of the organization will shape any research done in it. But we believe it is likely to be the case for *any* research topic. Engaging in the research, especially when you bring a group together, will reverberate content issues in the process as well. In many ways this is freeing – we do not have to run the group 'correctly', avoiding all conflict or distress or whatever is appropriate for our topic, but to be aware of the is-ness of what is happening and what issues are being touched.

And the story continues...

Our deliberate choice to offer a detailed description of the process thus far has forced us, given the limited space available, to render only a brief summary of the subsequent events which, at March 1988, were still unfolding. Following these we shall reflect on the overall project as an exercise in co-operative inquiry.

A first draft

Over the summer we (Judi and Adrian) reviewed the wealth of data and analysis that had been generated, and formulated a preliminary overview of the culture. We based this on the themes that had emerged from the two analysis days with the group. Inevitably we also noted other patterns, themes and interconnections in the material. The first attempt at capturing all of this in prose was shared between us, and we each went on holiday with a share of the assignment.

We sent our efforts direct to the members of the Culture Club, having arranged to reconvene as a group in July at our university offices. We wanted to act as hosts for a change, and laid on a posh lunch! We spent the day painstakingly working through the material. This was less relaxed than earlier meetings. We were anxious about our accounts and other members of the group seemed to be more defensive than usual. While they generally endorsed our efforts they also made many points of clarification and qualification, and occasionally directly challenged some interpretations. Particularly close scrutiny was given to any mentions of elected councillors and other politically sensitive matters. They were puzzled by some of our terminology, and at times alienated by the use of what they considered to be pretentious jargon. We heard all of this while struggling with our desire not to defend and justify. The whole group agreed that we (Adrian and Judi) should write a revised report and check this back with them prior to making the first presentation to the Chief Executive and Directors.

This duly happened in September. We met with the group for the morning prior to the presentation in the afternoon. Our meeting with the group was much more relaxed than our previous session, and they enthusiastically endorsed the final portrait of the culture. The entire group was present at the presentation to the senior managers and spoke to many of the points in the presentation which was led by Judi and Adrian. Afterwards we met as the Culture Club for what we thought would be the last time. The tone was a mixture of pride and celebration. Group members indicated their full support for the final form of the analysis, which in summary took the form of a web of interconnecting themes.

Since then there have been two further presentations to different audiences in the Authority, one of which was open to all employees. The group has continued to meet (minus Adrian and Judi), at the request of the Chief Executive, to assess the appropriateness of the cultural patterns to the changing circumstances which now confront the organization. We are continuing discussions with senior managers concerning their strategies for continuing the development of the culture.

Reflections

By way of conclusion we would like to reflect on the overall project as an example of co-operative inquiry and consolidate some of our learnings about the management of such a project.

We begin with the paradoxical realization that co-operative inquiry is not about equality. Throughout the project we were engaging with the inequalities between ourselves as experts who were undertaking a research initiative and a group of people who had been enlisted to help us. The discrepancy in expertise was considerable and inevitable. We were asking them to play our game. We considered ourselves to be exceptionally fortunate to be conducting this project in such a supportive and positive culture, but the fundamental discrepancy in knowledge and research experience represented a risk that all the key decisions and interpretations would come from us.

In the event we were gratified that our chosen strategy of acknowledging this expertise at the beginning, and taking a clear initiative early, had resulted in their empowerment later. In spite of our intermittent anxieties at not being fully in control of the process we were also delighted and impressed by their later independence and creative use of the research methods. The learning for us here is that by acknowledging our paradigmatic power, by being explicit in our use of the cultural metaphor, we provided a framework within which people could operate creatively and relatively independently.

The question this raises, however, is whether this is genuine co-operative inquiry. Is it necessary that an inquiry group should select or create its own paradigm as a part of the inquiry process? In this case we were prepared to proceed within our paradigm while seeking to be as explicit as possible about its partiality. Part of the reason for the compatibility of our approach in the Wrekin was that the cultural approach was sympathetic with their way of operating. However, we were not fully aware of this at the start of the venture and our deliberate decision not to open up the paradigmatic debate was largely for pragmatic reasons. There was not the time available to launch into such an uncertain and open-ended enterprise, and our co-researchers had little or no understanding of the realm of epistemology. Pragmatics aside, however, this was clearly one way in which the project might be seen as falling short of a co-operative ideal.

It did not escape our notice that as time became scarce we took an increasingly central and expert role by drafting the reports and fronting the presentations. While we consulted with other members of the group thoroughly over each draft there was an evident collusion on all our parts that we would lead this stage of the inquiry. It was expedient for all parties, given the time constraints and the unwieldy if not impossible alternative of doing it collectively. Clearly we began to diverge from a co-operative ideal at this point. In our view this was an expedient decision and we sought to guard against our forcing an analysis by the process of sharing each draft with the group. However, while the group expressed strong support for the final version of the report it still had been significantly shaped by us as experts familiar with the processes of writing and presenting ideas.

These, then, are some of the questions that reverberate after the inquiry has been completed. We come away from it thrilled by the commitment and excitement evident on the part of the members of the research group; at the quality and richness of the material generated; at the fact that the group is continuing to meet independently of us; at the interest and acknowledgement for the work from others within the organization; and at the fact that the organization is using the analysis as a basis for future action and policy. What is more, the learning generated in this exercise is still alive and present within the organization, not just in the form of a report and presentations but carried and kept alive by the members of the research group.

Reflections

Peter Reason

Having read and edited Chapters 5 to 10 I am left with my reflections about the enterprise of co-operative inquiry. In these closing pages I want to share these reflections, not as a definitive view, but in a way that I hope will help readers to articulate their own thoughts and feelings. In particular, I want to compare and contrast the different examples in terms of some of the issues raised in the Introduction and Part One of this book.

The purpose of inquiry

When I first discussed the contributions with the authors, and as the chapters arrived in their various drafts, I realized that, as well as representing inquiry in different fields of action, the examples also show the wide diversity of *purposes* of co-operative inquiry. I have identified five such different purposes; each inquiry emphasizes some purposes more than others.

Development of professional practice
The holistic medical inquiry, Bob Krim's work in City Hall and Ian Cunningham's work with learning facilitation, are all about developing new forms of professional practice. They are all seeking answers to questions about how to work effectively with the challenge of new times and new situations.

Liberation of disadvantaged groups
The woodfuel project is primarily liberationalist in intent, in that its concern is to help people at a grass-roots level take greater charge of their lives in the face of large-scale capital-oriented development policy and oppressive bureaucracy. Other purposes, in particular solving the woodfuel problem and meeting the needs of the sponsors, are important; but it is clear from the author's account that their first criterion for the success of the project was liberation, the achievement of greater space for the local people.

Other projects also have their liberationist aspects – the holistic medicine project being involved both with patient power and the liberation of doctors from the confines of their historical practice. The City Hall project is concerned with enhancing the quality of working life. The altered states of consciousness project, it could be argued, aims to liberate human awareness from the confines of ordinary consciousness. And so on. It would appear that co-operative inquiry is nearly always concerned, at some level, with the practice of freedom.

Exploration of human experience
The purpose of the altered states of consciousness project is quite simply to explore the wider possibilities of human experience in their own right. It is inquiry for the sake of human curiosity and personal development, with no immediate wider purpose. Other projects, particularly the medical project, are also concerned with this, but not so centrally.

Institutional change and development
Co-operative inquiry has often been used as a means of changing organizations; it is one way of gathering and acting on the collective wisdom of organizational members. The work with local authority organization culture, in the US City Hall, in Kenyan villages, and in a different way the holistic medical project, are all examples of this.

Development of theory
Most of the projects aim to develop new propositions and theories – we have a new model of medical practice, new understandings of learning, ways of articulating organization culture. None of the projects have developed what might be termed formal theory, rather they are all in the nature of theories of action and theories for action. I discuss this question of the nature of knowledge further below.

This range of purposes seems to me an important aspect of co-operative inquiry. It shows that human inquiry is not simply a way of generating academic knowledge, but is an approach to personal and professional practice – a way of learning through risk-taking in living. It again emphasizes the holistic purpose of human inquiry to develop understanding for worthwhile action in human situations.

The form of collaboration

As I pointed out in Chapter 1, the idea of co-operation does not mean that all those involved have to contribute in identical ways. In the chapters of Part Two we can see people working as initiators, as teachers, as facilitators, as formal researchers, as managers, and as consultants, all contributing to a process of co-operative inquiry.

John Rowan's research cycle can be used to illustrate the different kinds of relationships of the people involved in an inquiry. We can indicate by drawing lines round the research cycle the extent to which the co-researchers go round the whole cycle together, or simply engage together at different stages of the overall process. We can also show whether the relationship is fully collaborative (a solid line), alienated (a dotted line) or somewhere in between (a dashed line). I have attempted to use this convention loosely to illustrate the different kinds of relationships in the six different projects.

In the holistic medicine project (Figure 1), the participants came together at various points between being BEING and PROJECT – the broad form of the inquiry was developed in advance by the initiating facilitators, but most members had some say in the detail. At this stage relationships were undeveloped, as shown by the dotted line. The inquiry group worked together through PROJECT, ENCOUNTER, MAKING SENSE, and some of COMMUNICATION broadly in collaborative relationships with some alienation (shown by the occasional breaks in the line!), and went their separate ways during the COMMUNICATION phase.

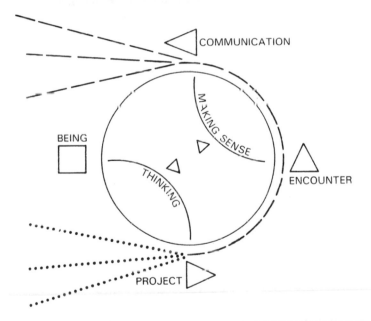

Figure 1

The woodfuel project seems rather different (Figure 2). While some of the villagers were involved in the PROJECT stage, most of the contact is at ENCOUNTER. Some are involved in MAKING SENSE and in COMMUNICATION (especially with other villages in the networking), but contact seems to cnd at about this stage. It would appear that great efforts are made to establish collaborative relationships at the points of contact. Indeed, in Chapter 6 the authors consider at some length the ambiguity of the concept of participation in a developmental situation, and argue that it is important that the participation is truly emancipatory, and not merely instrumental.

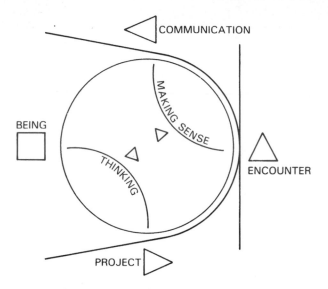

Figure 2

In City Hall (Figure 3) the aspects of the project reported here are almost entirely about Bob Krim's personal learning. He has many encounters with other organizational members, and with supervisors, as part of this. Some of these relationships are collaborative, most are not: indeed, the major issue of the research is the establishment of collaboration. I have indicated this with a series of question marks.

Practice to Theory (Figure 4) again centres very much on Ian Cunningham's personal development of theory and skills. He works with many people in different ways, and we have no evidence that these relationships were not on the whole collaborative. But since they were not involved in the whole project, I assume some degree of alienation, and have indicated this by breaks in the line.

The altered states of consciousness project appears (Figure 5) to be an example of a project with a high degree of collaboration in most stages. John Heron reports no particular problems of developing authentic relationships, and we can assume that this was facilitated by their being a fairly like-minded group of people. However, participants were only partially involved in MAKING SENSE and not at all in COMMUNICATION stage.

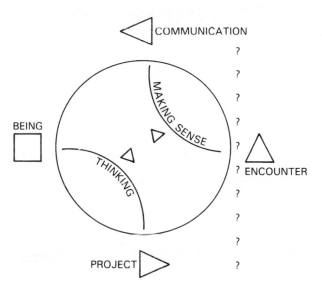

Figure 3

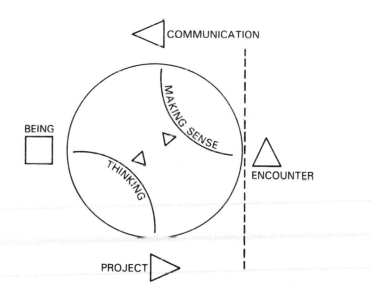

Figure 4

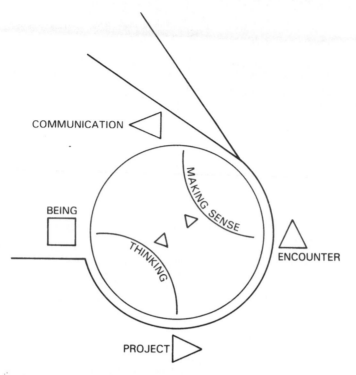

Figure 5

Finally, in the inquiry into culture (Figure 6) the group was organized as a part of someone else's larger PROJECT, and much of the design of their work and the ideas on which it was based was organized in advance. However, it is clear that they developed a high degree of collaboration during the ENCOUNTER and MAKING SENSE phases, and continued this to take ownership of much of the COMMUNICATION phase. Alone among the examples, this group continued to work at least for a while after the departure of the initiating facilitators.

I find that using Rowan's model in this way is helpful because it makes me think and stimulates debate. I initially sketched out Figures 1–6 and discussed the maps with a number of people, which raised several interesting issues and pointed to some of the inadequacies of this kind of mapping. First of all, it is evident that in co-operative inquiry there is never one simple inquiry. There will usually be an 'official' inquiry, with more or less formally agreed purpose and process; but to a greater or lesser extent all the participants will have their own purposes, their own questions and their own forms of engagement with them, and so in effect there will always be as many inquiry strands as there are participants.

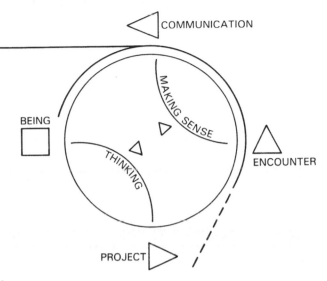

Figure 6

Randall and Southgate (1980), in their discussion of creative and destructive group processes, point out how a creative group needs to have a degree of fit between the 'official' purpose, the actual purpose, and the desires of members, these latter including unconscious desires. Similarly, for an inquiry to be valid, these separate private purposes need to be reasonably congruent with the group's actual and official purpose. This suggests another aspect of Heron's notion of authentic collaboration in Chapter 2: it would be helpful if inquiry groups could find some way of exploring the fit between their official purpose, the actual purpose, and the conscious and unconscious desires of members – some of the exercises in Randall and Southgate's handbook would be good starting points for this.

A second problem with Figures 1–6 is that they do not really show the development of the projects through their multiple cycles of action and reflection. They tend to show the inquiries as relatively simple, linear affairs, rather than as the complex and at times chaotic webs of action and reflection, reason and emotion, individuality and collectivity that they really are. This emphasizes for me the emergent quality of co-operative inquiry, how it may develop a life of its own which can take us by surprise, which I mentioned in Chapter 1. Judi Marshall and Adrian McLean offer us a map of their inquiry which shows this complexity and multiple cycling rather well.

A third problem with these maps lies in the notion of alienation itself. Several people suggested that the contrast between collaboration and alienation is too stark, and that we need broader ways of looking at human participation. We might, for example, follow Freire (1970; Randall and Southgate, 1980), and think in terms of dialogue on the one hand, and invasion and deprivation on the other. When dialogue is established there is a free flow of information and ideas, and people experience their ability to be self-directing; true dialogue can take a range of forms from informed consent through to full collaboration. On the other hand relations of invasion mean that people feel their personal space is encroached upon so they are unwillingly controlled – and deprivation means that the information and resources they need are withheld.

I also wonder whether the idea of co-operation necessarily contains within it the notion of authentic hierarchy: a form of genuinely enlightened and enabling leadership. However, this is question beyond the scope of these reflections.

So it seems that questions such as 'What do we mean by co-operation and participation?', and 'What is the relationship between participation and authority?' remain wide open for further exploration, and indeed must be explored in every co-operative inquiry so that appropriate choices can be made.

Issues of validity

A third theme that concerns me through the examples is about questions of validity. In some chapters these are addressed very fully, using some version of the procedures suggested in Chapter 2: the holistic medicine project demonstrates a reasonably thorough validity review; the altered states of consciousness project shows in particular an example of the devil's advocate procedure in use. The group exploring organizational cultures gives some consideration to the validity of their work. In other chapters questions of validity are discussed in passing; however, all the chapters show how co-operative inquiry involves systematic cycles of self-reflection and critique.

I feel that attention to questions of validity is of extreme importance. I say this first because if we wish to further the practice of co-operative inquiry we must counter the charge that our work is mere subjectivism. Our retort can be that we have been more carefully self-reflective and self-critical than most orthodox inquiries, and that a collaborative knowing is essentially more sound that a so-called objective view. We can only say this, I believe, if we have developed and used some systematic procedures for being self-reflective and maintaining a high level of collaboration. But far more important, we need to be systematically self-critical because the human capacity for delusion and collusion is quite enormous, and we are quite capable of fooling ourselves if we do not take care.

However, I also believe that there is no one way of getting it right – in the end applications of validity procedures come down to human judgement, what is practicable and what is 'good enough' given the aims and purposes of the project, the situation, and the existing state of practice. In human inquiry it is better to be approximately right than precisely wrong. It is also better to initiate and conduct inquiry into important questions of human conduct with a degree of acknowledged bias and imprecision, than to bog the whole thing down in attempts to be prematurely 'correct' or 'accurate'.

Styles of inquiry

I suggested in the Introduction that there are several 'schools' of co-operative inquiry, each of which emphasizes a different aspect of the whole. Of the examples, two (holistic medicine and altered states of consciousness) aim to establish a 'full-blown' co-operative inquiry group, and one (organizational culture) draws on the spirit of this practice, and combines it with more traditional forms of observation and participant observation. The woodfuel project is clearly in the tradition of participatory research, and City Hall that of action science.

In Chapter 8 Ian Cunningham offers an interesting combination of the different forms, which appears to suit his particular purpose. This is an approach which I personally welcome: again, there is no ideal form for inquiry, and certainly not a new orthodoxy; rather, there can be a variety of practices drawing on the ethos of collaboration and participation

The nature of knowing

I find myself pondering the question of the nature of the knowing that is the outcome of the inquiry. One framework for doing this is John Heron's extended epistemology involving propositional, practical, and experiential knowledge.

I think it is reasonable to say that the main outcome of the woodfuel project was practical knowledge: knowledge how to make more efficient and safer stoves, and knowledge how to mobilize the resources of a village to begin to solve its problems. Maybe we can say that to the extent the project fulfilled its liberationist ideals the outcome included the experiential knowledge of greater freedom and self-direction. In contrast, the outcome of Bob Krim's work seems to be mainly in the realm of experiential knowledge: he knows and understands himself as a practitioner, and is therefore a better practitioner, as a result of his work.

The other projects emerge with varied combinations of different knowings. The organizational cultures project seems to result in a more thorough understanding of their organization culture by those who participated (experiential knowledge). And it also appears to result in descriptions of the culture which communicate with other people, and contribute to the development of the theory of organizational culture (propositional knowledge). We have no evidence that participants are better able to act in the culture (practical knowledge). The holistic medicine project clearly resulted in all three forms of knowing: a model of holistic practice was developed; members were able to put it into practice; and in doing this developed certain tacit experiential understandings of themselves and the processes of holistic medicine (probably particularly concerning questions of power spirit and self-gardening). The altered states of consciousness project similarly appears to produce propositions about the other reality; practical skills in being in two worlds; and intense experience of this, which, as Heron points out, is an essential for inquiry into these unfamiliar areas of experience.

I think that because of these varied knowledge outcomes it is often difficult to communicate what we have learned in a particular inquiry to other people, especially those who expect clearly measurable results.

Critical subjectivity

I suggested in the Introduction that co-operative inquiry involves a state of awareness which integrates our subjective experience with our critical faculties so that we can develop a perspective on our discoveries and learning. I also suggested that to cultivate this 'critical subjectivity' co-researchers need to engage in activities both to work on the psychological distress which emerges through the inquiry, and which cultivate an expanded experience or 'mindfulness'. All the examples, with the exception of the woodfuel project, take steps in this direction. It is particularly evident in the holistic medicine project, in Bob Krim's personal struggles with City Hall, and in the altered states of consciousness research.

The report on the woodfuel project does not report such activity, nor do the authors appear concerned about these issues. I find myself wondering whether this is because of the more political tradition (as opposed to psychological and educational) in which they are working. Certainly they are involved with consciousness-raising (Freire used the term 'critical consciousness') but in a way that places greater emphasis on awareness of political oppression than of psychological restriction and the expansion of human awareness. And this may be appropriate in the situations where they are working.

These reflections make me want to expand the notion of countertransference in research, which Heron uses in Chapter 2 in purely psychological terms. Because it is clear that, just as effective research stirs up individual resistance, so it may often bring about comparable disturbance in the institutions in which it is set: in doctors' practices; in the local politics of Kenya; in City Hall. This means that co-operative researchers need to learn not only to manage their own processes, but to manage the collective distress of their institutions. Research is a personal process *and* research is a political process.

In conclusion

These, then, are my reflections. The reader will without doubt consider other issues in reading these accounts – what kind of research cycling is evident? have the co-researchers made arrangements for supervision? what is unsaid in this report? I think I can see their unacknowledged bias here! And so on. Some readers will want to adopt other frameworks through which to review and assess the contributions – for example, the questions posed by John Rowan (1981) offer a useful basis for scrutiny.

And so, where next? What seem to be the next directions for the development of human inquiry?

I find myself very interested in the political issues of getting this approach to inquiry more fully accepted. I have already quoted Gregory Bateson's statement that the most important task today is to learn to think in the new way – the new way for him being in terms of a holistic and interconnected world. It might be better to emphasize that the task is to *be* in the new way, and my belief is that human inquiry and the development of a collaborative consciousness is one way towards a sane human existence. I believe we meet the political challenge by taking our work into critical arenas of human action and working with the questions of being and action. All the examples in the book do this in their way.

A second issue which fascinates me is just doing it. As a teacher and supervisor I am lucky in that I get to see a lot of projects at second hand, as well as being involved in my own inquiries. The challenge seems to be to hold the ideas of co-operative inquiry firmly but lightly, and to find ways of using them *appropriately* for the situation. So co-operative inquiry is a continual invention of response to the possibilities offered by the situation. The next book in this field might well be called *The practice of human inquiry*, focusing in more detail on the joys, troubles, and above all dilemmas of actually doing co-operative inquiry. This leads to my third interest in the process of supervision, because if we include the personal and the political in inquiry, and if we see inquiry as an emergent and inventive process, then our work as supervisors becomes much more complex.

Finally, what is important is that human inquiry is a process of human experience and of human judgement. There are no procedures that will guarantee valid knowing, or accuracy, or truth. There are simply human beings in a certain place and time, working away more or less honestly, more or less systematically, more or less collaboratively, more or less self-awarely to seize the opportunities of their lives, solve the problems which beset them, and to understand the things that intrigue them. It is on the basis of this that they should be judged.

Bibliography

Argyris, C. and D. Schon (1974) *Theory and Practice: Increasing Professional Effectiveness.* San Francisco: Jossey-Bass.

Assagioli, R. (1965) *Psychosynthesis.* London: Turnstone Books.

Avens, R. (1980) *Imagination is Reality.* Irving (Texas): Spring Publications.

Balint, E. and J.S. Norell (1973) *Six Minutes for the Patient.* London: Tavistock.

Bandler, R. and L. Grinder (1975) *The Structure of Magic* (vols I and II). Palo Alto: Science and Behavior Books.

Bateson, G. (1972) *Steps to an Ecology of Mind.* San Francisco: Chandler.

Bateson, G. (1979) *Mind and Nature: a necessary unity.* New York: E.P. Dutton.

Bell, J. and R.J. Hardiman (1988) 'The Naturalistic Knowledge Engineer', in D. Diaper (ed.), *Knowledge Elicitation for Expert Systems.* London: Ellis Horwood.

Benedict, R. (1935) *Patterns of Culture.* London: Routledge.

Berenson, B.G., K.M. Mitchell and R.C. Laney (1968) 'Level of Therapist Functioning: Types of Confrontation and Type of Patient'. *Journal of Clinical Psychology,* 24(1): 111–13.

Berman, M. (1981) *The Reenchantment of the World.* Ithaca: Cornell University Press.

Berne, E. (1964) *Games People Play.* London: Penguin.

Bly, R. and K. Thompson (1985) 'What Men Really Want', in J. Welwood (ed.), *Challenge of the Heart; love, sex and intimacy in changing times.* Boston: Shambhala Publishers.

Bohm, D. (1980) *Wholeness and the Implicate Order.* London: Routledge and Kegan Paul.

Brew, A. (1988) 'Research as Learning'. PhD dissertation, University of Bath.

Brody, H. (1987) *Living Arctic: hunters of the Canadian North.* London: Faber and Faber.

Buber, M. (1958) *I and Thou.* New York: Schriber.

Burgoyne, J., T. Boydell and M. Pedler (1978) *Self Development: theory and applications for practitioners.* London: Association of Teachers of Management.

Capra, F. (1982) *The Turning Point.* London: Wildwood House.

Chambers, R. and J. Morris (1973) *Mwea: an irrigated rice settlement in Kenya.* München: Weltforum Verlag.

Churchman, C.W. (1971) *The Design of Inquiring Systems.* New York: Basic Books.

Colaizzi, P.F. (1978) 'Psychological Research as a Phenomenologist sees it', in R.S. Valle and R.V. King (eds), *Existential–Phenomenological Alternatives for Psychology.* New York: Oxford University Press.

Corfield, K. and M. Renney (1983) 'Action Learning in the Social Services', in M. Pedler (ed.), *Action Learning in Practice.* Aldershot: Gower.

Cornista, L.B. and E.F. Esqueta (1982) *Participatory Research in Village Studies.* Doc. M/715 (General), Marga Institute, Colombo.

Cousteau, V. (1973) 'How to Swim with Sharks: A Primer'. *Perspectives in Biology and Medicine,* 16(4): 525–8.

Cunningham, I. (1984a) 'Teaching Styles in Learner Centred Management Development Programmes'. PhD dissertation, Lancaster University.

Cunningham, I. (1984b) 'Planning to Develop Managers'. *Management Education and Development,* 15(2): 83–104.

Davies, G.F. (1986) 'Student Intentions and Institutional Experience: an evaluation of different psychological explanations of student behaviour'. PhD dissertation, University of Bath.

de Mello, A. (1985) *One Minute Wisdom*. Garden City, NY: Doubleday.

Devereaux, G. (1967) *From Anxiety to Method in the Behavioural Sciences*. The Hague: Mouton.

Diesing, P. (1972) *Patterns of Discovery in the Social Sciences*. London: Routledge and Kegan Paul.

Donnan, L. and S. Lenton (1985) *A Handbook for Women Starting Groups*. Toronto: The Women's Press.

EADI Bulletin (1987) *Participatory Action Research*. Tilburg: Executive Secretariat of the European Association for Development Research and Training Institutes.

Eckhartsberg, R.V. (1981) 'Maps of the Mind', in R.S. Valle and R. von Eckhartsberg (eds), *The Metaphors of Consciousness*. New York: Plenum.

Elmendorf, M. (1976) *Bura Irrigation Settlement Scheme; Social Impact Reconnaissance*. World Bank, Office of Environmental and Health Affairs.

Ernst, S. and L. Goodison (1981) *In Our Own Hands*. London: The Women's Press.

Fals-Borda, O. (1987) 'The Theory and Practice of Participatory Action Research: Issues from Fieldwork in Three Latin American Countries'. *EADI Bulletin*, 1: 41–47.

Ferguson, M. (1980) *The Aquarian Conspiracy*. Los Angeles: J.P. Tarcher.

Feyerabend, P. (1978) *Science in a Free Society*. London: Verso.

Freire, P. (1970) *Pedagogy of the Oppressed*. New York: Herder and Herder (also 1972, London: Penguin).

Geertz, C. (1973) *The Interpretation of Cultures*. New York: Basic Books.

Glaser, B.G. (1978) *Theoretical Sensitivity: advances in the methodology of grounded theory*. Mill Valley: Sociology Press.

Glaser, B.G. and A.L. Strauss (1967) *The Discovery of Grounded Theory*. Chicago: Aldine.

Goswell, M. (in preparation) PhD dissertation, University of Bath.

Greenall, A.J. (1982) Seminar paper, School of Management, University of Bath.

Greenberg, I. (1974) *Psychodrama: Theory and Therapy*. New York: Behavioral Publications.

Griffin, S. (1984) *Woman and Nature: the roaring inside her*. London: The Women's Press.

Gustafsson, A. amd M. Ouma (1979) 'Agricultural Development in Kenya'. Unpublished manuscript.

Hainer, R. (1968) 'Rationalism, Pragmatism, and Existentialism: perceived but undiscovered multi-cultural problems', in F. Glatt and M.S. Shelly (eds), *The Research Society*. New York: Gordon and Breach.

Hampden-Turner, C. (1970) *Radical Man*. London: Duckworth.

Harrison, R. and R. Hopkins (1967) 'The Design of Cross-Cultural Training: an Alternative to the University Model'. *Journal of Applied Behavioural Science*, 3(4): 431–60.

Hawkins, Peter (1980) 'In the Therapeutic Theatre, Reality and Illusion are One'. *Self and Society*, 8(9): 296–302.

Hawkins, Peter (1986) 'Living the Learning: an exploration of learning processes in primary learning communities and the development of a learning perspective to inform team development'. PhD dissertation, University of Bath.

Hawkins, P.J. (1986) 'Catharsis in Psychotherapy' PhD dissertation, University of Durham.

Heidegger, M. (1978) *Basic Writings* (edited by D.F. Krell). London: Routledge and Kegan Paul.

Heron, J. (1971) 'Experience and Method: an inquiry into the concept of experiential research'. Human Potential Research Project, University of Surrey.

Heron, J. (1977a) 'Dimensions of Facilitator Style'. Human Potential Research Project, University of Surrey.

Heron, J. (1977b) 'Catharsis in Human Development'. Human Potential Research Project, University of Surrey.

Heron, J. (1979) 'Co-counselling'. Human Potential Research Project, University of Surrey.

Heron, J. (1981a) 'Philosophical basis for a new paradigm', in P. Reason and J. Rowan (eds), *Human Inquiry: a sourcebook of new paradigm research*. Chichester: Wiley.

Heron, J. (1981b) 'Experiential Research Methodology', in P. Reason and J. Rowan (eds), *Human Inquiry: a sourcebook of new paradigm research*. Chichester: Wiley.

Heron, J. (1982) 'Empirical Validity in Experiential Research'. Human Potential Research Project, University of Surrey.

Heron, J. (1983) 'Education of the Affect'. Human Potential Research Project, University of Surrey.

Heron, J. (1984) 'Co-operative inquiry into Altered States of Consciousness'. Human Potential Research Project, University of Surrey.

Heron, J. (1986) 'Six Category Intervention Analysis' (second edition). Human Potential Research Project, University of Surrey.

Heron, J. (1987) *Confessions of a Janus Brain*. London: Endymion Press.

Heron, J. and P. Reason (1981) 'Co-counselling: a co-operative inquiry. I'. Human Potential Research Project, University of Surrey.

Heron, J. and P. Reason (1982) 'Co-counselling: a co-operative inquiry. II'. Human Potential Research Project, University of Surrey.

Heron, J. and P. Reason (eds) (1985) 'Whole Person Medicine'. British Postgraduate Medical Federation, University of London.

Hillman, J. (1975) *Revisioning Psychology*. New York: Harper Collophon.

Hoffman, E. (1976) *Huna: a beginners guide*. Rockport: Para Research.

Husserl, E. (1970) *The Idea of Phenomenology*. The Hague: Martinus Nijhoff.

Ihde, D. (1971) *Hermeneutic Phenomenology*. Evanston: Northwestern University Press.

ILACO (1975) 'Feasibility Study; Bura Irrigation Scheme'. The Netherlands, Final report.

Jantsch, E. (1980) *The Self-organizing Universe*. New York: Pergamon.

Jung, C. *Collected Works*. (R.F.C. Hull translation), 20 volumes. London: Routledge and Kegan Paul.

Kabir (1977) *The Kabir Book: forty-four ecstatic poems of Kabir*. Versions by Robert Bly. Boston: Beacon Press.

Kaplan, A. (1964) *The Conduct of Inquiry: methodology for the behavioural sciences*. San Francisco: Chandler.

Koestler, A. (1978) *Janus: a summing up*. London: Hutchinson.

Kolb, D.A. and R.E. Boyatzis (1984) 'Goal Setting and Self Directed Behaviour Change', in D.A. Kolb, I.M. Rubin, and J.M. McIntyre (eds), *Organizational Psychology: readings on human behaviour in organizations* (fourth edition). Englewood Cliffs: Prentice Hall.

Krim, R.M. (1986) 'The Challenge of Creating Organizational Effectiveness: Labor Management Cooperation and Learning Strategies in the Public Sector'. PhD dissertation, Boston College.

Kuhn, T. (1962) *The Structure of Scientific Revolutions*. Chicago: University of Chicago Press.

Kurtz, R.R. and J.E. Jones (1973) 'Confrontation: Types, Conditions and Outcomes', in J.W. Pfeiffer and J.E. Jones (eds), *Annual Handbook for Group Facilitators*. La Jolla: University Associates.

Lakoff, G. and M. Johnson, (1980) *Metaphors We Live By*. Chicago: University of Chicago Press.

Lessem, R. (1983) 'Building a Community of Action Learners', in M. Pedler (ed.), *Action Learning in Practice*. Aldershot: Gower.

Lewin, K. (1948) *Resolving Social Conflicts*. London: Souvenir Press.

Lincoln, S.Y. and E.G. Guba (1985) *Naturalistic Inquiry*. Beverly Hills: Sage Publications.

Long, M.F. (1948) *The Secret Science Behind Miracles*. Santa Monica: DeVorss.

Macmurray, J. (1957) *The Self as Agent*. London: Faber and Faber.

Marshall, J. (1981) 'Making Sense as a Personal Process', pp. 395–9 in P. Reason and J. Rowan (eds), *Human Inquiry: a sourcebook of new paradigm research*. Chichester: Wiley.

Maslow, A. (1966) *The Psychology of Science*. New York: Harper and Row.

Maxwell, N. (1984) *From Knowledge to Wisdom: a revolution in the aims and methods of science*. Oxford: Basil Blackwell.

McCall, M. (1987) 'Indigenous Knowledge Systems as the Basis for Participation, East African Potentials'. EADI General Conference, Amsterdam.

McLean, A. and J. Marshall (1988) *Working with Cultures: a workbook for people in local government*. Luton: Local Government Training Board.

McLean, A.J., D.P.B. Sims, I.L. Mangham and D. Tuffield (1982) *Organization Development in Transition*. Chichester: Wiley.

McMaster, M. and J. Grinder (1980) *Precision*. Beverly Hills: Precision Models.

Mellor-Ribet, E. (1986) 'Revisioning Group Process: towards a female perspective'. PhD dissertation, University of Bath.

Miller, D. (1981) *The New Polytheism*. Dallas: Spring Publications.

Mitroff, I. (1974) *The Subjective Side of Science*. Amsterdam: Elsevier.

Mitroff, I. and R. Kilmann (1978) *Methodological Approaches to Social Science*. San Francisco: Jossey-Bass.

Moreno, J. (1946) *Psychodrama*, Vol. 1. New York: Beacon House.

Moreno, J. (1969) *Psychodrama*, Vol. 3. New York: Beacon House.

Perls, F. (1969) *Gestalt Therapy Verbatim*. Lafayette: Real People Press.

Polanyi, M. (1958) *Personal Knowledge: towards a postcritical philosophy*. London: Routledge and Kegan Paul.

Postle, D. (1983) *The Nuclear State*. Central Television Production for Channel 4.

Prigogine, I. (1980) *From Being to Becoming*. San Francisco: Freeman.

Randall, R. and J. Southgate (1980) *Co-operative and Community Group Dynamics . . . . . or your meetings needn't be so appalling*. London: Barefoot Books.

Randall, R. and J. Southgate (1981) 'Doing Dialogical Research', in P. Reason and J. Rowan (eds), *Human Inquiry: a sourcebook of new paradigm research*. Chichester: Wiley.

Reason, P. (1984) 'Is Organizational Development Possible in Power Cultures?', in A. Kakabadse and C. Parker (eds), *Power, Politics, and Organizations: a behavioural science view*. Chichester: John Wiley.

Reason, P. (1986) 'Innovative Research Techniques'. Complementary Medical Research, 1(1): 23–39.

Reason, P. (1988) 'Experience, Action and Metaphor as Dimensions of Post-positivist Inquiry', in R. Woodman and W. Pasmore (eds), *Research in Organizational Change and Development*. Greenwich: JAI Press.

Reason, P. and J. Marshall (1987) 'Research as Personal Process', in D. Boud and V. Griffin (eds), *Appreciating Adults Learning: from the learner's perspective*. London: Kogan Page.

Reason, P. and J. Rowan (eds) (1981a) *Human Inquiry, a sourcebook of new paradigm research*. Chichester: Wiley.

Reason, P. and J. Rowan (1981b) 'Issues of Validity in New Paradigm Research', in P. Reason and J. Rowan (eds), *Human Inquiry, a sourcebook of new paradigm research*. Chichester: Wiley.

Reinharz, S. (1981) 'Implementing New Paradigm Research: a model for training and practice', in P. Reason and J. Rowan (eds), *Human Inquiry, a sourcebook of new paradigm research*. Chichester: Wiley.

Reinharz, S. (1983) 'Experiential Analysis', in G. Bowles and R. Duelli-Klein (eds), *Theories of Women's Studies*. Boston: Routledge and Kegan Paul.

Revans, R.W. (1971) *Developing Effective Managers*. London: Longman.

Revans, R.W. (1980) *Action Learning: new techniques for management*. London: Blond and Briggs.

Ricouer, P. (1981) *Hermeneutics and the Human Sciences*. Cambridge: Cambridge University Press.

Roberts, H. (1981) *Doing Feminist Research*. London: Routledge and Kegan Paul.

Robertson, G. (1984) *Experiences of Learning*. PhD dissertation, University of Bath.

Robertson, G. (1987) 'Learning and the Hidden Agenda', in D. Boud and V. Griffin (eds), *Appreciating Adults Learning: from the learner's perspective*. London: Kogan Page.

Rosenshine, B. and N. Furst (1973) 'The Use of Direct Observation to Study Teaching', in R.M.W. Travers (ed.), *Second Handbook of Research on Teaching*. Chicago: Rand McNally.

Rowan, J. (1979) 'Hegel and Self-Actualization'. *Self and Society*, 1(5): 129–38.

Rowan, J. (1981) 'A Dialectical Paradigm for Research', in P. Reason and J. Rowan (eds), *Human Inquiry: a sourcebook of new paradigm research*. Chichester: Wiley.

Rowan, J. and P. Reason (1981) 'On Making Sense', in P. Reason and J. Rowan (eds), *Human Inquiry: a sourcebook of new paradigm research*. Chichester: Wiley.

Ruigu, G. and D. Makanda (1987) *The Fuelwood Economy of the Bura Irrigation Settlement Project*. Draft Report, Institute for Development Studies, University of Nairobi.

Saha, S. (1982) 'Irrigation Planning in the Tana Basin of Kenya'. *Water Supply and Management*, 6(3): 261–79.

Schon, D.A. (1983) *The Reflective Practitioner: How Professionals Think in Action*. New York: Basic Books.

Schumacher, E.F. (1977) *A Guide for the Perplexed*. London: Jonathan Cape.

Schwartz, P. and J. Ogilvy (1979) *The Emergent Paradigm: changing patterns of thought and belief*. Analytical Report No. 7, Values and Lifestyles Program. Menlo Park: SRI International.

Shohet, R. and P. Hawkins (in preparation) 'Supervision: a humanistic, analytic, and organizational approach'. Milton Keynes: Open University Press.

Sir Malcolm MacDonald and Partners (1977) 'Bura Irrigation Settlement Project; Project Planning Report'. Government of Kenya.

Skolimowski, H. (1985) 'The Co-creative Mind as a Partner of the Creative Evolution'. Paper read at the First International Conference on the Mind–Matter Interaction. Universidada Estadual de Campinas, Brazil.

Skolimowski, H. (1986) 'The Interactive Mind in the Participatory Universe'. *The World and I*, February: 453–70.

Smith, P.B. (1979) Paper to Group Relations Training Association Conference, September.

Smith, P.B. (1980) 'The T-Group Trainer: Group Facilitator or Prisoner of Circumstance?'. *Journal of Applied Behavioural Science*, 16(1): 63–77.

Srivastva, S., S. L. Obert and E. Neilson (1977) 'Organizational Analysis through Group Processes: a Theoretical Perspective', in C.L. Cooper (ed.), *Organizational Development in the UK and USA*. London: Macmillan.

Stanley, L. and S. Wise (1983) *Breaking Out: feminist consciousness and feminist research*. London: Routledge and Kegan Paul.

Stavenhagen, R. (1971) 'Decolonizing Applied Social Sciences'. *Human Organization*, 30(4): 333–44.

Swantz, M-L. (1984) *Methodology of Non-traditional Research*. TECO Publication No. 4, Institute of Development Studies, University of Helsinki.

Tandon, R. (1981) 'Dialogue as Inquiry and Intervention', in P. Reason and J. Rowan (eds), *Human Inquiry: a sourcebook of new paradigm research*. Chichester: Wiley.

Teilhard de Chardin, P. (1959) *The Phenomenon of Man*. London: Collins.

Torbert, W. (1976) *Creating a Community of Inquiry: conflict, collaboration, transformation*. New York: Wiley.

Torbert, W. (1981a) 'Why Educational Research Has Been So Uneducational: the case for a new model of social science based on collaborative inquiry', in P. Reason and J. Rowan (eds), *Human Inquiry: a sourcebook of new paradigm research*. Chichester: Wiley.

Torbert, W. (1981b) 'Empirical, Behavioural, Theoretical and Attentional Skills Necessary for Collaborative Inquiry', in P. Reason and J. Rowan (eds), *Human Inquiry: a sourcebook of new paradigm research*. Chichester: Wiley.

Torbert, W. (1983) 'Executive Mind, Timely Action'. *ReVision*, (6)1: 3–21.

Torbert, W. (1986) *Managing the Corporate Dream: Restructuring for Longterm Success*. Homewood: Dow-Jones/Irwin.

Traylen, H. (in preparation) MPhil dissertation, University of Bath.

Vainio-Mattila, A. (1987) *Bura Fuelwood Project: Domestic Fuel Economy*. Institute of Development Studies, University of Helsinki.

Valle, R.S. and R.V. King (1978) *Existential–Phenomenological Alternatives for Psychology*. New York: Oxford University Press.

von Franz, M.L. (1982) *An Introduction to the Interpretation of Fairy Tales*. Irving: Spring Publications

Wilber, K. (1981a) *Up from Eden: a transpersonal view of human evolution*. Garden City: Doubleday/Anchor.

Wilber, K. (1981b) 'Reflections on the New Age Paradigm: an interview with Ken Wilber'. *ReVision*, 4(1): 53–74.

Index